Manufactured in the United States of America

To the Memory of
My Brother

PREFACE

SINCE 1931 the world's international pecuniary transactions have been subject to an increasing degree of social control. Government regulation of the international flow of goods and capital has achieved a complexity and finesse which would have made a thoroughgoing Mercantilist envious. A major aspect of these controls has been the growth of the principle of bilateralism; that is, the "channelization" of trade, as well as other economic transactions, directly between pairs of countries.

In line with this tendency, Argentina in 1933 adopted a new foreign commercial policy based upon the principle of bilateralism and preferential treatment, in contrast to her previous foreign economic policy which for a hundred years had been based upon equality of treatment. The adoption of this new policy of bilateralism by Argentina brought to a close, temporarily at least, an era of expanding economic intercourse with the United States which was inaugurated upon the outbreak of the World War.

The present inquiry, therefore, is a description and analysis of the international economic relations of Argentina during the years since 1914, particularly with reference to the United States. Since the years 1914 and 1933 mark two important milestones in the economic relations between Argentina and the United States, the study was originally planned to cover the twenty-year period beginning in 1914. Marked changes have occurred in Argentina's economic position since 1934, however, so that consideration has been given, so far as practicable, to developments during the past two years.

The obligations incurred in the preparation of this study are extensive. My graduate studies at the University of Pennsylvania have been under the general direction and constant encouragement of Professor Ernest Minor Patterson. Grateful acknowledgment is also made for the criticisms and suggestions

received from Professors Roland L. Kramer and Ralph Young. I am particularly indebted, however, to Professor G. G. Huebner, under whose guidance and quiet inspiration this study has taken form.

In the collection of materials Mr. C. E. Babcock, Librarian, Columbus Memorial Library, Pan-American Union, Washington, D.C., and Sr. C. Alonso Irigoyen, Financial Attaché, and Dr. Carlos Garcia-Mata, Commercial Attaché, Argentine Embassy, Washington, D.C., were especially helpful.

Acknowledgment is also due Dr. Amos E. Taylor, Dr. Paul Dickens, and Mr. James C. Corliss, of the Finance Division, and Mr. George Wythe, Chief, Latin-American Section, Division of Regional Information, Bureau of Foreign and Domestic Commerce, Washington, D.C., for placing data at my disposal, as well as reading portions of the manuscript.

A year's residence in Washington was made possible through a fellowship granted by The Brookings Institution, in coöperation with the University of Pennsylvania. Dr. Leo Pasvolsky, of the Brookings staff, in his capacity as adviser, has offered important criticisms. Dr. Cleona Lewis and Dr. C. O. Hardy, also of the Brookings staff, have read parts of the manuscript and made valuable suggestions.

My greatest obligation, however, is to my wife, without whose constant encouragement and untiring efforts the study could not have been completed.

V. L. P.

Washington, D.C.
July 1937.

CONTENTS

TABLES

APPENDICES

CHARTS

I

INTRODUCTION

This study covers, in general, the period since the outbreak of the World War. The year 1914 was of great significance in the economic history of Argentina, since the conflagration which struck Europe at that time had a profound influence on the international economic relations of the country. It marked the shift, to a considerable degree, of the foreign economic orbit of Argentina from Europe to North America, or more specifically, to the United States.

Prior to 1914 the economic relationships between Argentina and the United States were relatively insignificant. During the first century of its independent history Argentina had relied upon Europe to buy its surplus production, and also as the source of both goods and capital. Of the European nations, Great Britain was by far the outstanding leader in this economic intercourse.

Not only was Argentina dependent economically upon Europe, but culturally and intellectually European influence was predominant, although in this sphere France, Italy, and Spain were of greater significance than Great Britain. Since most Argentinians were European immigrants, or children of such immigrants, this affinity is not difficult to understand. Only in the political sphere were the ideals of North America predominant; and even here the question may be raised as to whether French influence was not as dominant as that of the United States.

This does not mean, however, that so far as the United States was concerned, Argentina failed to exist prior to 1914. Argentina's economic dependence upon Europe was relative, not absolute. Commercial relations between Argentina and the United States had existed from the earliest days of the southern

republic; in fact, prior to the formal declaration of Argentine independence. One of the first shipments of manufactured exports from the United States was a cargo of furniture sent in the bark *Superior* in 1801 from Providence to Buenos Aires.[1]

The earliest commercial contacts of the United States with Argentina were largely incidental to the China trade, since American vessels would merely stop at Buenos Aires going to or from the Orient. American trade with the La Plata area grew rapidly, however, during the Napoleonic Wars, largely at the expense of the British.[2] By 1806 five American firms had been established for the purpose of trading with Argentina, and advertisements for River Plate hides and wool appeared in various United States newspapers. In 1807 forty-two American vessels entered the port of Buenos Aires.[3]

That the increasing commercial importance of this area was recognized by the State Department of the United States is evidenced by the fact that within a month of the establishment of the "Provisional Junta of the Provinces of the Rio de la Plata," President Madison appointed Joel R. Poinsett as commercial agent to Buenos Aires. Although the formation of the "Junta" on May 25, 1810, marked the beginning of self-government in La Plata,[4] the formal declaration of independence of "Argentina" did not occur until six years later.

On Nov. 15, 1811, Wm. Gilchrist Miller of Philadelphia was recognized by the Argentine Government as Vice-Consul, and was said to have been the first foreign representative ever officially recognized by the Argentine Government. The first

[1] Julius Klein, *The Frontiers of Trade,* Century Company, 1928, p. 305.

[2] E. J. Pratt, "Anglo-American Commercial and Political Rivalry on the Plata, 1820-1830," *Hispanic-American Historical Review,* August 1931, pp. 302-325.

[3] Address at Chicago by Argentine Consul-general, Sr. E. Gruning Rosas, as reported in *Argentina,* Vol. VII, No. 42, May 1932, p. 9.

[4] Harold F. Peterson, *Diplomatic Relations between the United States and Argentina, 1810-1870,* an unpublished Ph.D. thesis, Duke University, 1933; see also Paul DeWitt, "The Commercial Relations between the United States and Argentina," *The Southwestern Political and Social Science Quarterly,* Vol. XI, No. 2, Sept., 1930.

American Consul in Buenos Aires was Thomas Lloyd Halsey, who was appointed by President Madison in May 1813.[5]

Although official commercial relations with Argentina date, therefore, from 1810, diplomatic recognition of the new nation by the United States was not granted until 1823; and, although intermittent efforts were made to negotiate a commercial treaty, particularly following the announcement of the Anglo-Argentine commercial treaty in 1825, treaties of commerce and navigation were not consummated until 1853, after the fall of the Rosas régime.[6]

Notwithstanding these early developments, trade between the two countries grew slowly during the nineteenth century, as evidenced by the following figures:

UNITED STATES TRADE WITH ARGENTINA

(in thousands of dollars)

	Imports	*Exports*
1830	1,432	630
1840	294	369
1850	2,654	1,065
1860	4,020	1,000
1870	6,414	2,479
1880	6,215	1,883
1890	5,402	8,887
1900	8,114	11,558
1910	33,463	40,695

Source: United States Department of Commerce, *Foreign Commerce and Navigation.*

[5] Chas. Lyon Chandler, "The First Yankee Consul in Buenos Aires, Interesting Activities of Thomas Lloyd Halsey from 1813 to 1818," *Comments on Argentine Trade,* official publication of the United States Chamber of Commerce in Argentina, Buenos Aires, July 1922, pp. 3-7.

[6] The negotiation of the treaties, as well as the reasons for the thirty-year delay, are described in Harold F. Peterson, and Paul DeWitt, *op. cit.;* W. Stewart, "United States-Argentine Commercial Negotiations of 1825," *Hispanic-American Historical Review,* Vol. 13, August 1933, pp. 367-71; H. B. MacKenzie, "Commercial Treaties between the United States and Argentina," *Comments on Argentine Trade,* December 1926, pp. 9-11.

Furthermore, the total investment of United States capital in Argentina in 1913 probably did not exceed 40 million dollars.[7] Other items in the balance of payments between the two countries were also relatively insignificant.

In the decade prior to 1914, however (as the above statistics indicate), increasing attention was being given in the United States to the Argentine market. This was, of course, a natural corollary of the growing industrialization and economic maturity of the former country. The War simply accentuated and accelerated, therefore, a development which ultimately would have occurred on a more gradual scale. This economic evolution of the United States applied not only to its relations with Argentina, but was world-wide in scope; it has been described too many times to need elaboration here.

The purpose of this study has been then to investigate the effect of the European War and its aftermath in the years since 1918 upon the international economic position of Argentina, particularly with reference to the country's economic relations with the United States. The basic data for such a study are found in Argentina's international financial transactions; that is, in the items which make up its international accounts, or balance of payments.

In such a study one is immediately confronted with the problem of obtaining reliable estimates of such transactions. Even with respect to "visible" commodity trade, reliable statistics are of recent origin in most countries. In England reliable trade statistics, computed from actual valuations of the exports and imports, were not compiled until late in the nineteenth century.[8] Even today official trade statistics are frequently subject to a wide margin of error, the major reasons for which are smuggling, omissions, undervaluations by importers, use of arbitrary official valuations by some countries, as well as variations between countries in the use of foreign (f.o.b.) or delivered (c.i.f.) values for imports. Anyone who attempts to match official statis-

[7] See Appendix II, pp. 250-51.

[8] Jacob Viner, "Balance of Trade," *Encyclopaedia of the Social Sciences*, Vol. II, p. 402.

tics between countries (i.e., exports of one country with imports of another) is soon painfully aware of these discrepancies.

With such discrepancies arising for those international transactions for which official attempts have been made to keep an accurate check, the difficulties attached to, and the wide margin of error resulting from, the attempts to calculate the "invisibles" in the international accounts are readily appreciated. In this connection it is interesting to observe that the governments of many countries keep a very careful check on the movement of individuals across their borders, but seem much less concerned regarding the movements of capital to and from the national area. Of course individuals are much more tangible; a "flight" of individuals is much easier to measure than a "flight" of capital.

Except for the years 1916 and 1917 no official compilation of Argentina's balance of payments was attempted prior to 1932. Fortunately, however, a private estimate was compiled annually[9] from 1911 to 1931 by Sr. Carlos A. Tornquist, until recently head of one of the oldest banking firms in Argentina.[10] Sr. Tornquist's statements constitute, therefore, the basic sources for that portion of this study dealing with the Argentine international accounts prior to 1932.

Following the institution of exchange control by Argentina in 1931, the Exchange Control Commission published figures covering the official purchases and sales of foreign exchange. These statistics did not constitute a complete balance of payments, however, since they failed to include transactions in the "black" or "bootleg" market,[11] nor the volume of "blocked" pesos accumulated in Argentina which were not remitted. Estimates of the total Argentine balance of payments for the years 1932-35 inclusive have been compiled by the new Central Bank of Argentina, however, and constitute the statistical basis for this portion of the present study.

[9] With a few exceptions when two years were grouped together. See Appendix I.

[10] See Appendix I.

[11] Legalized "free" market since November 1933.

One of the outstanding characteristics of the international economic relations of recent years has been the growth of bilateralism, the "channelization" of international economic transactions between pairs of countries.[12] The network of international bilateral agreements through which this "channelization" has been attempted since 1931 requires no elaboration here.[13]

Many of the commercial reciprocity agreements negotiated during recent years have included consideration of the "invisible" transactions, as well as actual commodity movements between the two countries concerned. The basic data upon which to base such negotiations requires a knowledge of the volume and character of the respective countries' financial transactions with each other. Up to the present very little has been accomplished in the way of bi-country balance of payments studies.[14] The annual League

[12] The use of the bilateral method of regulating contractual international trade relations is of course not new; on the contrary, historically, the customary way of negotiating commercial treaties or agreements has been between pairs of countries. The term "bilateralism" may be used, however, to describe a variety of circumstances. A careful distinction has been drawn recently, therefore, between "formal" as contrasted with "substantive" bilateralism. "Formal" bilateralism is defined as an arrangement between two countries, the provisions of which may be widely generalized to other nations through the use of the most-favored-nation clause, thus maintaining equality of treatment. "Substantive" bilateralism, in contrast, is defined as those arrangements the purpose of which is to affect the balance of trade or payments between the negotiating countries through the medium of preferential treatment. (Leo Pasvolsky, "Bilateralism in International Commercial Relations," *Harvard Business Review*, Spring Number, 1936, pp. 279-86.) It is in this latter more restricted sense in which the term "bilateralism" is used above, and will be used throughout the present study.

[13] The significance of this development was officially recognized in the United States with the adoption of a new foreign trade policy as reflected in the Trade Agreements Act of June 1934, thus legalizing a procedure for the negotiation of bilateral trade agreements with other nations. The passage of, and the subsequent negotiations and agreements consummated under, the Trade Agreements Act has not meant that the United States has subscribed to the policy of "substantive" bilateralism, i.e., bi-country balancing of trade. On the contrary, the declared purpose of the operation of the Trade Agreements Act has been primarily to increase the *total volume* of trade through the use of the unconditional interpretation of the most-favored clause; i.e., generalization of concessions granted to all countries which do not discriminate in the regulation of their foreign trade against the United States.

[14] One significant study of this nature which has come to the writer's atten-

of Nations Memorandum on Balances of Payments for the year 1933 contained an extended discussion of the world's bilateral trade. Yet *The Economist,* in referring to this discussion, makes the following significant comment:

"Unfortunately very few countries make estimates of their balances of payments with individual foreign countries, so that the investigation had to be confined to merchandise trade alone."[15]

One reason for this situation is the fact that many students of international economics decry the whole "bilateralism" movement, and believe (or devoutly hope) that it is only a temporary phenomenon of the depression period. Perhaps a more important reason is the paucity of data upon which to base such studies. After all, as indicated above, the calculation of the international accounts of a given country with the entire world in any systematic fashion is a comparatively recent development, and even such statements still leave much to be desired.[16]

Since the inauguration of exchange control in 1931, supplemented since 1933 by a series of reciprocal exchange and trade agreements, Argentina has adopted a new foreign commercial policy based upon the doctrine of bilateralism.[17] The adoption of this policy of balancing her international payments by countries places the United States in an unfavorable position with respect to increased sales of goods to Argentina, since Argentine payments to the United States, in recent years, have exceeded payments from the United States to Argentina. The negotiation of a trade agreement by the United States with Argentina under the provision of the Trade Agreements Act of 1934, in so far as it might provide for increased purchases of Argentine products by the United States, would tend to relieve the pressure

tion is a bi-country breakdown of the international accounts of Germany for the period 1924-33, in *Wirtschaft und Statistik,* Sonderheft No. 11, 1934.

[15] *The Economist* (London), Feb. 2, 1935, p. 251.

[16] Recognized as outstanding in the field of international statistical technique are the annual statements which have been compiled during the past decade by the Finance Division, United States Bureau of Foreign and Domestic Commerce, under the supervision, successively, of Mr. Ray Hall and Dr. Amos Taylor.

[17] I.e., "substantive" bilateralism.

against the importation of United States goods into Argentina.

The basis for such negotiations rests upon the existing economic relations between the two countries; that is, the status of the international accounts between Argentina and the United States. The latter part of this study is, therefore, an evaluation of the present competitive position of the United States in its economic relations with Argentina, including an attempt to compile rough estimates of the major balance of payments items between Argentina and the United States, as well as Great Britain, the latter's major competitor.

The importance of Argentina in the international market for both goods and capital funds, as well as its potentialities for the future, are indicated in the following summary of the general characteristics of the Argentine economy.

THE ARGENTINE ECONOMY

Due to its remarkable development during the past fifty years, Argentina now occupies a position of economic leadership in South America. In many lines of economic activity, as the accompanying table indicates, Argentina accounts for nearly half of the total activity of the entire southern continent. Furthermore, until the recent depression, Argentina had over seventy per cent of the continent's gold stock, her gold reserves being among the half dozen largest in the world.

Argentina enjoys a wide variation in climate, since its area of approximately 1,153,000 square miles extends between the twenty-second and fifty-fifth parallels of south latitude, a total distance of some 2,300 miles. Its total area is about one-third that of the United States, or slightly larger than that part lying east of the Mississippi River.

If the area occupied by Argentina in the southern hemisphere were transferred to the same relative position in the northern hemisphere, its rough triangular area would have its base extending from a point approximately 150 miles south of the Texas-Mexican border midway between the Pacific and Atlantic oceans, southeastward into the Gulf of Mexico nearly to the Honduran peninsula some three to four hundred miles south of

New Orleans; its apex would rest approximately at the southern extremity of Hudson's Bay. Buenos Aires would rest close to Oklahoma City.

Geographically, Argentina may be divided into three great

TABLE I

ECONOMIC ACTIVITY IN ARGENTINA RELATIVE TO THE REST OF SOUTH AMERICA

Activity	*Percentage of all South America*
Exports, 1932	41
Imports, 1932	47
Total Foreign Trade, 1932	43
Railroads, mileage, 1930	40
" freight tonnage, 1930	40
" passengers carried, 1930	44
Automobile vehicles, 1935	55
Petroleum Consumption, 1935	50
Telephones, instruments, 1930	49
" messages, 1930	35
Radios	66
Postal Service, pieces of mail, 1930	63
Telegrams sent, 1930	60
Educational expenditures, 1930	65
Print paper consumed, 1924	57

Source: *Revista de Economía Argentina*, Vol. XXXV, No. 214–216, April–June, 1936 (Buenos Aires), pp. 47–49. George Wythe, "Manufacturing Developments in Argentina," *Trade Information Bulletin* No. 820, Bureau of Foreign and Domestic Commerce, Washington, D.C., 1934; H. K. Norton, *The Coming of South America*, New York, 1932.

plains—the sub-tropical, hilly Gran Chaco in the north, the temperate flat Pampa of the central region, and the sub-arctic plateau district of Patagonia in the south.[18] The bulk of the territory lies within the temperate zone, however, and here the great centers of population and economic activity are to be found.

[18] In addition, there is the Andes region stretching along the western boundary, interspersed with several important "oases," the most important being the sugar and wine producing regions of Mendoza and Tucuman.

Within this wide area, with such diversified climatic and topographical features, there has been developed during the past century, and particularly since 1880, a tremendous volume of wealth, based primarily on agricultural and pastoral pursuits. In 1895 the population totaled four million persons; at the outbreak of the World War it had doubled, approximating eight million people. During the same period the population of Buenos Aires increased from 664,000 to 1,585,000 persons. From 1900 to 1913 the railway mileage of the country was doubled, increasing from 10 to 20 thousand miles, roughly speaking.[19] As late as 1900 the total exports were only 154.6 million gold pesos,[20] and the total imports 114.0 million pesos, where-

[19] In 1920 the railway mileage was approximately 21,000, and in 1934, 25,000.

[20] Equivalent to $.9648 (U. S.) at par of exchange. From 1899 to November 1933, Argentina had a dual currency system which was the outgrowth of a period of currency depreciation between 1885 and 1899. The monetary unit of Argentina as established by law in November 1881 was the gold peso of 100 centavos, representing 1.6129 grams of gold 0.900 fine (1.4516 grams of fine gold), the equivalent of five French pre-war gold francs. Its par value in United States currency prior to March 1933, was therefore $.9648. Conversion was suspended in 1885 and was not reëstablished until the passage of the currency reform law of November 4, 1899. By this law the value of the paper peso, which had been the real circulating medium during the preceding fifteen years, was fixed officially at 44 per cent of the gold peso, or approximately $.42 in United States currency. In order to maintain this ratio the Caja de Conversion (Conversion Office), an independent government agency charged with maintaining convertibility, was authorized to pay out gold in exchange for legal tender notes at the rate of 44 centavos for one paper peso. In practice all domestic transactions continued to be conducted on the basis of paper pesos, while foreign trade statistics and transactions with foreign countries were made on the basis of the gold peso. In fact, conversion generally meant the sale of gold at a fixed rate solely for the purpose of making foreign payments; gold coins never circulated to any extent, the major portion of the country's gold stock being held by the Conversion Office, the Banco de la Nación (Bank of the Argentine Nation), and other private banks. The gold peso was, in effect, very largely an abstract monetary unit. Since November 1933 the gold peso has not been used, all statistics being now quoted in paper pesos, including foreign exchange rates and foreign trade figures. Since the gold peso was the official currency for international transactions throughout most of the period covered by this study, plus the fact that it approximated the United States dollar in par value (one gold peso equivalent to $.96 U. S.), the writer has retained it for most of his data, rather than converting them to paper pesos. The official statistics used since 1933 have generally been converted from paper to gold pesos.

as by 1913 they had reached 485.5 million and 421.3 million gold pesos, respectively, or an increase of over three hundred per cent. A vital factor in this development has been the utilization of foreign capital, the growth of which, especially since 1913, is described below in Chapter V.

As indicated in the preceding paragraph, the basis of the national wealth and prosperity is preponderantly agricultural. This concentration of economic activity results of necessity in a large volume of foreign trade. A relatively small group of agricultural products is exported to pay for a diversified list of imports. As recently suggested, however, this simplicity in the national economy has been excessive; such a concentration of activity in a small group of related products is a bad risk.[21] When grains and meats are in demand, Argentina is prosperous; a cessation of this demand, and the effect is felt throughout the entire Argentine economy. The country's entire economic life has hinged upon the export trade; all branches of the national economy have been organized to promote that trade and its corollary, the import trade. Add to this the importance of foreign loans to Argentina, with their accompanying debt service, and the dependence of the Argentine economy upon international forces is clearly depicted.

Table II (on page 12) indicates the relative importance of foreign and domestic goods in the economic life of Argentina. Of particular significance are the declining ratios of domestic production exported, and foreign goods consumed, in recent years.[22]

Supplementing the data presented in Table II, Table III gives per capita exports and productivity for Argentina, together with comparative figures for the United Kingdom and the United States.

Although the land area under cultivation in Argentina in-

[21] H. E. Peters, *The Foreign Debt of the Argentine Republic*, Johns Hopkins Press, 1934, p. 50.

[22] See below, p. 15 for discussion of this point. The figures in Table II do not accurately reflect changes in the physical volume of production and consumption, of course, due to the changes in the value of the peso between 1912 and 1936. Cf. Chart V, p. 97.

TABLE II

ESTIMATED VALUE OF ARGENTINE PRODUCTION AND CONSUMPTION, SELECTED YEARS, 1912–1936
(in millions of paper pesos)

	Production				Consumption				
Year	*Total*	*Consumed*	*Exported*	*Per Cent Exported*	*Total*	*Produced*	*Imported*	*Per Cent Imported*	*Per Capita*
1912	2,601	1,461	1,140	43.8	2,477	1,461	1,016	41.4	347
1914	2,666	1,750	916	34.4	2,483	1,750	733	29.5	312
1927	5,460	3,166	2,294	42.0	5,113	3,166	1,947	38.0	481
1933	4,383	3,262	1,121	25.6	4,159	3,262	897	21.5	346
1936	5,352	3,700	1,652	30.8	4,817	3,700	1,117	23.2	384

Source: Alejandro Bunge, "Situación económica actual de la Argentina," *Revista de Economía Argentina*, Oct.-Dec., 1935, pp. 285-309; *The Times of Argentina*, Mar. 22, 1937, p. 17.

TABLE III

PER CAPITA EXPORTS AND PRODUCTIVITY, ARGENTINA, UNITED KINGDOM, AND UNITED STATES
(in U. S. dollars)

	Per capita exports	*Per capita productivity*	*Ratio*
Argentina	$85.30	$213.25	40%
United Kingdom	89.27	297.57	30
United States	43.15	435.86	9.9

Source: Adapted from George J. Eder, "Current Trends in the International Trade of Argentina," *International Conciliation*, No. 271, June 1931, pp. 375–76. Argentine data are the average for 1923–27 of Bunge's figures, *op. cit.*; United Kingdom and United States data are for 1927, the former figure being the estimate of A. W. Flux, President of the Royal Statistical Society, *Journal of the Royal Statistical Society*, Vol. XCII, 1929, part I, the latter from the *United States Commerce Yearbook*, 1931.

creased from 12 million acres in 1895 to 57 million in 1913, and to 59 million in 1927, yet in the latter year only 13.7 per cent of the tillable soil had been utilized.[23] In 1934, 68 million

[23] *Times Year Book on Argentina*, London, 1927, p. 210.

acres were under cultivation, or about 14.6 per cent.[24] Stock raising, on the other hand, has more nearly approached its limit, since existing pasture land is well stocked. As will be described in more detail in Chapter VI, one of the major trends in agricultural production and exports in recent years has been the shift from pastoral to agricultural products, that is, to a less extensive type of agriculture.

Notwithstanding the large unutilized agricultural resources of the country, increasing attention is being given to industrial pursuits. Particularly since 1931, the realization has been forced upon Argentina that, due to the attempts at national self-sufficiency on the part of many of the industrial nations of the world, its markets for agricultural products are being perhaps permanently curtailed. The result has been increasing emphasis upon the fostering of domestic manufacturing and a more diversified, well-rounded, national economy.[25]

The industrialization of Argentina has gone through two important stages of development.[26] In the half century prior to the World War Argentina was considered as an excellent example of a country whose economy consisted primarily of the exchange of raw materials for the manufactures of Europe (and to a small, but increasing degree, of the United States). Although there was considerable industrial development in certain lines, particularly in the processing of foodstuffs, as well as in the manufacture of certain other articles, largely consumers' goods, yet in

[24] Rafael Garcia-Mata and Emilio Llorens, *Geografía Económica Argentina*, 1936, p. 19.

[25] Cf. George Wythe, "The New Industrialism in Latin America," *Journal of Political Economy*, University of Chicago Press, April 1937, pp. 207-28.

[26] George Wythe, "Manufacturing Developments in Argentina," *op. cit.*; "Argentine Industrial Development," *Comments on Argentine Trade*, *op. cit.*, January 1934, pp. 19-39. For details of industrial development in 1914, see "Investments in Latin America," *Special Agents Series* No. 169 and "Investments in Latin America: I-Argentina," *TIB* No. 362, Bureau of Foreign and Domestic Commerce, Washington, D.C.; also *The South American Handbook*, 1914, Ch. 14, "Manufactures and Minor Industries." For a brief statement of development prior to 1914, see "Wearing Apparel in Argentina," *Miscellaneous Series* No. 68, United States Bureau of Foreign and Domestic Commerce, Washington, D.C., 1918, pp. 120-22.

comparison to the volume of pastoral and agricultural production and export it was relatively unimportant.

During the World War, however, the manufacture of many articles developed rapidly, due to Europe's inability (as well as that of the United States) to supply them. Following the War, some of these new industries were liquidated, but others continued and were even expanded. The War also brought home to Argentina for the first time the handicaps of relying upon other countries for many of the necessities and conveniences of life.

TABLE IV

ARGENTINE INDUSTRIAL DEVELOPMENT 1914 AND 1934

	No. of establishments	*Capital*[a]	*Value of production*[b]	*No. of employees*
1914	48,779	1,787,662	1,861,790	410,201
1934	20,696	4,876,505	2,687,298	380,066

[a] In thousands of paper pesos. One paper peso equivalent to 42 cents (U. S.) at par of exchange prior to 1929. During 1934 the Argentine official selling rate for the dollar averaged 29 cents per peso.

[b] Value of production understood to include value of raw materials. In 1933 it was estimated that the total value of all national physical production was 4,383 million paper pesos, of which the value added by manufacture was 2,062 million paper pesos or forty-one per cent. *Revista de Economía Argentina*, October-December, 1935, p. 300, cited by Wythe, "The New Industrialism in Latin-America," *op. cit.*, p. 214.

The second important stage in industrialization dates from 1931, and is still going on. No industrial census has been taken since 1914, so that official current statistics on this development are not available.[27] A tabulation of Argentine industrial development at the beginning of 1934 was made in connection with the study referred to above,[28] however, which provided the basis for the summary figures in the above table.

[27] On June 15, 1934, a bill was transmitted from the Argentine Congress to the President providing for an industrial census, which was taken in October 1935. The results are not yet available.

[28] "Argentine Industrial Development"; also reproduced in Wythe, "Manufacturing Developments in Argentina," pp. 7-8.

The figures in Table IV for 1914 and 1934 are not strictly comparable, since many small establishments are not included for 1934, due to lack of accurate statistics. The table, therefore, understates, rather than over-emphasizes, the industrial development during the twenty-year period.

Whether this current trend is simply a temporary phase of the depression, or is likely to become permanent, is possibly debatable. The weight of evidence, however, points to the latter view. Regarding this point, the following opinion is significant:

> This period [since 1931] may be considered as one of the most significant turning points in Argentina's economic history, and as representing a definite shift of emphasis from the heretofore all-important export market toward balanced internal development. Although this change in direction cannot be said to have been entirely voluntary on Argentina's part, since it was forced upon her by the growing agrarian self-sufficiency of Europe and by the policy of British Imperial preference that found expression in the Ottawa pacts, the new road has been accepted as one from which there is no turning back. As Great Britain is Argentina's best customer, and normally takes around 84 per cent of that country's exports of livestock products, the signing of the Ottawa agreements on August 20, 1932, made a profound impression on the Argentines and intensified the sentiment in favor of developing a broader basis for the economic life of the nation.[29]

The development of manufacturing since 1931 has been stimulated both by the use of import duties and currency depreciation plus exchange control.[30]

An interesting comparison may be drawn between the Argentine of today and the United States of a century ago. The United States at that time, like the Argentine Republic of today, was largely an agricultural country, with a population increasing rapidly through immigration and native growth. The United States of 1830, like present-day Argentina, exported raw materials and imported manufactured goods. Argentina's foreign

[29] Wythe, "Manufacturing Developments in Argentina," *op. cit.*, p. 3. See also "The New Industrialism in Latin-America," *op. cit.*

[30] See Chapter IV of this study.

trade in recent years, however, was more than ten times that of the United States in the earlier period. This difference is attributable chiefly to the increased productivity of agriculture and the improvement in transportation facilities during the last hundred years. The 25,000 miles of railroad that move Argentine products to the seaboard had no counterpart in the United States a hundred years ago; likewise, modern shipping represents as great an innovation in contrast with the vessels of that period. Argentina is closer to her principal foreign markets in freight-carrying time than New York was to Charleston in 1830.

In decided contrast to the United States of a hundred years ago, Argentina lacks many of the resources essential to the achievement of a very high degree of economic self-sufficiency. Economic supplies of coal and iron are relatively unimportant; the same is true of most of the other industrial minerals.[31]

A notable exception is petroleum, which has helped to offset the dearth of other fuel and power resources. Prior to 1914 practically all of the fuel requirements were met by coal imports.[32] During the War, due largely to the inability of Great Britain (the major source) to continue its supply of coal, Argentina was compelled to use wood as its major fuel supply. It has been estimated that in 1918 74.8 per cent of the fuel supply came from this source.[33] At the same time, the use of petroleum increased gradually (except during 1918). After the War, the use of petroleum increased rapidly, with imports supplying about two-thirds of the total consumption until 1925, when increased domestic production supplied over one-half of the total. This

[31] Lead, tin, copper, silver, gold, and certain other minerals are produced on a minor scale.

[32] In 1913, the total fuel and power supply was equivalent to 3.9 million tons of coal, of which imported coal accounted for 96 per cent, oil fuel three per cent, and water power less than one per cent. Wythe, "Manufacturing Developments in Argentina," *op. cit.*, p. 4.

[33] Carlos Garcia-Mata, "El consumo de combustibles en la Argentina," *Revista de Economía Argentina*, Vol. XVIII, No. 107, May 1927, p. 391. This article presents a complete statistical and graphical statement of Argentina's fuel supply and consumption for the period 1912-1925. See also H. F. Bain and T. T. Read, *Ores and Industry in South America*, Harper & Brothers, 1934, p. 178. Chapter VIII, "Argentina," of this book contains an excellent discussion of the mineral resources of Argentina.

increasing output of petroleum has decreased the dependence on imported fuels, although both coal and fuel oils are still imported in considerable quantities. Under a large measure of government exploitation the country now supplies about one-half of its domestic consumption, of which about two-fifths is produced by the Government; that is, the Government produces some 20 per cent of the nation's total petroleum requirements.[34]

Considerable potential hydro-electric power exists (notably the Apipe Falls on the Parana River and the Iguassu Falls on the northeastern boundary, as well as extensive potential water-power resources in Patagonia), but it is at present too far distant from sources of demand to be, under present power-transmission technique, economically profitable.[35]

Lacking iron ore to support blast furnaces, Argentina has developed, from the scrap metal supplies accruing largely from the railroads, a small but important industry in the remelting, recasting, and reworking of iron and steel. Large quantities of iron and steel, however, are also imported in raw or semi-finished form for domestic fabrication.[36]

Minerals have been then, as a whole, of minor importance in the development of Argentina. Fuel and petrolum products, machinery and vehicles largely made of steel, and steel manufactures, account for nearly half of the country's total imports; and, as far as can be foreseen, must continue to do so, since the mineral industry will probably continue to be "strictly subordinate."[37]

So far we have emphasized the physical resources of Argen-

[34] In 1928 coal supplied 45 per cent, oil fuel 52 per cent, and water power a little over two per cent, of a total fuel supply equivalent to 6,732,000 tons of coal; in 1931 total fuel consumption amounted to the equivalent of 6,603,000 tons of coal, of which coal supplied 39.2 per cent, oil fuel 58.9 per cent, and hydraulic energy 1.9 per cent. Wythe, "Manufacturing Developments in Argentina," *op. cit.*, p. 5.

[35] The Apipe and Iguassu Falls are approximately 800 miles from Buenos Aires, and economic transmission of electricity does not at present exceed 400 miles.

[36] For a detailed picture of the Argentine iron and steel industry, see "The Argentine Iron and Steel Industry and Trade," *TIB* No. 776, U. S. Bureau of Foreign and Domestic Commerce, Washington, D.C., 1931.

[37] Bain and Read, *op. cit.*, p. 204.

tina. We turn now to a brief description of the human element in the Argentine economy.

Argentina occupies second place among the South American republics both as regards area and population. Out of an estimated total for the entire continent of 84 million people, Argentina has between 12 and 13 million, or approximately 14 per cent.[38]

The rapid growth of Argentina's population is indicated by the returns of the three national censuses, as follows:

First Census	1869	1,736,923
Second Census	1895	3,954,911
Third Census	1914	7,885,237

That Argentina had ample room for this rapid expansion, however, is evidenced by the fact that in 1914 population density was still 7.3 per square mile; by 1935 it was approximately 10.7 per square mile.[39] In contrast, comparative figures for the United States were 33 and 42 respectively.

An important factor in this growth was, of course, the heavy immigration, mostly from Europe. During the period 1910 to 1913 the average net annual increase in population from immigration, according to official statistics, was 169,304 persons.[40] The net overseas immigration from 1857, when records were first compiled, to 1913 (inclusive) was 3,373,292 persons.

There was a net loss of 209,753 during the war period, 1914-1918; a net gain of 962,374 from 1919 to 1931, and a further net loss of 18,317 during 1932 and 1933. In 1934 there was

[38] Brazil's population is estimated at one-half of the total for the continent.

[39] The total population in 1934 was estimated to be 12,200,531 persons, and for the following year 12,372,965, an increase in one year of 168,871 persons. Although no official census of population has been taken since 1914, the Office of National Statistics publishes annual estimates of population growth. See *El Comercio Exterior Argentino* (annual). These estimates are based upon the assumption, however, that the vital statistics since the last census in 1914 are 100 per cent accurate, whereas undoubtedly there have been many unrecorded births, as well as deaths. Dr. Carlos Garcia-Mata, who has made a careful study of his country's population growth, informed the writer that, in his opinion, the total population of Argentina as of July 1, 1936, was not less than 12.7 million persons.

[40] *El Comercio Exterior Argentino, op. cit.*, 1934, p. 88.

again a net increase of 4,080, making a net gain of 4,111,676 from 1857 through 1934.[41] In nearly every year of the decade prior to 1914 the migrational increase in the population exceeded that of the natural increase. This immigration was more than the country could assimilate, however, and was a factor in the crisis of 1913-14.[42] The 1914 census showed that of the 7,885,000 inhabitants, 2,358,000, or about 30 per cent, were foreign born, a proportion twice as large as that in the United States in 1910 when it reached its maximum.[43]

Another significant aspect of this population movement has been the size of the return stream, the relatively large percentage of emigration. This was due to the so-called "floating immigration," the *golondrinas* (swallows); that is, European laborers, primarily Italians, who, due to differences in the seasons between the two hemispheres, spent the northern winters in the harvest fields of Argentina, and returned in the spring with their savings to cultivate and harvest another crop on the stony hillsides of the homeland.[44] This movement disappeared in 1914 due to the War, and since then has not been revived on anything like the pre-war scale. Approximately 50 per cent of this emigration was made up of Italians.

[41] *Ibid.* This trend was continued in 1935, the total net immigration for the year being 21,160 persons. For more comprehensive studies of Argentine immigration, see (a) *International Migrations,* National Bureau of Economic Research, New York City, Vol. I, "Statistics," pp. 539-47, based upon Argentine official sources of the Department of Immigration, Ministry of Agriculture, primarily *Resumen Estadístico del Movimiento Migratorio en la República Argentina, años 1857-1924,* Ministry of Agriculture, Buenos Aires, 1925; Vol. II, "Interpretations," Ch. IV, "Argentina," by Alejandro E. Bunge and Carlos Garcia-Mata, and (b) Mark Jefferson, *Peopling the Argentine Pampa,* American Geographical Society Research Series No. 16, 1926, especially Figure 18, pp. 40-41, showing annual total net immigration and population, 1857-1924. Regarding the accuracy of official statistics, see especially *International Migrations,* Vol. II, pp. 144-146.

[42] See Chapter II below, pp. 22-25.

[43] At the beginning of 1936, it was estimated that 20 per cent of the population in Argentina was foreign-born. *Revista de Economía Argentina,* Vol. XXXV, No. 214-216, April-June, 1936, p. 44.

[44] See Jefferson, *op. cit.,* Figure 66, p. 191, showing *monthly* immigration and emigration, 1893-1924, which graphically illustrates the seasonality of this movement.

During the period 1857-1926, Italians also constituted nearly half (47.4 per cent) of the total immigration of the country. The other dominant nationality was Spanish, accounting for 32.3 per cent during the same period.[45] From 1910 to 1935, the classification of Argentina's immigration by nationality was as follows:[46]

Spaniards	1,178,510
Italians	1,047,527
Poles	145,517
Germans	97,343
Russians	82,340
French	48,885
Portuguese	47,788
Others	452,455
Total	3,100,365

By far the greater percentage of the immigrants have been Latins, Italians and Spaniards constituting nearly 80 per cent of the total. In recent years, however, the situation has been somewhat modified; non-Latin immigrants now constitute more than one-fourth of the total.[47] This shift is due to both a negative and a positive factor; negative in that since the spring of 1927 the Italian government has discouraged emigration; positive in the rapid increase in German immigration during the middle twenties.[48]

As indicated above, however, during recent years immigration into Argentina has been reduced to a negligible figure. In 1932 and 1933 there was a net emigration following the issuance of a decree by the Argentine Government in 1932 placing certain restrictions upon free immigration, in order to prevent further augmentation of unemployment. In recent months, however, the unemployment problem has very largely disappeared in Argentina, and with renewed prosperity the influx of immi-

[45] *International Migrations, op. cit.*, p. 153.

[46] *Revista de Economía*, p. 45.

[47] *Ibid.*, p. 152.

[48] See *Survey of International Affairs*, Royal Institute of International Affairs, Oxford University Press, London, 1927, p. 531.

grants may be expected to revive. Furthermore, Argentina has at present one of the highest rates of natural increase in population of any country in the world. In 1933 the natural rate of increase per 1,000 inhabitants for selected countries was as follows:[49]

Argentina	14.3	Italy	10.0
Japan	13.7	U. S.	5.7
Poland	12.3	Germany	3.5
Canada	11.3		

The location and distribution of Argentina's population requires brief comment. Out of the total population of nearly 13 millions, over 50 per cent is urban,[50] with nearly three million persons living within the metropolitan area of Buenos Aires.

During the 19 years between the census of 1895 and that of 1914, there was a very rapid growth of the urban population at the expense of the rural, since the former grew from 43 per cent of the total population in 1895 to 58 per cent in 1914. There were at least two major reasons for this: (1) improvement and increasing use of agricultural machinery reduced the need for farm labor; (2) industrial development in the cities attracted increasing numbers of persons.

The economic disadvantages, as well as the political and social problems, which this population distribution entails cannot be elaborated here. The solution of the problem may be rendered easier, however, by the decline in the number of immigrants in recent years.

With this brief description of the Argentine economy, we turn in the succeeding pages to a more detailed consideration of the effect of the World War upon the international economic position of Argentina.

[49] League of Nations, *Statistical Yearbook, 1934-35*, p. 53.

[50] Estimated at 60 per cent in 1936. *Revista de Economía Argentina*, p. 44.

II

THE ARGENTINE INTERNATIONAL ACCOUNTS

1914-20

1. 1914-17: ECONOMIC READJUSTMENTS UPON THE OUTBREAK OF THE WORLD WAR

THE OUTBREAK of the World War in August 1914 found Argentina particularly unprepared to withstand the impact of the economic forces which that catastrophe loosed. Especially susceptible to international economic influences, because of its close commercial and financial relations with Europe, Argentina was bound to be severely affected by the outbreak of such a struggle, even under a normal domestic economic situation. But in 1914 Argentina was already in the depths of a depression which had culminated a decade of extremely rapid economic expansion and development. The immediate cause of this reaction was traceable to the Balkan War, which tended to check the flow of European capital into Argentina that had characterized the preceding decade, and which was a major factor in the prosperity which ensued.[1] This decline of new foreign capital put a stop to much constructive work and brought an end to the land boom and period of real estate speculation, since a great deal of the funds for this speculation had originated abroad.[2]

[1] "The great sensitiveness of Latin American countries to disturbances in Europe and the close interrelation which has existed between the two sections were graphically illustrated two years ago, when trouble in the Balkans, involving directly only a few small nations in the east of Europe, was sufficient to cause a decided depression over practically all of Central and South America." Edward Ewing Pratt, Chief, Bureau of Foreign and Domestic Commerce, "Trade Conditions in Latin America as Affected by the European War," *Annals of American Academy of Political and Social Science*, Vol. LX, July 1915, pp. 72-3. See also George E. Roberts, "Investments in Central and South America," *The Americas* (published by the National City Bank of New York), Vol. I, May 1915, p. 3; Gordon Ross, *Argentina and Uruguay*, 1916, p. 93.

[2] An estimate of the *Economist's* (London) correspondent put the figure at

There was much sound basis for the economic expansion during this pre-war decade; but, like many such expansions, it was carried too far—at least too far, in view of subsequent events. As previously indicated, the land area under cultivation increased from 12,230,000 acres in 1895 to 57 million acres in 1913. Trade and commerce witnessed a corresponding expansion. In 1900 exports were valued at 154 million gold pesos; in 1913, 519 million. This rapid land development encouraged speculation in anticipation of large profits. Such speculation was not restricted to agricultural lands; urban real estate boomed also as a result of the accompanying increased commercial and financial activity. Although this resulted in the building up of many large fortunes, values were inflated beyond the point at which even the rapid progress of the country could sustain them.

This wave of prosperity increased the demand for imported articles to such an extent that the export surplus which had characterized the country's foreign trade since 1890 was considerably reduced. In fact, in the calendar year 1911, there was an import surplus of 63 million gold pesos. This meant, therefore, that the annual foreign debt service of some 150 to 170 million gold pesos on capital already invested in the country was met increasingly from the proceeds of new foreign loans. That these new loans were forthcoming has already been indicated. Table V, summarizing Argentina's international accounts for the two-year period, October 1, 1911 to September 30, 1913, is presumably typical of the entire period after 1900, since during most of this time the rates of exchange were favorable to Argentina and there was a steady net inflow of gold. The total excess of gold imports over exports from 1900 to 1912 inclusive was approximately 305 million gold pesos.[8]

---

400 million paper pesos, or 176 million gold pesos, as the sum which Europe invested in cedulas, or mortgage bonds, between 1910 and 1914, a demand which disappeared, however, in the latter year. *The Economist*, 1914, I, p. 831, cited by H. E. Peters, *op. cit.*, footnote, p. 66. This was approximately 60 million gold pesos annually. The *total* import of new capital during the last three years before the War was estimated to have averaged 200 million dollars annually. See Appendix II, p. 243.

[8] "There is little doubt that in the great majority of years since 1900 the

The pre-war decade so far described was then, briefly, a period of great prosperity resulting in over-expansion, the continuation of which was contingent upon continuing loans from Europe. The decline of these loans led to a forced liquidation, which became pronounced about the beginning of 1913, and in-

TABLE V

THE ARGENTINE INTERNATIONAL ACCOUNTS, SUMMARY STATEMENT, "ECONOMIC" YEARS, 1911/12–1912/13
(in millions of gold pesos)

	1911–12	*1912–13*
Commodity Trade:		
Exports	428.50	512.20
Imports	409.00	460.40
Export Surplus	19.50	51.80
Service Items: (net)		
Debt Service	167.90	160.50
Other Services	87.00	87.00
Total Service Items	254.90	247.50
Balance of Payments	−235.40	−195.70
Add Net Gold Imports	34.45	24.20
Estimated Net Increase in Foreign Indebtedness	269.85	219.90

Note: For source and definition of Argentine "economic" year, see Appendix I, p. 233.

creased in severity during the ensuing months. That the worst was over, in the opinion of many, was evidenced by the fact that the banks were increasingly lenient in their loan policy over the year-end, 1913-14, in anticipation of the crop yields in the fall (i.e., the first half of 1914, since the Argentine seasons of the southern hemisphere are the opposite of those in the United

balance of payments has shown a considerable surplus in Argentina's favor." John H. Williams, *Argentine International Trade Under Inconvertible Paper Money, 1880-1900*, Harvard University Press, 1920, pp. 155-6. By "surplus" Williams meant that the export surplus plus new investments exceeded debt service.

States).[4] But the worst was yet to come—the 1913-14 crop was a failure. During the growing season there was a lack of sufficient rainfall; during the harvesting and marketing season there was too much rainfall, and by the time the roads were dried and the grain was fit to ship, the War had broken out and shipping was not available. The following figures for the "economic" years 1911/12-1913/14 covering total exports show the effect of this crop failure:

ARGENTINE TOTAL EXPORTS

(in millions of gold pesos)	
1911-12	428.5
1912-13	512.2
1913-14	404.2

The crop failure had a still further disastrous effect on land values.

By the end of July 1914 the depression was at its lowest ebb, when the outbreak of the War accentuated the country's economic difficulties.[5] Nearly all business activity came to a halt, and for weeks trade and commerce were practically paralyzed. A banking holiday which lasted eight days was declared on August

[4] Cf. Emilio Hansen, *The Argentine Financial Emergency Measures on the Outbreak of the European War*, Buenos Aires, 1915, p. 6. This monograph is a critical analysis of the period.

[5] An interesting commentary, in view of developments in recent years in the United States, was the public reaction in Argentina to the situation just described. When the Argentine Congress met in May 1914, the public hoped it would "do something."

"The popular feeling, as in all times of stress, was that the government must have something 'up its sleeves' which would at once sweep away the depression. Financial nostrums were commonly propounded, mostly compounded either with emission of "cedulas" for the National Hypothecary Bank, or else a similar emission of paper money for the Banco de la Nación and its lending department. But vice-president Plaza, acting as interim president, had a surer grasp of the situation, and the method of facing it, and he came boldly forward, stating that the situation could not justify any such exceptional measures. . . . The government considered that the trouble all came from one single cause—the abuse of credit. The root of the evil lay . . . in [this] abuse of credit, and this abuse had battened on the land speculation. In 1904 there had started a mild boom, checked in time by a passing depression the next year, and recommenced with increased vigor after the American crisis of 1907." Emilio Hansen, *op. cit.*, p. 7.

2, 1914, and a financial moratorium covering all of August. Gold payments were suspended by the closing of the Conversion Office and the placing of an embargo on gold exports.[6] Removal of gold imports from the risks of ocean shipping was also provided for by a decree which permitted gold acquired abroad to be held in Argentine legations. It was also provided that the Conversion Office might rediscount commercial paper in exchange for currency, providing the gold reserves did not fall below 40 per cent.[7]

Rediscounting was not resorted to, however, during the War, so that, although gold payments were suspended, currency was not issued except against the deposit of gold.[8]

Although these emergency measures prevented a panic during the early days of the War, foreign trade came to a virtual standstill. Temporarily, there was an almost total cessation of both exports and imports, since much of the shipping that had been en route when the War broke out came in and remained in port. Imports in 1914 declined in value over 30 per cent compared with 1913. This decline was due in part, of course, to the reduced purchasing power resulting from the general depression prior to the outbreak of the War. Later, lack of shipping facilities, blockade of some of Argentina's suppliers, as well as the inability (or unwillingness) of the allied nations to maintain their exports to Argentina, all contributed to the decline. European war needs, however, soon revived the export trade. By the end of January (1915) the volume of all exports except linseed had about reached normal proportions.

The immediate shifts wrought by the War in the international economic position of Argentina are best reflected in the country's international accounts which, for the period 1913-17, are summarized in Table VI.

As indicated in the table, the commodity export surplus in

[6] This was opposed by Socialists on the grounds that it would increase the cost of living and weigh heavily upon the working class.

[7] Since the establishment of the Conversion Law in 1899, paper currency had been issued only in exchange for gold. See footnote 20, p. 10.

[8] In 1931 the measure was revived to meet the emergency which arose at that time. See below, footnote 59, p. 92.

TABLE VI

THE ARGENTINE INTERNATIONAL ACCOUNTS, SUMMARY STATEMENT, "ECONOMIC" YEARS, 1913/14–1916/17
(in millions of gold pesos)

	1913–14	*1914–15*	*1915–16*	*1916–17*
Commodity Trade:				
Exports	404.25	556.90	508.50	612.40
Imports	392.10	268.00	365.70	357.50
Export Surplus	12.15	288.90	142.80	254.90
Service Items: (net)				
Debt Service	139.30	138.10	146.20	148.50
Other Service	38.00	35.00	17.00	13.00
Total Service Items	177.30	173.10	163.20	161.50
Balance of Payments:	−165.15	+115.80	−20.40	+93.40
Covered by:				
Net Changes in				
Foreign Indebtedness:				
Increase	+132.55		+31.01	
Decrease		− 41.40		−61.58
Net Gold Movements:				
Exports	+ 32.60			
Imports		− 74.40	−10.61	−31.82
	+165.15	−115.80	+20.40	−93.40
Net Change in				
Foreign Indebtedness: (details)				
A. Receipts: (Income)				
1. Borrowing from foreigners	132.55	35.20	59.60	11.70
2. Repayments by foreigners	—	8.00	—	5.50
Total receipts	132.55	43.20	59.60	17.20
B. Payments: (Outgo)				
1. Repayments to foreigners	—	84.60	19.59	70.28
2. Loans to foreigners	—	—	9.00	8.50
	—	84.60	28.59	78.78
Net Increase (+) or Decrease (−) in Foreign Indebtedness	+132.55	− 41.40	+31.01	−61.58

Source: See Appendix I, Table I, opposite p. 238.

1913-14 was only 12.15 million gold pesos, because of the low volume of exports resulting from the crop failure alluded to above, accompanied by the failure of imports to contract correspondingly. Since the total of service items due to foreigners[9] was 177.3 million gold pesos, there remained a balance of payments against Argentina on current items of 165.15 million pesos. This was covered by an estimated net increase in foreign indebtedness of 132.55 million gold pesos,[10] plus a net gold export of 32.6 million gold pesos.

The marked effect of the outbreak of the World War upon the international transactions of Argentina is clearly shown in the condition of the international accounts for the succeeding "economic" year (1914-15), when the export surplus reached a total of 288.9 million gold pesos, as a result of an increase in the value of exports over 1913-14 of approximately 150 million pesos, coupled with a decline in imports of 125 million pesos. This completely reversed the balance of payments compared with 1913-14, since it left a balance in favor of Argentina of 115.8 million pesos. This balance was covered by a net increase in gold imports (including gold deposited in legations abroad) of 74.4 million pesos,[11] plus an estimated decrease in foreign indebtedness of 41.4 million pesos,[12] in striking contrast to the previous year when foreign indebtedness increased by 132.55 million pesos, which figure was probably less than the average net annual capital imports for several years immediately preceding the War.

This sudden cessation of foreign loans, coupled with the

[9] See Appendix I, Table I, "International Income Account of Argentina, 1913-1934," opposite p. 238, for details of these items.

[10] For more detailed description, i.e., gross changes in foreign indebtedness, see Table II, "Estimated International Capital Transactions of Argentina, 1913-1934," Appendix II, pp. 240-41.

[11] Tornquist, in his 1914-15 statement, deprecates the fact that the entire "favorable" balance was not applied to debt repayment, since the large gold imports made possible an "excessive" circulation of paper money, "encouraging us to spend more than we ought to."

[12] It was estimated that at the opening of the War Argentina was probably a short-term debtor to Europe on account of bills outstanding of some 60-70 million gold pesos. Hansen, *op. cit.*, p. 82.

necessity of repaying foreign credits, continued nevertheless as a depressing factor on the Argentine economy. Except for a boom in industries receiving war orders, business stagnation continued with a high rate of business failures during 1915.

In 1915-16, however, we find Argentina again with a small "adverse" balance of payments totaling 20.4 million gold pesos. With respect to current items, this was the result of a reduction in the export surplus of approximately 150 million pesos which, in turn, was due both to lessened exports[13] and increased value of imports. Service remittances remaining relatively fixed, however, amounting to 163.2 million pesos, the export surplus of 142.8 million pesos left an "adverse" balance of 20.4 million gold pesos. Notwithstanding this fact, there was a net increase in gold holdings (including gold in legations abroad) of 10.61 million pesos, so that the estimated net increase in foreign indebtedness was 31.01 million pesos.

A major factor in this increase was the negotiation of short-term loans by the National Government with New York bankers. Already in the previous "economic" year the stringency of foreign funds had been alleviated by short-term borrowing abroad. In December 1914, a short-term loan of 15 million dollars was effected in New York; in May 1915, five million pounds more was obtained in London and 25 million dollars in New York, but since these loans were largely for refunding purposes, the net amount received by Argentina from all three loans was approximately 15 million gold pesos. During 1915-16 this tapping of a new capital source was continued by the negotiation of additional short-term loans from New York bankers,

[13] The decline in the value of exports in 1915-16 was partially offset by the increase of the next year, 1916-17. The decline was caused primarily by a drop in cereal prices plus the scarcity of shipping with its corollary of high freights. The drop in cereal prices early in 1916 was the result of anticipated large harvests in the United States and Canada, as well as in Argentina. This situation, together with the lack of shipping facilities, retarded exports so that a relatively large stock remained available in the country. When the upward reaction of prices occurred in the fourth quarter of 1916, exports increased greatly over 1915, jumping from 117.5 million pesos in the fourth quarter of 1915 to 185.2 million pesos in the corresponding period of 1916; in other words, a portion of the 1915-16 crop really appears in the 1916-17 export figures.

netting Argentina some 48 million gold pesos. These loans then, coupled with other capital transactions, resulted in an estimated net increase in foreign indebtedness of 31.01 million pesos, as indicated in the preceding paragraph.

Greatly increased prices for her exports in the following year (1916-17), however, again enabled Argentina to effect a "favorable" balance of payments; a situation which was to continue until 1920. This shift again in the balance of payments in 1916-17 was the result of a change in only one item, exports. With the value of imports remaining at approximately the same figure as in the preceding year, exports increased in value slightly over 100 million pesos,[14] thus increasing the export surplus to 254.9 million pesos. With estimated service remittances again at approximately the same figure (161.5 million pesos), this left a "favorable" balance for 1916-17 of nearly 100 million pesos. As indicated in Table VI, this balance was covered by a further net increase in gold holdings of 31.82 million pesos, plus an estimated net decrease in foreign indebtedness of 61.58 million gold pesos. A major item in this latter figure was the repayment of approximately 53 million pesos of short-term bankers' loans in New York.

The shifts in Argentina's international accounts during this period are also reflected in the foreign exchange rates, as shown in Chart I.[15] During the early months of 1914 sterling ruled

[14] This was notwithstanding the crop failure; that is, the increase resulted entirely from higher prices and not from increases in the volume of exports.

[15] The dollar rate was not clearly indicative of the situation since, prior to the War, there was no active market for dollar exchange, and bills on New York were usually at a disparity of from one to one and one-half per cent as compared with exchange on London.

The data used in Chart I were computed from rates obtained from the following sources:

United States:

1914-19: United States Federal Reserve Board, *Federal Reserve Bulletin*, June, 1920, p. 598.

1920-27: *Ibid.*, January, 1928, pp. 60-61.

1928-33: Banco de la Nación, *Economic Review*, April-June, 1934, p. 45.

1934-36:

Official Rates:

República de Argentina, Dirección General de Estadística de la Nación,

CHART I. AVERAGE MONTHLY FOREIGN EXCHANGE RATES IN BUENOS AIRES, PERCENTAGE OF GOLD PARITY, 1914-36

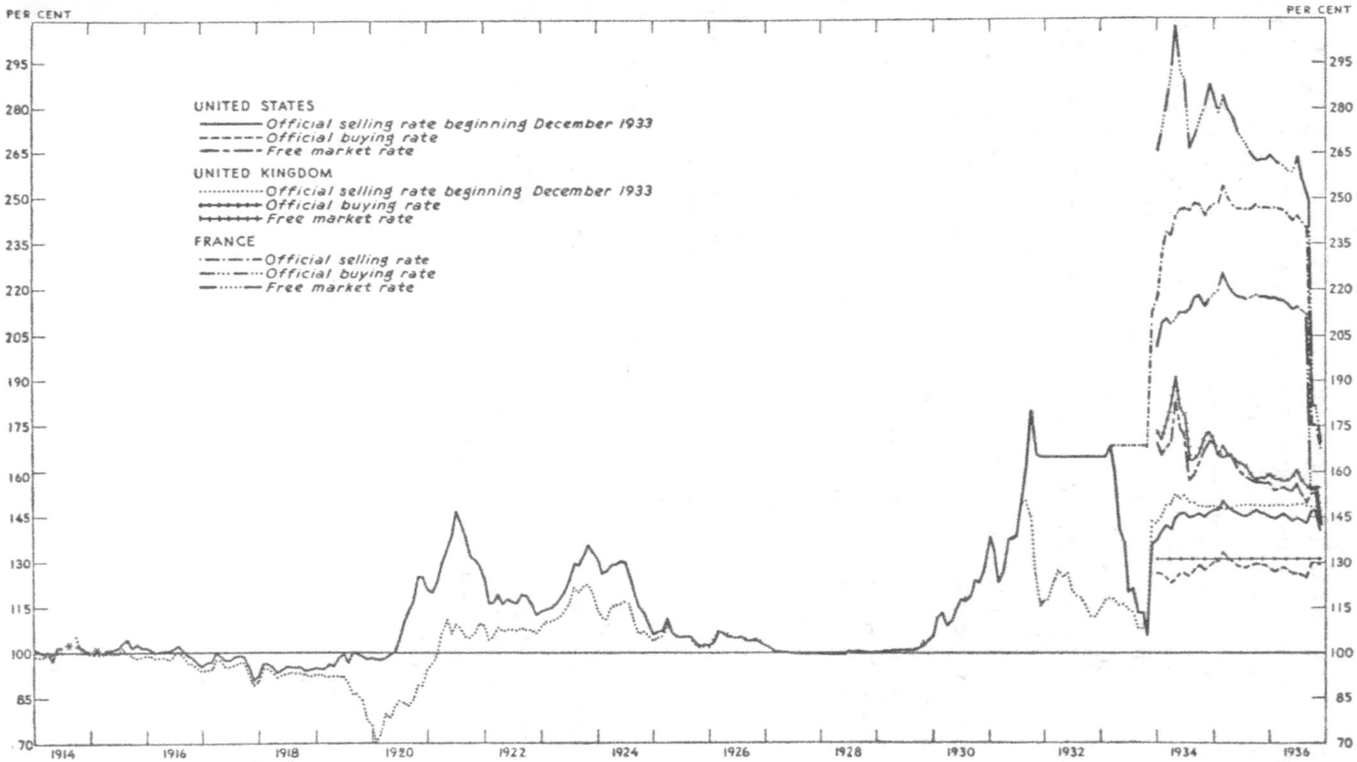

* Data not available

Sources: Computed from exchange rates obtained from sources cited in footnote 15, opposite page.

below par, leading to gold imports. The accompanying table, showing the quarterly movements, indicates more clearly than the annual data the shifts in the gold flow during these months. By June, however, sterling reached the gold export point, leading to a gold outflow which totaled 18,819,430 pesos for the second quarter of 1914, or a net export (less imports) of 17,433,696 pesos. Gold exports continued during the third quarter until the embargo of August ninth prohibited further shipments. The result was a net gold export for the twelve months, October 1, 1913 to September 30, 1914 of 32,600,000 gold pesos, which was indicative of the "adverse" balance of pay-

---

El Comercio Exterior, Boletíns No. 217, 219.
Free Market Rates:
Files of Finance Division, Bureau of Foreign and Domestic Commerce, Washington, D.C.

Great Britain:

1914–Mar. 1920: United States Federal Reserve Board, *op. cit.*, p. 598. Figures are rate as of tenth of each month (or nearest day for which quoted, i.e., ninth or eleventh) taken from *La Prensa*, Buenos Aires, and *Buenos Aires Herald.*

Apr.–May, 1920: Ernesto Tornquist and Company, *Business Conditions in Argentina*, No. 165.

June, 1920-Dec., 1922: London and Cambridge Economic Service, *Monthly Bulletin*, Vol. I, No. I, p. 18 (Jan. 23, 1923).

1923-25: Royal Economic Society, *Report on Current Economic Conditions*, Memorandum No. 2, p. 15 (July 1927).

1926-33: Banco de la Nación, *op. cit.*

1934-36:
Official Rates:
Dirección General de Estadística de la Nación, *op. cit.*
Free Market Rates:
League of Nations, *Monthly Bulletin of Statistics*, Jan. 1935, p. 30; Jan. 1936, p. 32; Jan. 1937, p. 32.

France:

1933: República Argentina, Dirección General de Estadística de la Nación, *op. cit.*, Boletín No. 217.

1934-36:
Official Rates:
Ibid.
Free Market Rates:
Argentine Republic, *Prospectus*, Sinking Fund External Conversion Loan Four Per Cent Bonds, April 22, 1937.

ments, and the decline in foreign borrowing. Upon resumption of foreign exchange transactions following the financial moratorium in August and September 1914, sterling continued above par, reaching its peak in October, after which it declined rapidly, going below par in January 1915. Since August 1914, gold exports from the United Kingdom had been prohibited.

TABLE VII
ARGENTINE GOLD EXPORTS AND IMPORTS
QUARTERLY FIGURES, 1912–14
(thousands of gold pesos)

	Imports	*Exports*	*Import Surplus*	*Export Surplus*
1912				
First Quarter	19,228	140	19,088	
Second "	9,610	140	9,470	
Third "	4,994	440	4,554	
Fourth "	2,246	5	2,241	
1913				
First Quarter	35,270	3	35,267	
Second "	10,251	12	10,239	
Third "	1,822	25,372		23,550
Fourth "	599	18,031		17,432
1914				
First Quarter	14,149	264	13,885	
Second "	1,386	18,819		17,433
Third "	635	12,211		11,576
Fourth "	1,790	—	1,790	

During most of the following "economic" year, 1914-15, sterling remained below par. The dollar was maintained at par, or close to it, until 1917, by the transfer of gold to Argentina.[16] Thus, in 1914-15, gold movements and exchange rates reflect

[16] A large portion of this gold was not actually shipped, however, but was deposited with the Argentine Legation in Washington. Similar deposits were made with the Argentine Legations in Europe during the War, reaching a total in 1918 of approximately 100 million pesos. As indicated in Table I, "International Income Account of Argentina, 1913-1935," Appendix I, opposite p. 238, of the total net increase in Argentine gold stocks in 1914-15 of 74 million gold pesos, only 3.4 millions were actually transferred, the balance being left with legations abroad.

again the shift to a "favorable" balance of payments, in contrast to the "adverse" balance of the previous year.

The "economic" year 1915-16 was a period of approximate equilibrium in Argentina's balance of payments.[17] Tornquist's

[17] I.e., "equilibrium," or equality, of current, or trade and service, transactions. There appears to be no consistent usage of the term "equilibrium" as applied to a country's international balance of payments. This lack of consistency is closely associated with the lack of a common definition of the term "balance of payments." If a country's "balance of payments" is defined as a "complete inventory of all payments passing the frontiers in either direction" (Carl Iverson, *Aspects of the Theory of International Capital Movements*, Copenhagen, 1935, p. 32), or as "embracing all the international transactions that must be settled during a definite period" (Bertil Ohlin, *Interregional and International Trade*, Cambridge, 1933, p. 381) then obviously the inward or "credit" payments of any period must be equal to the outward or "debit" payments, and thus the balance of payments may be said to be *always* in "equilibrium."

Parenthetically, it may be mentioned that this lack of consistency in the use of the term "equilibrium" is well illustrated in Iversons's recent study just cited. Although in his formal definition in Chapter I Iverson states emphatically that the "balance of payments is always in equilibrium" (p. 32), yet, when he analyzes the "classical" as contrasted with the "modern" theory of international capital transfers, he refers to "means of correcting *permanent disequilibrium*" (footnote 2, pp. 199-200—the writer's italics), and "exports necessary to re-establish the equilibrium" (p. 200); later, in discussing the paper standard mechanism of capital transfer, Iverson mentions "other possible disturbances of a given state of equilibrium" (p. 302), "disturbances upsetting a previous equilibrium in the balance of payments" (p. 313), "the disequilibrium in the balance of payments" (p. 319), "adjustment of price and income structures necessary to maintain equilibrium between gold-standard countries" (p. 321).

The term "balance of payments" is used also, however, to designate the "balance" of current transactions; that is, the difference between total payments and total receipts on trade and service items in a country's international accounts. This "balance" is covered then by gold (if gold is excluded from other commodity transactions) and capital movements. ("The balance of payments is . . . kept in equilibrium through international capital transactions." Ohlin, *op. cit.*, p. 507.) These capital movements are of two types, "real" and "equalising" (Iverson, *op. cit.*, p. 81). "Real" capital movements are "normal" international capital transactions (usually, but not always, long-term loans) which are "carried out for reasons unconnected with the state of the balance of payments" (J. L. K. Gifford, *The Devaluation of the Pound*, London, 1934, Chapter II, "General Theory of International Price Equilibrium and Equilibrium in the Balance of Payments," p. 11). "Equalising" capital movements, on the other hand, are those which are caused by, and tend to offset, a temporary deficit or difference in current transactions.

Under this terminology, when current transactions plus "normal" capital movements are equivalent, thus necessitating no gold or "equalising" capital

data, showing a relatively small "adverse" balance of 20.4 million pesos, are supported by the gold and exchange movements. Sterling, as well as the currencies of the warring nations, declined below par, because of the gold export embargoes. The dollar fluctuated closely about parity throughout the year. Net gold imports totaled 21.31 million pesos, but were offset partially by a decline in gold held abroad in legations of 10.7 million pesos, which left a net increase in the country's gold stock of 10.61 million gold pesos.

As previously indicated, during the succeeding "economic" year, 1916-17, the balance of payments turned again definitely in favor of Argentina, a condition which was to continue throughout the remainder of the War period. The net increase in gold stocks in Argentina totaled 36.86 million pesos, being partially offset again, however, by a net decrease in gold held abroad by legations of 5.04 million pesos, so that the estimated net increase in the country's gold stock was 31.82 million pesos.[18]

Argentina's international economic position during the four-year period from October 1913 to October 1917 may be summarized, then, as follows:

---

transactions, a country's international accounts may be considered as in a state of "equilibrium." Gifford (*op. cit.*, p. 11) uses the word "neutral" to describe this "even balance in the fundamental items," meaning thereby trade and service transactions plus "normal" capital movements. In the present study it has been statistically impossible, however, to segregate "real" from "equalising" capital movements, although it is probable that a major portion of such transactions between 1929 and 1934 were of the latter type. Therefore, for want of a less cumbersome term, throughout this study the term "equilibrium," as applied to Argentina's international accounts, will signify a condition of equality between current outgo (debit) and income (credit) items (excluding gold). Gold and capital movements, both "real" and "equalising," are then the "balancing" items. Strictly speaking, it might be contended that gold should be included with commodities as a current item, particularly under the "non-gold standard" conditions which were operative in Argentina during most of the period covered by this study. Due to its importance as a short-term balancing item, however, plus its significance as a monetary factor in influencing the ratios among the trade and service items, it has seemed expedient to include gold with capital movements.

[18] Most of these gold imports came from the United States, and as the following quarterly figures show, entered the country prior to the declaration of war and imposition of a gold embargo by the United States in April, 1917.

1. In the last year before the outbreak of the World War, Argentina's balance of payments was "adverse" to the extent of approximately 165 million pesos. This resulted in a net export of gold of 33 million pesos, plus an estimated increase in foreign borrowing of 132 million pesos, which was, however, probably some 50 to 75 million pesos less than the average annual foreign borrowing during the years just preceding. This decline in foreign borrowing was the result (part cause and part effect) of a combination of circumstances traceable to the Balkan War which reduced the willingness of European nations to lend freely to Argentina; this, in turn, accentuated a domestic liquidation and readjustment, following upon a decade of rapidly increasing expansion and prosperity, which had culminated in excessive land speculation and highly inflated land values.

Faced with an estimated "adverse" balance of payments, then, of 165 million gold pesos and with additional new loans not forthcoming from abroad to cover it in full, Argentina was forced to export gold to the extent of 33 million pesos for the balance.[19]

2. The impact of the outbreak of the War brought not only a cessation of long-term loans from abroad, but a demand for repayment of commercial and other short-term credits, which resulted in an estimated net decrease in foreign indebtedness of 41.40 million pesos in the "economic" year 1914-15. This shutting off of commercial credits, together with lack of shipping facilities and inability of Europe longer to supply imports previ-

GOLD IMPORTS INTO ARGENTINA

	gold pesos
Last quarter of 1916	6,772,000
First quarter of 1917	24,021,000
Second quarter of 1917	2,301,000
Third quarter of 1917	49,000

In this connection, see the discussion by John H. Williams in the *Quarterly Journal of Economics*, Vol. XXXIII, No. 3, May 1919, pp. 428-438, "Latin American Foreign Exchange and International Balances During the War."

[19] Any such causal interrelationships among various balance-of-payments items must, of course, be used and interpreted with extreme caution, since the interrelationships are so complex as to make it impossible to isolate a change in any one factor as being necessarily causal in changing another item.

ously obtained, resulted in a marked decrease in imports. Coupled with expanding exports (i.e., export values—volume increased only slightly) the result was to increase the export surplus to 288.9 million pesos, leaving Argentina with a "favorable" balance of payments of 115.8 million gold pesos. The difference between this balance and the estimated decrease in net foreign indebtedness of 41.4 million pesos was received in the form of gold imports (net) of 74.4 million pesos.

3. Increased imports in 1915-16 coupled with short-term borrowing abroad again resulted, however, in a slight "adverse" balance of payments.

4. By 1916-17 the balance again turned "favorable," as the value of exports increased rapidly, enabling Argentina to reduce her net foreign indebtedness by 62 million gold pesos, as well as to add 32 million pesos to her gold stock.

II. 1917-20: WAR-TIME PROSPERITY

The international economic position of Argentina during and immediately after the War was dominated by the tremendous European demand for foodstuffs which constitute the basis of Argentina's export trade. As with other neutral countries during the War, these were prosperous years for Argentina, and this prosperity is reflected in the country's international accounts.

Continuing the trend which became apparent in 1916-17, Table VIII (page 39) shows that Argentina's balance of payments was decidedly "favorable" in every year during this period. For the time being, Argentina even became an international lender, since, as shown in this table, the estimated net decrease in her foreign indebtedness took the form not only of repayments to foreigners of previous borrowings, but also of actual new loans by Argentina to foreigners.[20]

[20] These loans were largely of two types: (1) a governmental loan to Great Britain and France for 100 million gold pesos each, the proceeds of which were to be used in the purchase of Argentine grain; and (2) subscriptions to War loans, largely by European emigrants resident in Argentina.

A "credit exchange" agreement was also negotiated with the United States in January 1918 for 100,000,000 pesos. See John H. Williams, "Argentine Foreign Exchange and Trade Since the Armistice," *Harvard Review of Economic Statis-*

In 1917-18 exports were valued at over 150 million pesos greater than the preceding year, and by 1919-20 had reached an all-time record of over a billion pesos. These are value increases, it must be emphasized, however, and not volume.[21] Rapidly increasing prices for imports as well as for exports, however, largely offset increasing export values, so that the net export surplus remained relatively stable, averaging approximately 250 million pesos annually during the four-year period 1916/17–1919/20.

Although the annual debt service also remained relatively constant, other service remittances increased rapidly during the period, thus tending to reduce the balance in favor of Argentina. Notwithstanding this increase in service remittances, the "favorable" balance averaged approximately 100 million pesos annually during these four years. Of this "favorable" balance totaling 413 million gold pesos for the four years, nearly half was taken in the form of gold imports (176 million pesos or forty-two per cent), whereas the remaining 58 per cent constituted a reduction in Argentina's net international debtor position.

In each of his annual reports, beginning in 1916, Sr. Tornquist urged upon the leaders of his country the necessity for fundamental reforms in the administration of Argentina's economic life, pointing out that the abnormal war-time conditions could not survive the termination of the War. More specifically, he emphasized the fact that Argentina's markets for exports

tics, 1921, Vol. III, pp. 47-56, for a description of this agreement, duration, repayment, and effect on exchange rates. See also Williams, "Latin-American Foreign Exchanges and International Balances During the War," *Quarterly Journal of Economics*, Vol. XXXIII, May 1919, pp. 422-25. Williams erred, however, when he referred to this as a capital export, considering it the same type of transaction as the Anglo-French agreement. The latter was a genuine lending (debtor-creditor) transaction, but the former was simply an increase in ear-marked gold held abroad by Argentina, against which domestic peso currency was issued to the extent of 260 million gold pesos by the Bank of the Nation. Peters also implies that it was a capital lending transaction (H. E. Peters, *op. cit.*, p. 90). It does not appear as such (and correctly so) in Tornquist's Balance of Payments Statements, but is included in the figure for ear-marked gold (i.e., gold in legations abroad).

[21] See Chapter VI for detailed comparison of value and volume statistics of foreign trade.

TABLE VIII

THE ARGENTINE INTERNATIONAL ACCOUNTS, SUMMARY STATEMENT, "ECONOMIC" YEARS, 1917/18–1919/20
(in millions of gold pesos)

	1917–18	*1918–19*	*1919–20*
Commodity Trade:			
Exports	764.10	901.75	1,172.04
Imports	479.40	599.35	844.20
Export Surplus	284.70	302.40	327.84
Service Items: (net)			
Debt Service	145.60	148.90	144.44
Other Service	21.70	66.50	66.40
Total Service Items	167.30	215.40	210.84
Balance of Payments:	+117.40	+87.00	+117.00
Covered by:			
Net Decrease in Foreign Indebtedness	− 59.36	−75.10	− 38.48
Net Gold Imports	− 58.04	−11.90	− 78.52
	−117.40	−87.00	−117.00
Net Decrease in Foreign Indebtedness: (details)			
A. Receipts: (Income)			
1. Borrowing from Foreigners	180.19	21.90	109.79
2. Repayments by Foreigners	3.15	57.40	7.10
Total Receipts	183.34	79.30	116.89
B. Payments: (Outgo)			
1. Repayments to Foreigners	52.70	141.80	111.50
2. Loans to Foreigners	190.00	12.60	43.87
Total Payments	242.70	154.40	155.37
Net Decrease in Foreign Indebtedness:	− 59.36	−75.10	− 38.48

Source: See Appendix I, Table I: opposite p. 238.

would probably be curtailed. Furthermore, the reopening of more normal trade relations would probably bring a great increase of imports to meet a pent-up demand resulting from war-

time shortages. This influx of imports coupled with declining exports would produce a reversal in the international accounts of the country, unless remedies were adopted to prevent, and here Tornquist urged the adoption of a program of greater national self-sufficiency through the imposition of tariff protection for Argentine industries.[22]

That Sr. Tornquist's predictions were fully realized is, of course, now history, and is evidenced by the condition of Argentina's international accounts in the "economic" years following 1919-20. The beginning of the post-war liquidation and precipitous decline in prices is found, however, in the trade figures for the last three months of the "economic" year 1919-20; that is, the third quarter of the calendar year 1920. Quarterly figures of Argentina's foreign trade for the "economic" year 1919-20, as well as for the fourth quarter of 1920, are shown in the following table:

TABLE IX

ARGENTINA'S FOREIGN TRADE, OCTOBER 1919–DECEMBER 1920
QUARTERLY FIGURES
(in millions of gold pesos)

Quarter	*Imports*	*Exports*	*Balance*
4th 1919	191.17	311.79	+120.62
1st 1920	191.25	276.83	+ 85.58
2nd 1920	215.79	347.61	+131.82
3rd 1920	266.69	234.94	− 31.75
4th 1920	261.23	185.70	− 75.53

Source: República Argentina, Dirección General De Estadística, *El Comercio Exterior Argentino*, Boletín No. 211.

The accentuation of this trend is described in the next chapter, in which we shall find that Argentina's international accounts return to their pre-war status, that is, the balance again becomes "unfavorable," and continues so throughout every succeeding year until 1934, excepting 1930-31.

[22] Sr. Tornquist also advocated monetary and banking reform to relieve the rigidity of the currency system, and a policy of fostering immigration of foreign capital, rather than increasing social legislation which tended to reduce profits from capital and frighten away the foreign capitalists.

The movements of the foreign exchanges again support the conclusions reached above with respect to Argentina's balance of payments during the period October 1917-October 1920 (See Chart I, p. 49). As stated in the previous section, during the closing months of 1917 the peso value of both dollar and sterling exchange depreciated rapidly to a low point of some ten per cent below par. The marked recovery shown in January of 1918, and the relative stability throughout the suceeding year was largely the result of the loan of 200 million pesos granted to Great Britain and France by the Argentine Government.[23]

The removal of the peg on sterling in New York in March 1919, however, ended the close correspondence in the fluctuations of the dollar and sterling rates which had existed throughout the War, and was followed by a marked improvement in dollar exchange. The wide divergence between dollar and sterling exchange after the middle of 1919 was due primarily to the removal of the embargo on gold exports by the United States in June of that year, whereas British currency remained inconvertible.

That the balance of payments continued in Argentina's favor throughout 1919 and the first half of 1920 is evidenced by the heavy gold shipments during this period from the United States to Argentina, as well as the continued depreciation of both dollar and sterling exchange, the latter falling early in 1920 to

[23] Williams, *op. cit.* Tornquist, in his balance-of-payments statement for 1916-17, points out that these "grain conventions" (see footnote 20, p. 37 above) were highly desirable from Argentina's viewpoint for the following additional reasons: (1) they would encourage exports at remunerative prices, since they tended to raise the price of foreign currencies in terms of pesos; (2) they would help build up a "creditor position" which could be used after the War in buying necessary imports; (3) they would prevent further "serious perturbations in the monetary circulation" of Argentina by reducing the quantity of gold held abroad, against which paper pesos might be issued and injected into the domestic monetary circulation of Argentina. With respect to this point, Tornquist emphasized that the Anglo-French agreement was preferable to that with the United States, since the latter provided that paper money might be issued against the credits granted in the United States. In other words, as indicated above, the agreement with the United States was not a capital loan, as was the Anglo-French, but a gold ear-marking arrangement. Argentina simply held part of its gold reserves in New York.

a low point of 31 per cent below par. From June 1919 to June 1920, gold exports from New York to Buenos Aires totaled some 150 million dollars.

The overturn of the trade balance which occurred during the summer of 1920, and which presaged the development of a large "adverse" balance of payments for the succeeding "economic" year, 1920-21, is clearly reflected in the exchange rates.[24] During 1920 both sterling and the dollar appreciated rapidly, with the dollar reaching par in June, and touching a maximum of 25 per cent above par by November. This appreciation of the dollar (depreciation of the peso) occurred, notwithstanding the fact that during the summer of 1920 some 75 million pesos of funds in New York, held by the Banco de la Nación accruing from the "credit-exchange" agreement of 1918, were released to pay for Argentine imports. The exhaustion of these funds, together with the fact that Argentina's embargo on gold exports was not lifted, resulted in a further rapid appreciation of foreign currencies in terms of the peso, a situation which continued throughout the succeeding post-war period, as we shall see in the following chapter. The failure of the Argentine government to reopen the Conversion Office and remove the gold embargo during the period was severely criticized by certain groups, particularly by those who were interested in the import trade, since the high price of foreign currencies greatly increased the cost of imported articles.

[24] During this period, the trade balance was the dominating factor in the international accounts.

III

THE ARGENTINE INTERNATIONAL ACCOUNTS

1920-29

1. 1920-24: POST-WAR READJUSTMENTS

THE EFFECT of the post-war liquidation, which set in throughout the world late in 1920, upon the international economic position of Argentina is reflected in Table X, a summary of Argentina's balance of payments from 1920 to 1924. Beginning with the "economic" year 1920-21, the international accounts show a complete reversal of the war-time surpluses available for reduction of Argentina's foreign indebtedness.

Exports declined in value from 1,172.04 million pesos in 1919-20 to 716.31 million pesos in 1920-21, or roughly 39 per cent, the decline being a result of greatly diminished prices as well as reductions in volume. Imports failed to contract, however, to offset the decline in exports, resulting in a negligible export surplus totaling only 4.29 million pesos.[1] With service remittances remaining relatively constant, however, and thus requiring slightly over 200 million pesos, the result was an estimated "adverse" balance of 197.21 million pesos. Since Sr. Tornquist estimated a net reduction in the gold stock of 17.25 million pesos,[2] there was left a remainder of 179.96 million

[1] See Table X, footnote (a).

[2] The official embargo on gold exports was not lifted until May 1925, when Great Britain resumed the gold standard, and the Conversion Office was not reopened until August 1927. During this period, however, there had been a slight decline in the gold stocks held by the banks which Tornquist assumed as having been smuggled from the country, except for a very small sum carried by travelers and paid for ocean passage. According to official statistics, this latter sum in the calendar years 1921 and 1922 was, respectively, only 4,925 pesos and 6,600 pesos. República Argentina, Dirección General De Estadística de la Nación, *El Comercio Exterior Argentino en 1934 y 1933*, Boletín No. 215,

TABLE X

THE ARGENTINE INTERNATIONAL ACCOUNTS, SUMMARY STATEMENT, "ECONOMIC" YEARS, 1920/21–1923/24

(in millions of gold pesos)

	1920–21	*1921–22*	*1922–23*	*1923–24*
Commodity Trade:				
Exports	716.31	677.45	767.00	947.74
Imports[a]	712.02	567.74	761.00	822.59
Export Surplus	4.29	109.71	6.00	125.15
Service Items: (net)				
Debt Service	145.50	115.58	157.50	169.33
Other Service	56.00	45.50	44.00	49.00
Total Service Items	201.50	161.08	201.50	218.33
Balance of Payments:[a]	−197.21	− 51.37	−195.50	− 93.18
Covered by:				
Net Increase in Foreign Indebtedness	+179.96	+ 49.92	+193.60	+ 53.18
Net Gold Exports	+ 17.25	+ 1.45	+ 1.85	+ 40.00
	+197.21	+ 51.37	+195.50	+ 93.18
Net Increase in Foreign Indebtedness: (details)[b]				
A. Receipts: (Income)				
1. Borrowing from foreigners		211.16	213.10	231.43
2. Repayments by foreigners		91.20	—	—
Total Receipts		302.36	213.10	231.43
B. Payments: (Outgo)				
1. Repayments to foreigners		70.18	18.70	19.70
2. Loans to foreigners		2.30	.80	—
Total Payments		72.48	19.50	19.70
Net Increase in Foreign Indebtedness:		+229.88	+193.60	+211.73

[a] See Appendix I, p. 236, for the writer's estimated adjustments of the official import statistics for this item. Using official figures, Tornquist's "unfavorable" balance is much greater than the above, his figures for each year being respectively as follows: 1920–21, 322.21 million pesos; 1921–22, 151.37 million pesos; 1922–23, 280.50 million pesos; 1923–24, same as above, 93.18 million pesos.

[b] Tornquist gives figures for 1920/21–1921/22 and for 1923/24–1924/25 together. No breakdown has been attempted of the capital items. At best, they are highly conjectural.

Source: See Appendix I, Table I, opposite p. 238.

pesos presumably accounted for by an increase in net foreign indebtedness. Major items in this net change in foreign indebtedness were the repayment to Argentina of 84 million pesos of the British and French loans, plus a new short-term loan from New York bankers amounting to 66 million pesos.

The liquidation continued throughout 1921; early in 1922 healthier symptoms appeared, and by the end of the year marked improvement in industrial and business conditions was apparent. For the "economic" year 1921-22, exports were valued at 677.45 million pesos, only slightly less than the figure of 716.31 million pesos for the preceding year. Imports reflected, however, the effect of decreased purchasing power in Argentina, declining by approximately 150 million pesos, which left an export surplus of 109.71 million pesos.[3] There was, moreover, a marked decline in the sums required for service remittances, the estimated debt service decreasing from approximately 145 million pesos to 115 millions, and other service remittances from 56 million pesos to 45 million pesos. With total service items amounting to 161.08 million pesos, there remained a balance against Argentina on current items of 51.37 million pesos, which was covered very largely by an increase in net foreign indebtedness, since the decrease in the gold stock was estimated at only 1.45 million gold pesos.

By the end of 1922 the period of liquidation and readjustment was largely complete. Large stocks of exportable cereals had been disposed of, and the year closed with a steady demand for Argentina's basic products at improved prices. The gradual improvement which continued in 1923 we find reflected in the export statistics for the "economic" year 1922-23, exports being valued at 767 million pesos, an increase of approximately 90 million pesos over the preceding year. This increase was ac-

p. 83. For details of decrease in stocks of gold in the banks, see Appendix III, p. 263.

[3] As in the preceding year, the figure for imports is considerably under the official figure, having been reduced 100 million pesos to cover allowances for the loss on goods imported plus over-valuation in the official statistics. If one uses the official figure, the export surplus is practically wiped out. See Appendix I, p. 236.

companied, however, by a corresponding expansion in the import trade, so that the trade balance was again reduced to a negligible figure.[4] The strength of this demand for foreign merchandise is all the more significant since the peso was still depreciated in the foreign exchange market some 15 to 20 per cent.[5] An important factor offsetting peso depreciation which greatly stimulated imports during 1923, however, was a projected increase in Argentine customs duties which caused importers to purchase exceptionally large stocks in anticipation of the higher duties. Although the law was proposed in December 1922, it did not pass Congress until December of the following year. The effect of these abnormal imports is also indicated by the decline in the official statistics of imports in the following "economic" year 1923-24, in the face of rapidly increasing exports.

Notwithstanding Argentina's failure to develop a large export surplus in 1922-23, the debt service payments increased by upwards of 40 per cent, most of the increase being accounted for by enlarged railway revenues. This brought the total of estimated service remittances to 201.5 million gold pesos, which left an "adverse" balance on current items of 195.5 million pesos. With the official embargo on gold exports still in effect, this meant that the major portion of this balance must have been covered by a further increase in foreign indebtedness. Presumably a large part of this increase was in the form of short-term commercial credits to cover the unusual increase in imports.

During 1924 a general revival of business throughout the world increased the European demand for Argentina's products. Notwithstanding excellent crops which resulted in a new record for export volume, prices remained steady. This continued improvement is reflected in the international accounts for 1923-24

[4] According to official statistics, imports were valued at 846 million pesos, which gives an import surplus of 79 million pesos. This figure has been reduced by ten per cent, or 85 million pesos, to allow for over-valuation of imports plus losses suffered by foreigners on their sales in Argentina. During this period, large quantities of goods were shipped to Argentina on consignment, upon which foreign sellers often suffered large losses. See Carlos A. Tornquist, *Balance of Payments of the Argentine Republic, 1923-25*, Buenos Aires, p. 5.

[5] See Chart I, p. 31.

which show that the disastrous post-war period of liquidation had been largely completed. The value of exports reached nearly 950 million pesos, approaching again the war-time peak of 1,170 million pesos. Service remittances continued to increase, however, as business conditions improved, reaching a total of 218.33 million pesos. Because of the greatly increased export surplus, however, the "adverse" balance on current items was reduced to 93.18 million pesos, which was covered approximately one-half by gold exports and one-half by an increase in net foreign indebtedness.[6] Once again Argentina was approaching the "pay-as-she-goes" stage in her international transactions, a situation which was not to last long, however, since in the next "economic" year 1924-25, we shall find her again with a large "adverse" balance of payments which was met entirely by an increase in her net foreign obligations.

Reference again to Chart I, p. 31, shows that the fluctuations in peso exchange during this period were in accordance with Argentina's international economic position as indicated by the country's international accounts. The extreme depreciation of the peso in terms of the dollar during 1920-21 was reflected in the large "adverse" balance of payments totaling approximately 200 million pesos. The marked improvement in exchange rates in 1921-22 corresponds with the estimated reductions in the "adverse" balance of that year to some 50 million pesos. The reversal of this downward trend in the dollar rate during the "economic" year 1922-23 accords with the estimated increase in the "adverse" balance of payments again to nearly 200 million pesos. The downward trend in the exchange rates which was resumed again in 1923-24 corresponds with the reduction in the "unfavorable" balance of payments in that year to 45 million pesos. The release of 40 million pesos of gold for export was also a favorable factor. Sterling exchange, although still inconvertible, ruled above par throughout the period, parallelling to a

[6] A large portion of these gold exports was made by the government to pay foreign debt service. The restrictions on gold exports by private individuals was not removed until the following year (May 1925), when Great Britain returned to the gold standard.

marked degree, except during 1921, the fluctuations in dollar exchange. The extreme appreciation of the dollar, in terms of the peso, during 1921 was indicative of the large "adverse" trade balance which existed with the United States. Both sterling and the dollar continued to reflect seasonal fluctuations, falling during Argentina's spring and summer (October-May) when the crops are moved, and rising during the fall and winter months (May-October).

II. 1924-29: THE "NEW ERA" IN ARGENTINA

The prosperity of 1923-24 was short-lived. The "economic" year 1924-25 brought another poor crop, the adverse effect of which was accentuated by declining cereal prices. Both 1925 and 1926 were depression years in Argentina. As shown in Table XI, exports declined in 1924-25 to approximately 900 million gold pesos, or nearly 50 million pesos less than the total of 948 millions for the previous "economic" year. As has been generally true in Argentina, however, a lag resulted between the decrease in exports and a corresponding decline in imports; in fact, in this instance, imports actually increased. The result was a reduction in the export surplus to approximately 50 million pesos. With estimated service remittances declining only slightly (from 218.33 million to 202.77 million pesos), the country was again faced with an "adverse" balance of payments of nearly 150 million gold pesos. But, interestingly enough, notwithstanding this "adverse" current balance, we find Argentina with a slight increase in gold stocks totaling nine million pesos. The explanation of this anomalous situation is found in the fact that Argentina was embarking again upon a period characterized by extensive foreign borrowing, financed to a large degree by the New York money market.[7]

[7] The Argentine national debt (both long and short term) outstanding in the United States increased from 95 million pesos in 1923 to 339.8 million pesos in 1930. Increases in other government debt (i.e., provincial and municipal) plus estimated new private investments by the United States in Argentina during the same period of 413 million pesos, brought the total borrowings from the United States by 1930 to approximately 800 million gold pesos. See Chapter V, "Growth of Foreign Investments in Argentina," pp. 102-4.

Table XI

The Argentine International Accounts, Summary Statement, "Economic" Years, 1924/25–1928/29
(in millions of gold pesos)

	1924–25	*1925–26*	*1926–27*	*1927–28*	*1928–29*
Commodity Trade:					
Exports	903.56	792.50	960.95	1,048.90	1,001.05
Imports	850.84	744.70	816.60	843.50	881.70
Export Surplus	52.72	47.80	144.35	205.40	119.35
Service Items: (net)					
Debt Service	165.27	153.35	177.55	187.75	197.10
Other Service	37.00	37.00	59.00	54.00	51.00
Total Service Items	202.27	190.35	236.55	241.75	248.10
Balance of Payments:	−149.55	−142.55	− 92.20	− 36.35	−128.75
Covered by:					
Net increase in Foreign Indebtedness	+158.55	+144.20	+128.00	+186.85	+ 4.25
Gold Exports (net)					+124.50
Gold Imports (net)	− 9.00	− 1.65	− 35.80	−150.50	
	+149.55	+142.55	+ 92.20	+ 36.35	+128.75
Net Change in Foreign Indebtedness: (details)					
A. Receipts					
1. Borrowing from foreigners		166.20	162.40	165.35	62.60
2. Repayments by foreigners		—	—	35.20	—
Total Receipts		166.20	162.40	200.55	62.60
B. Payments					
1. Repayments to foreigners		5.70	23.20	13.70	40.65
2. Loans to foreigners		16.30	11.20	—	17.70
Total Payments		22.00	34.40	13.70	58.35
Net Increase in Foreign Indebtedness:		+144.20	+128.00	+186.85	+ 4.25

[a] See footnote (b), Table X, p. 44.

Source: See Appendix I, Table I, opposite p. 238.

The result was an estimated increase in net foreign indebtedness of about 160 million pesos in the "economic" year 1924-25.

As indicated in Table XI, this increase in foreign indebtedness continued throughout the four-year period, 1924/25-1927/28. In 1925-26 exports were still at a relatively low ebb, being valued at 792.5 million pesos. Lessened imports also, however, left an estimated export surplus of 47.8 million pesos.[8]

A slight reduction in service remittances left an estimated "adverse" balance for the year on current items of 142.55 million pesos. Nevertheless, as was true to an increasing degree throughout this four-year period, there was a slight net increase in gold stocks, so that the estimated net increase in foreign indebtedness was 144.20 million gold pesos.

The following year 1926-27 was one of excellent crops, which, although marketed at lower prices, increased the total value of Argentina's exports to 960.95 million pesos. This resulted in an export surplus of nearly 150 million pesos. Increasing prosperity, however, brought a marked increase in external service remittances. Tourist expenditures plus immigrant remittances were estimated to have increased from 45 to 65 million pesos. The increased public indebtedness incurred in previous years also increased the external public debt service by nearly 25 per cent over the preceding year (from 47 to 58 million pesos). Estimated total service remittances were increased, therefore, to 236.55 million pesos, leaving an estimated "adverse" balance of payments of 92.2 million pesos. The rapid growth of foreign borrowing, however, resulted in an estimated increase in net foreign indebtedness of some 40 per cent greater than was necessary to cover this "adverse" balance on current items. The surplus accruing from these foreign borrowings was accepted by Argentina in the form of increased gold imports, the addition to the country's gold stock being 35.8 million pesos.

These same trends in the international accounts were ac-

[8] According to official figures, these imports were valued at 844.7 million pesos resulting in an import surplus of 52.2 million pesos. The writer has again reduced the official figure to allow for estimated over-valuation and losses on imported merchandise suffered by foreign sellers. See Appendix I, p. 237.

centuated in 1927-28. The value of exports exceeded one billion pesos for the first time since 1920. Excellent crops were sold at relatively high prices, so that the value of exports gained over the preceding year by some 90 million pesos. Imports also increased (by 27 million pesos) but to a lesser degree, resulting in an export surplus slightly in excess of 200 million pesos, the first time it had exceeded that figure since the War. With total service remittances increasing only some five million pesos, the estimated "adverse" balance on current items was reduced to 36.35 million pesos, the lowest figure since 1915-16. But foreign borrowings continued to expand, increasing from 128 million pesos (net) in 1926-27 to 186.85 million pesos (net). With an "adverse" balance on current items of only 36.35 million pesos, Argentina received the balance of the proceeds of these loans in the form of an increase in the country's gold stock of 150.5 million pesos.[9]

The large gold imports since 1926 furnished the basis for an increased purchasing power and acceleration of domestic business activity. A further expansion of commodity imports during 1928-29 resulted,[10] total imports being valued at 881.7 million pesos, so that the export surplus was reduced from 205.4 million pesos to 119.35 millions, or by approximately 85 million pesos. Debt service, however, continued to increase, because of the increased borrowing of previous years, by some ten million pesos. This increase was offset by a slight decrease in other remittances, so that total net service remittances equaled slightly less than 250 million pesos. This sum was again, however, more than twice as great as the export surplus, thus producing an estimated "adverse" balance of payments of 128.75 million pesos. But, in marked contrast to the preceding years, this balance was not covered by an increase in net foreign indebtedness which, as

[9] Strictly speaking, of course (as previously indicated), no such causal relationship exists between any two items in a country's international accounts. In any given period all credit or income items are offset by an equivalent total of debit or outgo items, but it is difficult in most cases to allocate any specific credit item as being offset by a specific debit item.

[10] The lag referred to above should again be noted—i.e., exports reached their peak in 1927-28; imports, a year later.

shown in Table XI, dropped to the negligible figure of 4.25 million pesos. To meet this "adverse" balance a decrease in the country's gold stock of approximately 125 million pesos was required, thus canceling a large part of the increase in gold stocks of the previous "economic" year 1927-28, which had totaled 150.5 million pesos. This shift in the gold movement had begun in 1928. In the first half of the calendar year 1928 net gold imports amounted to 99.5 million pesos, whereas in the second half there was a net export of 13.2 million pesos.

In other words, the international accounts for 1928-29 reflected another turning point in Argentina's international economic transactions. The wave of new foreign borrowing of the previous four years which was largely fostered by the "new era" of plentiful funds in the United States came abruptly to a close. Public borrowing practically ceased; new private borrowings (estimated at approximately 60 million pesos and largely in the form of direct investments from the United States) were largely offset by repayments and loans to foreigners. These latter were in part the remittances of short-term funds to New York to take advantage of the high interest rates prevailing there during 1928-29.

The foreign exchange rates again corroborate the position of Argentina's international accounts just described, covering the five-year period 1924-29 (see Chart I, p. 31). Although the balance of payments on current items during the "economic" year 1924-25 was "adverse" to the extent of nearly 150 million pesos, the volume of foreign borrowings was sufficient to offset this pressure on the foreign exchanges, so that the trend of both dollar and sterling exchange was downward throughout the year, allowance being made again for the seasonal fluctuation. This trend continued throughout the following year, 1925-26, during which Argentina's "adverse" balance of payments on current items (excluding gold) was again exceeded slightly by net new borrowings.

By 1927 the plethora of foreign loans exceeded the "adverse" balance on current items. During the early part of the year, the peso rose above par (i.e., dollar and sterling exchange went

below par in Buenos Aires); gold imports increased which led to the reopening of the Conversion Office in August; in other words, the complete restoration of the gold standard, since the embargo on gold exports had been removed in May 1925, upon the resumption of specie payments by Great Britain.

During 1927-28 this situation became still further accentuated, as already described; new foreign borrowings greatly exceeded the "adverse" balance on current account, foreign gold currencies continued below par, and gold flowed in to the extent of over 150 million pesos. By June 1928, however, dollar and sterling exchange again rose above par and the gold flow was reversed, a condition which continued throughout the succeeding "economic" year, 1928-29, during which net gold exports totaled 124.5 million pesos.

Notwithstanding these large exports, both the dollar and sterling continued to appreciate throughout the year 1929, culminating in the suspension of gold payments in December, further reference to which will be made in the succeeding chapter.

IV

THE ARGENTINE INTERNATIONAL ACCOUNTS

1929-35

I. 1929-31: THE "GREAT DEPRESSION"

NEVER has the dependence of the Argentine economy upon world economic conditions been more clearly reflected than in the changes which occurred in her international accounts in the years subsequent to 1928. These changes are summarized in Table XII covering the "economic" years 1929-30 and 1930-31.

Exports in 1929-30 were valued at 661.3 million pesos, a decline of 339.75 million pesos over the previous "economic" year, or roughly 34 per cent. This precipitous decline (which was world-wide in scope and too familiar to require elaboration here) first became noticeable late in 1928, was accentuated in 1929, and continued through 1933. Although the following season brought excellent crops again, exports for the "economic" year 1930-31 were valued at 606.1 million pesos, some 50 million pesos less than the preceding year, thus reflecting the continued price decline. In fact, with the exception of the "economic" year 1929-30, the decline in the total value of Argentina's exports after 1928 was due almost entirely to falling prices, as the statistics in Table XIII indicate.

Imports failed again to contract sufficiently to offset the continued decline in exports, so that for the "economic" year 1929-30, we find Argentina with an "adverse" trade balance totaling 117.6 million gold pesos. This lag in the decline of imports during periods of recession which characterized Argentine foreign trade during the period covered by this study has already been alluded to in connection with the post-war decline of 1920-21 and again in the somewhat less severe reaction of 1924-25.

TABLE XII

THE ARGENTINE INTERNATIONAL ACCOUNTS, SUMMARY STATEMENT, "ECONOMIC" YEARS, 1929/30–1930/31
(in millions of gold pesos)

	1929–30	*1930–31*
Commodity Trade:		
Exports	661.30	606.10
Imports	778.90	546.60
Export Surplus		59.50
Import "	117.60	
Service Items: (net)		
Debt Service	180.00	163.00
Other Service	43.00	30.00
Total Service Items	223.00	193.00
Balance of Payments:	−340.60	−133.50
Covered by:		
Net Change in Foreign Indebtedness:		
Increase	+276.60	
Decrease		− 37.50
Gold Exports: (net)	+ 64.00	+171.00
	+340.60	+133.50
Net Change in Foreign Indebtedness: (details)		
A. Receipts: (Income)		
1. Borrowing from foreigners	283.20	59.00
2. Repayments by foreigners	16.80	50.10
Total Receipts	300.00	109.10
B. Payments: (Outgo)		
1. Repayments to foreigners	3.40	106.60
2. Loans to foreigners	20.00	40.00
Total Payments	23.40	146.60
Net Change in Foreign Indebtedness:		
Increase	276.60	
Decrease		37.50

Source: See Appendix 1, Table I, opposite p. 238.

The sequence of events causing this lag was, briefly, as follows. During periods of increasing export surpluses (frequently paralleled by new borrowing from abroad) bank reserves tended to increase, credit expanded, and imports were stimulated, but with a lag between expanding exports and increased imports. Later, when exports were restricted, credit was not always restricted at once to offset the decline in exports. In this period in Argentina (1929-31), credit was not restricted as a result of two

TABLE XIII

QUANTITY AND VALUE OF ARGENTINE EXPORTS, 1927–34

Calendar year	*Thousands of tons*	*Millions of gold pesos*	*Millions of gold dollars*[a]	*Millions of current dollars*[a]
1927	18,740	1,009	974	
1928	17,029	1,055	1,017	
1929	16,703	954	908	
1930	11,027	614	514	
1931	18,477	641	427	
1932	15,826	567	344	
1933	13,777	493	276	359
1934	15,252	633	253	474

[a] Converted at average annual rate of exchange.

Source: Dirección General de Estadística, *El Comercio Exterior Argentino*, Boletín No. 211, pp. 7 and 32; Boletín No. 215, p. 42.

important factors, both interrelated; namely, the suspension of gold payments in December 1929, and the large volume of government short-term borrowing outstanding in the form of bank credits.

Had gold payments been maintained, presumably the continued gold exports would have brought a further decline in the means of payment within Argentina, both as a result of the necessary contraction of currency in circulation, as well as a reduction in bank credits which reduced gold reserves would have required. Such a reduction in purchasing power would have been reflected in decreased imports, leading to a restoration of equilibrium in the balance of payments.[1] As explained in greater

[1] See pp. 75-76 below for more detailed discussion of this point.

detail below,[2] Argentina's currency system was extremely inelastic, inasmuch as the withdrawal of gold from the Conversion Office meant the retirement of an equivalent sum of paper money from circulation. Fear that this inelasticity would (if permitted to exert its effect) lead to a rapid internal deflation resulted, however, in the suspension of gold payments, thus freeing the Conversion Office of the requirement of exchanging gold for paper notes, and removing the necessity for further currency contraction.[3] Furthermore, additional emergency measures were taken in 1931 and in 1932 looking to an expansion of the currency.[4]

Under a régime of inconvertibility, the restoration of equilibrium in the balance of payments comes as a result of the changes in the external value of the currency, that is, the depreciation of the currency tends to increase the cost of imports and other external payments, and thus brings about a reduction in their volume.[5] That this failed to occur with greater rapidity in Argentina during 1930, notwithstanding a rapid decline in the foreign exchange value of the peso, was due in large part to the second factor mentioned above; namely, the large volume of government short-term paper held by the banks which was the accumulated result of continued government budgetary deficits. These deficits were caused by large public-works expenditures, as well as other government expenses. The policy had been to allow these credits to accumulate, and then to fund them in a long-term loan, usually from abroad, but the cessation of foreign lending had, for the time being, prevented such a policy. This government floating debt, totaling approximately one-third of the bank credit outstanding, was also a factor in the decision to suspend gold payments; since the government floating debt could not be liquidated, the further decline in bank credit, which gold exports would have necessitated, would have meant that the contraction of bank loans would have fallen entirely upon private borrowers

[2] P. 89.

[3] Gold exports were not prohibited.

[4] See below, footnote 59, p. 92, for a description of these measures.

[5] See below, pp. 76-77.

with presumably disastrous results.[6] Furthermore, budgetary deficits continued to increase. This utilization of bank credit by the government continued to pump purchasing power into circulation, thus maintaining the demand for imported goods in excess of what it might have been had the budgetary deficits not existed.[7] This failure of imports to contract more rapidly led to still greater depreciation of the peso.[8]

Regardless of what might have happened under other circumstances, with estimated foreign service remittances declining only from their peak of 248.1 million pesos in 1928-29 to 223 million pesos in 1929-30, the international accounts of Argentina showed a deficit on current items for the latter year of approximately 340 million pesos, an "adverse" balance greatly exceeding that of the post-war decline in 1920-21, when the estimated deficit was slightly under 200 million pesos. Thus was the "New Era" in Argentina succeeded by the "Great Depression."

With net gold exports reduced to 64 million pesos, the remainder of the deficit amounting to 276.6 million pesos was presumably covered by an increase in Argentina's net foreign indebtedness, primarily by foreign borrowing of the "forced" variety, a considerable portion of which was public.[9]

By 1931, however, significant readjustments were developing, so that for the "economic" year 1930-31, the balance of payments, as shown in Table XII, was much less "unfavorable" than that

[6] See Peters, *op. cit.*, p. 156.

[7] Banco de la Nación, *Economic Review*, September 1930, p. 124.

[8] With gold prices falling throughout the world, however, the internal deflation in Argentina was less severe than if the country were still on a gold basis. See more detailed discussion of this point below, pp. 92-94.

[9] Lawrence Smith, "Suspension of the Gold Standard in Raw Material Exporting Countries," *American Economic Review*, September 1934, p. 436. By "forced" borrowing, Smith meant that remittances due abroad simply were not made, since current supplies of foreign currencies available for such remittances were inadequate. The result was curtailment of interest and dividend remittances in many cases; that is (in effect), "forced" temporary borrowing plus the negotiation of public short-term loans. The most important of these public loans were a six-months' 50 million peso loan placed in the United States in April 1930 (renewed for one year in October), plus one for 85 million pesos negotiated with Baring Brothers in London in June 1930. According to Peters, *op. cit.*, p. 158, these loans were unwise, since renewal was refused in 1931 when the situation had become worse rather than better.

for the preceding year. Although the value of exports declined still further, as already indicated,[10] imports contracted rapidly, the decline from the previous "economic" year being some 232 million pesos, or roughly 30 per cent. During 1931 the effect of the depression on internal purchasing power became increasingly severe. It was a year of great monetary stringency, and bank credit was finally beginning to contract.[11] Furthermore, the accumulated maladjustment in the balance of payments caused the peso to depreciate rapidly in the foreign exchange markets. This decline in the external purchasing power of the peso, aided by increased customs duties, restricted imports sufficiently to give Argentina an export surplus for the year 1930-31 of approximately 60 million pesos. At the same time, estimated external service remittances declined from 223 million pesos to 193 millions.[12]

The net result was a reduction in the "adverse" balance on current items in Argentina's international accounts to 133.5 million gold pesos, in contrast to the "adverse" balance of the previous "economic" year (1929-30) of some 340 million gold pesos. This "adverse" balance of 133.5 million pesos was more than offset by gold exports, which totaled 171 million pesos (net).[13]

In other words, if gold exports are included with commodity exports as an "income" item, Argentina closed the year with a "favorable" balance of payments, that is, an estimated decrease in net foreign indebtedness of 37.5 million pesos.

[10] The volume of exports increased 67 per cent in 1931 over 1930.

[11] *Economic Review*, *op. cit.*, April-June, 1934, p. 52.

[12] Estimated railway interest and dividend payments remitted abroad declined from 70 million pesos in 1929-30 to 56 million pesos in 1930-31, or by 14 million pesos. Other service items (immigrant remittances and tourist expenditures) also declined 15 million pesos.

[13] Approximately 100 million pesos of these gold exports were used to cover interest payments on the public debt held abroad; the remaining 70 million was used for exchange operations in an attempt to stabilize the foreign exchange rate of the peso. It will be recalled that gold exports were not prohibited in 1929, merely the paying out of gold by the Conversion Office. In October 1930, however, a government decree provided for the withdrawal of gold from the Conversion Office to be used in meeting interest payments abroad on the national debt, a provision which was extended on December 31 to cover local government units and exchange stabilization.

II. 1931-35: THE "NEW DEAL" IN ARGENTINA

As stated previously, the 1930-31 balance of payments for Argentina was the last statement to be compiled by Sr. Tornquist. Since October 1931, Argentina's foreign exchange transactions have been subject to the regulation of an Exchange Control Commission (Comisión de Control de Cambios), with reference to which Sr. Tornquist, in his last Balance of Payments statement, made the following comment:

Before analysing the result of the study of the Balances of Payments of these two economic years [1929-30 and 1930-31], it is necessary to point out that the data required for these ends are becoming more and more accessible and that the information required from public offices and private institutions is obtainable in a more complete form than heretofore.

At the present time, more people are devoting themselves to this class of study, and there is a constantly increasing interest in the composition of Balance of Payments, this owing to the influence of the economic and financial factors which are agitating the world and which are exacting the application of legislative measures in respect of which it is particularly useful to know the composition and definite outcome of the Balance of Payments.

The intense reaction on economic and financial affairs caused by the exceptional happenings affecting the world at large has greatly increased in recent times the tendency to study economic and financial problems. This class of study has been taken up by a large number of people engaged in scientific or practical tasks.

It is to be hoped that in the future it will be possible to draw upon even more and better material for the compilation of the Balance of Payments, once the Exchange Control Committee created in October of last year has given out all the information in its possession. In the Balance of Payments, there are, however, still certain items which cannot be reckoned with any great degree of certainty. There is reason to believe that in this respect the details accumulated by the Exchange Control Committee will fill the gap and will throw light on certain remittances abroad which it has been only possible in the past to calculate approximately on the strength of banking and other information. It will then be possible to draw up a balance of payments with a minimum of errors and without items of any importance

which, as at present, cannot be represented in figures as a part of the Balance of Payments. This applies to the transfer of capital by private individuals in the ways and for the ends which are known.[14]

The Exchange Control Commission has published statements showing the purchases and sales of foreign exchange since October 18, 1931. These statements are not a true balance of payments, however, since they include only actual purchases and sales of exchange by the Commission. They do not include free market operations (both official and "bootleg"), nor do they take into account the claims for foreign currencies which are not covered, that is, the piling up of blocked funds in Argentina.

Estimates of the Argentine balance of payments for the calendar years 1932-35 have been compiled by the new Central Bank of Argentina, however, and are summarized in Table XIV.[15]

During the fourth quarter of 1931, Argentina's official trade figures showed an export surplus of 64 million pesos, which was presumably sufficient to cover external service remittances. As indicated in Table XII, such remittances had totaled 193 million pesos during the preceding twelve months, or a quarterly average of 48 million pesos. Furthermore, for the "economic" year 1930-31, Argentina's balance of payments, it will be recalled, showed an estimated net decrease in foreign indebtedness of 37.5 million gold pesos. Notwithstanding an estimated "favorable" balance of 14 million pesos on current items for the last three months of 1931, Argentina exported 24 million pesos in gold during the quarter, thus reducing her estimated net foreign indebtedness by an additional 38 million pesos. From October 1, 1930, to December 31, 1931, this was an estimated total decrease of 76 million pesos. During 1931 Argentina repaid short-term loans

[14] Carlos A. Tornquist, *Balance of Payments of the Argentine Republic in the Economic Years 1929-30 and 1930-31*, Buenos Aires, 1932, p. 3.

[15] These estimates were placed at the writer's disposal through the courtesy of Sr. C. Alonso Irigoyen, Financial Attaché, Argentine Embassy, Washington, D.C. They have since been published by the Institute of International Finance, New York City, in Bulletin No. 86, *Credit Position of Argentina*, June 1, 1936. An estimate of Argentina's foreign exchange requirements for 1933 also appeared in Banco de la Nación, *Economic Review*, Buenos Aires, January-March 1934, pp. 4-5.

TABLE XIV

THE ARGENTINE INTERNATIONAL ACCOUNTS, SUMMARY STATEMENT, OCTOBER 1, 1931–DECEMBER 31, 1935 (in millions of gold pesos)

	Oct.–Dec., 1931[a]	*1932*	*1933*	*1934*	*1935*
Commodity Trade:					
Exports		574[b]	500	730	766
Exporters' Profits		18	15	22	23
Total Exports[a]	165	592	515	752	789
Imports	101	368	395	484	524
Export Surplus	64	224	120	268	265
Service Items: (net)					
Debt Service		211	191	221	215
Other Services		73	38	47	45
Total Service Items	50	284	229	268	260
Balance of Payments:	+14	−60	−109	000	+ 5
Covered by:					
Net Change in Foreign Indebtedness:[c]					
Increase		+52	+ 90		
Decrease	−38			−7	−12
Gold Exports: (net)	+24	+ 8	+ 19	+7	+ 7
	−14	+60	+109	000	− 5

[a] For the period Oct.–Dec., 1931 trade statistics are from *El Comercio Exterior Argentino*, Boletín 211; service items are estimated on basis of figures for the previous "economic" year; statistics of gold exports from *Economic Review*, Jan., 1932, p. 15.

[b] Official statistics of exports are less than the figures contained in the "Balance of Payments" of the Central Bank, as follows:

(in millions of gold pesos)

	1932	*1933*	*1934*	*1935*
Balance of Payments	574	500	730	766
Official statistics	567	493	633	690
Difference	7	7	97	76

The large discrepancy in 1934 and 1935 was due to the calculation of exports in the official statistics at the official buying rate of exchange, whereas the figure in the balance of payments was reached by converting the foreign exchange at the official

in New York and London totaling 50 million pesos. Furthermore, Tornquist estimated the "flight of capital" for the "economic" year 1930-31 at 40 million pesos.[16]

In the calendar year 1932, exports declined in value to 592 million gold pesos, including estimated exporters' profits of 18 million pesos. Excluding exporters' profits, this was a 12 per cent decrease from the preceding calendar year when exports totaled 641 million pesos. Imports declined in value, however, from 516 million pesos in 1931 to 368 million pesos in 1932, or roughly 29 per cent. This decline in the value of imports in 1932 was the result, in part, of the action of the Exchange Control Commission in restricting sales of exchange to necessary imports, and the unwillingness of many foreign exporters to permit additional blocked funds to pile up in Argentina.

This relatively greater decline in imports gave Argentina an export surplus for 1932 of nearly 224 million gold pesos. With

---

selling rate, which averaged about 14 per cent above the official buying rate. The 1932 and 1933 figures were converted at the average official rates.

[a] Includes figure for unestimated, or residual item, as follows:

(in millions of gold pesos)

	1932	*1933*	*1934*	*1935*
Residual	+54	+99	−74	−70
Net change omitting residual	− 2	− 9	+67	+58
	+52	+90	−7	−12

Source: See Appendix I, Table I, opposite p. 238.

[16] Purchases and sales of exchange by the Exchange Control Commission for the period October 13-December 31, 1931, were as follows:

Purchases	(millions of gold pesos)
Exports	140
Miscellaneous	38
Total	178
Sales	
Imports	149
Service Items	36
Total	185

The excess of sales was covered by gold exports of ten million pesos. The balance of gold exports of 14 million pesos (see Table XIV) was exported directly by the Banco de la Nación to cover debt service in the United States.

total service remittances estimated at 284 million pesos, this left Argentina with an "adverse" balance on current items for 1932 of 60 million pesos. Since gold exports for the year equaled only eight million pesos, there resulted an estimated net increase in foreign indebtedness of 52 million pesos.[17]

This reappearance of disequilibrium in Argentina's balance of payments during 1932 was accentuated in 1933. As indicated in Table XIV, the total value of exports in 1933 (including exporters' profits) equalled 515 million pesos; this was a decline of approximately 15 per cent from the 1932 total of 592 million pesos. At the same time, imports increased in value from 368 million pesos in 1932 to 395 million pesos, or roughly seven per cent. The result was a decline in the export surplus to 120 million pesos, or approximately 100 million pesos less than in 1932. This meant that once again Argentina's trade balance fell far short of

[17] The balance of payments figures for imports and other remittances for 1932, compared with actual purchases and sales of exchange for these items, were as follows:

(millions of gold pesos)

	Balance of Payments	*Exchange Purchases and Sales*	*Difference*
Exports	574[a]	554	—20
Imports	368	320	+48
	206	234	+28
Other Items: (net)	266[a]	233	+33
Balance	—60	+1	+61

[a] Exporters' Profits included with "Other Items."

For 1932, then, exchange allocations for imports were 48 million pesos less than actual imports (as recorded in the official statistics). This sum is offset by the amount by which recorded exports exceeded exchange purchases derived from exports, or 20 million pesos. Disregarding transactions in "bootleg" exchange and lags, presumably there was a net increase in blocked pesos on "visible," i.e., commodity transactions, of some 28 million pesos. In addition, estimated "invisibles" due abroad for the year exceeded exchange allocations for these items by 33 million pesos, or a combined total on both "visible" and "invisible" items of some 60 million pesos. Deducting gold exports for the year of eight million pesos, we arrive at an estimated total of slightly over 50 million gold pesos as representing the net increase in blocked funds in Argentina for the year 1932.

meeting her other current external obligations in the form of debt and other service remittances, which for 1933 were estimated at 229 million gold pesos (net).

An important factor in this reappearance of disequilibrium in Argentina's balance of payments was the rate at which the peso had been pegged since the institution of exchange control in October 1931. From November 26, 1931 to March 4, 1933, the peso was pegged to the dollar at 171 pesos per 100 dollars, or 58.4 cents (old U. S. gold dollars) per gold peso.[18]

When the United States went off the gold standard in March 1933, the peso peg was shifted to the French franc at 14.69 francs per gold peso (equivalent to 57.4 cents, U. S. old gold dollar). This rate was maintained until November 1933, at which time, due to the unfavorable factors which arose during the preceding months, the exchange control system was revised to provide for prior exchange permits and the auctioning of available foreign exchange, to which we shall refer in more detail shortly.

Apparently, this rate of 14.69 francs per gold peso at which the peso was pegged was too high, since imports continued to increase, and blocked funds to accumulate in Argentina.[19] In

[18] Former par was approximately 96.48 cents per gold peso. See Chart I, p. 31.

[19] The comparative figures for Argentina's estimated balance of payments and foreign exchange transactions for the year 1933 are as follows:

(millions of gold pesos)

	Balance of Payments	*Exchange Purchases and Sales*	*Difference*
Exports	500*	459	+ 41
Imports	395	285	—110
	105	174	— 69
Service Remittances	214*	174	— 40
	—109	0	—109

* Exporters' Profits included with Service Remittances.

For 1933, exchange allocations for imports were 110 million pesos less than recorded imports (excluding that portion of financial remittances which went for fuel and equipment of public utilities). Deducting the excess of actual exports from the total exchange derived from exports, that is, 41 million pesos, there remained an estimated *net* increase in blocked funds on "visible" trade

other words, as long as the price of foreign currencies was maintained at a (relatively) low level, the cost of imports to the Argentine importer was held down, thus encouraging him to continue to make purchases abroad. On the other hand, if the peso had not been held at the pegged level set by the Exchange Control Commission, that is, if the increasing volume of blocked pesos in Argentina could have been effective in a free market, the exchange rate would have been depressed, thus increasing the cost of new imports. Eventually the accumulation of blocked pesos would have curtailed imports (due to unwillingness of foreign sellers to leave their funds in Argentina), but this might have been a slow process, since importers had adopted the policy of using the exchange they obtained in the payment of old debts, and then incurring new external obligations in the hope of obtaining exchange later to meet them.

The increase in imports during 1933 was probably fostered not only by the high external value of the peso, but also by: (1) the increase in note circulation resulting from the payment of salaries and other government accounts in arrears from the proceeds of a large internal loan (the so-called Patriotic Loan of 1932), a large portion of which was obtained by the deposit of the bonds as collateral—that is, simply currency expansion;[20] (2) funding during 1933 of some 143 million gold pesos (325 million paper pesos) of blocked funds which, no doubt, alleviated the position of many dealers in foreign goods.

The foreign exchange problem which confronted the Argentine government late in 1933 was, then, twofold, involving first, the liquidation of the large volume of blocked pesos which had accumulated, and which was weighing heavily upon the market, plus, secondly, the task of preventing renewed accumulations of unpaid external obligations in the future.

---

of 69 million pesos. Again, estimated service remittances due in 1933 were 40 million pesos more than actual exchange allocations, making the estimated total increase in blocked funds 109 million pesos. Subtracting the gold exports of 19 million pesos for the year, there remained an estimated *net* increase in blocked funds of 90 million pesos, which was equivalent to the estimated net increase in foreign indebtedness for 1933 in Table XIV.

[20] See Appendix III, p. 263.

The first problem was solved by the negotiation of foreign loans with her creditors during 1933, as stated above, totaling some 143 million gold pesos,[21] a sum which approximated the estimated "adverse" balance of payments (including gold) for the two-year period 1932-33 of 142 million pesos.[22]

The second aspect of the problem, that of preventing renewed accumulation of blocked funds, was met by a reorganization of the exchange control system, the chief provisions of which were as follows:

(1) A free, as well as an official, exchange market was established; that is, the proceeds of specified exports and other foreign transactions, such as capital investments, were not required to be sold to the Exchange Control Commission, but could be disposed of in the open market.[23]

[21] These funding loans were distributed as follows:

	(in millions of pesos)	
	gold pesos	*paper pesos*
Sterling	82.8	188.2
Dollar	26.6	60.4
Others: (French, Dutch, German, Swiss, Belgian, Italian)	33.6	76.4
Total	143.0	325.0

[22] See Table XIV above, p. 62.

[23] These products were in general those whose export it was desired to encourage. Such items totaled, however, only about five per cent of Argentina's total exports. The principal products excepted, including those added subsequent to the original list, were as follows:

Butter	Cotton linters	Tanned hides
Casein	Corn bran	Yerba maté
Wool[a]	Skins of wild animals	Mica
Frozen turkeys and ducks	Broom straw	Alfalfa seed
Onyx	Garlic	Tobacco
Honey	Fish guano and fish meal	Fruit in general
Millet	Wine	Glands

[a] Sale of wool permitted at seventeen paper pesos to the pound sterling, less five per cent to cover possible exchange fluctuations, instead of 15 pesos to the pound sterling, effective Oct. 25, 1934—a compromise upon petition by wool producers and exporters for exchange at the free market rates. This special rate was later reduced, and on Dec. 10, 1936 was abolished.

(2) All other exchange was still required to be turned over to the Exchange Control Commission at its official buying rate, which on November 28, 1933, when the new system was inaugurated, was raised 20 per cent; that is, from 14.69 francs to 12.38 francs per gold peso. In terms of gold currencies, this lowering of the pegged or official rate for the peso was equivalent to a total depreciation since 1929 of approximately 47 per cent, or equivalent to $.51 (U. S. old gold dollars) per gold peso. On January 19, 1934, the peg was changed from the franc to the pound sterling; the official buying rate for exporters' bills being set at the rate of 15 paper pesos per pound, which rate is still (May 1937) maintained.[24] This was equivalent in gold currencies to a depreciation which averaged approximately 49 per cent for the month of January 1934.

(3) These purchases of exchange by the Exchange Control Commission were to be sold thereafter, however, through the medium of a daily auction based upon a system of prior permits; that is, in order to be eligible to bid for exchange in the official market, it was necessary to obtain permits prior to the importation of goods. Bids were accepted daily, and filled, beginning with the highest, until all the exchange available that day was disposed of; the average rate and the lowest bid accepted were then published, and served as a guide for bids on subsequent days. Those persons lacking official permits were forced to buy their exchange in the free market, where the rate has ruled above the official selling rate.[25]

That the peso had been pegged too high is evidenced by the course of the selling rate for pesos subsequent to November 1933. A spread immediately arose between the buying rate (which was fixed abitrarily) and the selling rate (which was determined by supply and demand forces).[26] The average official selling rate during the week ending December 9, 1933 was 15.97 paper pesos per pound sterling, a spread of 3.9 per cent. By the second week in March this rate had increased to 17.13, or a spread of 14.2 per cent. Furthermore, the free market rate held well above the

[24] See Chart I, p. 31.

[25] *Ibid.*

[26] *Ibid.*

official rate, averaging from (approximately) 19 to 21 pesos during the first three months of 1934.

With respect to the pegged rate prior to November 28, 1933, these selling rates were equivalent to a depreciation in the official market ranging from 18.9 per cent during the first week in December, 1933 to 30.4 per cent during the second week in March, and in the free market ranging from 37.8 per cent for the week ending December 30, 1933 to 40.5 per cent for the week ending March 10, 1934. In terms of the old gold par (pre-December, 1929), this was a depreciation ranging roughly from 52 to 58 per cent in the official market, and from 63 to 65 per cent in the free market.

How far the peso might have depreciated during 1932 and 1933 had exchange control not been instituted in October, 1931, and the rate subsequently pegged, is, of course, impossible to say. In terms of gold currencies, however, the trend of rapid depreciation during 1930 and 1931 (to October), as shown in Chart I, if projected through 1932 and 1933, is continued in the official and free rates for the franc in 1934, when the peg was removed. In terms of dollar and sterling currencies, their respective rates in the official and free markets during 1934 are perhaps significant with respect to their possible rates during 1932 and 1933, had the peso not been pegged.

The spread which immediately arose between the official buying and selling rates for exchange has continued, resulting in large profits accruing to the Exchange Profits Fund (Fondo de Beneficios de Cambio).[27] These profits during 1934, 1935, and 1936 were as follows:

[27] During 1934 the official selling rate for sterling exchange ranged from (monthly averages) 16.44 paper pesos to 17.44 paper pesos per pound sterling, compared with the pegged buying rate of 15 paper pesos per pound. Other currencies showed a similar spread. Furthermore, the Exchange Control Commission made some sales in the free market, where the sterling rate for 1934 ranged from 18.66 to 21.88 pesos per pound. During 1935 the official rate for sterling ranged from 16.91 to 17.03 paper pesos per pound, and the free rate from 18.04 to 19.48 pesos per pound.

On January 2, 1936, the auctioning of exchange by bids was abolished. Since that date the Central Bank determines the selling rates for exchange on the following basis: Sales up to 1,000 pesos are made at a selling rate fixed each morning by the Central Bank. On sales over 1,000 pesos, holders of permits

	(millions of pesos)	
	paper	*gold*
1934	119.2	52.4
1935	118.1	52.0
1936	91.5	40.3
Total	328.8	144.7

It was precisely for the purpose of having these profits accrue to the Argentine Government that the auction system was introduced in November 1933, since at that time it was the stated purpose of the Government that the modification of the exchange regulations, accompanied by a further depreciation of the peso, was not only to effect a better equilibrium in the balance of payments, but also to improve the prices of agricultural and pastoral products which would result from the increased value in paper pesos of the foreign drafts obtained from their sale abroad.[28] It was feared, however, particularly with respect to the international grain markets, that as a result of the higher prices on pesos, growers in Argentina might flood the markets, temporarily at least, thus forcing down prices and nullifying the higher prices resulting from peso depreciation. Furthermore, it was realized that, even though the rushing of offers on the world markets could be avoided, world grain prices might continue to fall, so that the effects of peso depreciation on local prices would have been temporary.[29]

---

must apply through a bank or authorized broker and the rate is fixed by the Central Bank at time application is submitted.

During 1936 the official sterling selling rate approximated 17 pesos per pound until December 10, when it was reduced to 16 pesos per pound. The free rate also declined during the year to an average in December of 16.42 pesos per pound. Thus in recent months the profit margin of the Exchange Control Office on sales in the official market has been greatly reduced. Profits on sales in the free market remain substantial, however, since, according to a decree promulgated in April 1935, purchasers of exchange in the free market must pay a surcharge equal to the difference between 120 per cent of the official selling rate as determined by the Central Bank and the free market rate.

[28] *Economic Review*, "The Balance of Payments and the Value of the Argentine Peso," January-March, 1934, p. 13.

[29] *Ibid.*, pp. 13-14.

In order to make certain that higher prices would accrue to the grain growers, a Grain Regulating Board was created by the Government (by decree of November 28, 1933) which was to purchase all the wheat, linseed, and maize offered at basic prices to be fixed from time to time. The prices established on November 28 were approximately 20 per cent above those ruling in the market at that time.[30] These purchases by the Grain Board were not to be held, but were to be sold by the Government to exporters at ruling prices for disposal abroad. Any difference between purchase and sale price was to be covered from the profits obtained by the Exchange Control Commission.

According to the official report of the Grain Regulating Board, about one-third of its total deficit of 8.7 million paper pesos covering its first year's operation was for operating expenses and interest on advances. The difference between the purchase and sale prices of grains handled was only 5.9 million paper pesos, most of which was incurred in wheat operations, since there was a profit of 1,850 paper pesos on linseed transactions.[31] Favorable prices resulting from crop shortages in the northern hemisphere were significant factors in this favorable showing. In 1936, as indicated below, the Grain Board showed a surplus over and above expenses of 2.6 million pesos.

The Grain Regulating Board is the most important of a whole series of government agencies which have been inaugurated in Argentina during recent years. These agencies have resulted in

[30] The basic prices established at Port of Buenos Aires were as follows (in paper pesos per 100 kilos): wheat, 5.75; maize, 4.40; and linseed, 11.50 (equivalent in dollars at current rate of exchange, to approximately \$.63, \$.49, and \$1.26, respectively). These basic prices were maintained until late in 1935, when the price of wheat was raised to 10 pesos per quintal and linseed to 14 pesos per quintal, equivalent in dollars to \$.90 and \$1.26 per bushel, respectively. Early in 1936 the basic price of maize was also raised from 4.4 pesos to 5.0 pesos per quintal, or \$.45 per bushel. Following marked increases in the market prices of grains during the latter part of 1936, these minimum price guarantees on wheat and linseed were removed in December 1936. It is also reported that the basic price on corn is also to be removed. *Latin American Financial Notes*, No. 215, March 14, 1937.

[31] United States Bureau of Foreign and Domestic Commerce, *World Economic Review*, 1934, p. 219. See also, Simon G. Hansen, "The Argentine Grain Board," *Journal of Political Economy*, April 1936, pp. 240-47.

Distribution of Exchange Profits
1934–36
(millions of pesos)

	paper			*gold*		
	1934	*1935*	*1936*[a]	*1934*	*1935*	*1936*[a]
Transferred to Treasury to cover exchange differences on National external debt	22.8	34.9	26.8	10.0	15.4	11.8
Exchange differences on other Government remittances	1.5	23.7	5.0	0.6	10.5	2.2
Expenditures and deficits of Grain Board	8.7	20.3	[b]	3.8	8.9	[b]
Expenditures and advances to Grain Board	—			—		
Expenditures and deficits of Dairy Board	2.0	1.4	2.2	0.9	0.6	1.0
Expenditures and deficits of Cotton Board	—	0.5	1.1	—	0.2	0.5
Expenditures and deficits of Meat Exports Board	—	3.0	—	—	1.3	—
Administrative expenditures of Exchange Control Office	0.2	0.2	0.2	0.1	0.1	0.1
Total expenditures	35.2	84.0	35.3	15.4	37.0	15.6
Allocation of balance:						
Foreign currencies fund (gold, securities, and devisen)	72.9	9.7	81.4	32.1	4.3	35.8
Cash in banks (including in 1934, temporary investments)	11.1	24.4	−25.2	4.9	10.7	−11.1
Total profits	119.2	118.1	91.5	52.4	52.0	40.3

[a] Provisional figures.

[b] In 1936 the Grain Board showed a surplus of 2.6 million paper pesos which was credited to the Exchange Profits Fund and included in the total profits of 91.5 million paper pesos for that year.

Source: Argentine Government, *Prospectus*, $35,000,000 Sinking Fund External Conversion Loan, 4% Bonds, April 22, 1937, p. 27.

an increasing degree of social regulation of the country's economic activity, particularly since 1933. As early as 1928 a National Sugar Commission was established; in January 1931 it was given price-controlling powers. During 1933 a National Meat Board and a National Commission for Quebracho Extract were established, in addition to the aforementioned Grain Regulating

Board. During 1934 there were established a Dairy Industry Regulating Board, an Edible Oil Commission, a Cotton Board, a Commission for National Foodstuffs Products, and measures aimed to help the wine and fruit industries. In September 1935 a "Regulating Committee for the Production and Sale of Yerba Maté," and a National Grain and Elevator Commission were added to the list.[32] Any detailed analysis of these government agencies or their activities is beyond the scope of this study. The keystone of the whole system, however, is the Exchange Control Office (formerly Commission), since the operations of these numerous agencies are financed largely from the profits derived from exchange control. Exchange control profits have also been utilized to cover the additional cost in pesos of the service on the public debt held abroad, caused by the increased peso depreciation. Data showing the distribution of exchange profits, totaling 328.8 million paper pesos (144.7 million gold pesos) during 1934, 1935, and 1936, are given on page 72.

The exchange control system as at present administered operates under the control of the Ministry of Finance which exercises its control through the Central Bank and the Exchange Control Office. The balance of the profits derived from the Exchange Profits Fund, after the deductions indicated above, plus the income obtained from the surcharge payable in foreign currencies by importers without prior import permits, is transferred to the Foreign Currencies Fund.

Pending international stabilization of the leading currencies of the world, this Foreign Currencies Fund is operated as a stabilization fund. A substantial portion of the fund has been converted into gold which on December 31, 1936, was held on deposit in London.[33]

Ultimate transfer of exchange control, the Exchange Profits Fund, and the Foreign Currencies Fund to the Central Bank is anticipated in the legislation and decrees establishing the new Central Bank early in 1935 (Law No. 12,160 and Decree No. 61,127 of May 18, 1935). The Foreign Currencies Fund is now

[32] *Revista de Economia Argentina, October-December,* 1935, pp. 285-309.

[33] Argentine Government, *Prospectus, op. cit.*

administered by the Central Bank for the account of and in consultation with the Government.[34]

Partly as a result of this revision of exchange control (including further marked depreciation of the peso), Argentina succeeded in 1934 in balancing its international accounts without any increase in its net foreign indebtedness. The estimated income from exports (including exporters' profits), as shown in Table XIV, increased from 515 million gold pesos to 752 million gold pesos, or roughly by 46 per cent. Imports also increased from 395 million pesos to 484 millions, or by 22 per cent. The relatively greater expansion of exports resulted in an export surplus, however, of 268 million pesos which was estimated to just cover total service remittances due abroad. With net gold exports totaling seven million pesos, there resulted an equivalent estimated decrease in net foreign indebtedness.

This equilibrium was achieved at the expense of a drastic reduction in all external remittances (balance of payments debits), excepting public debt service, which, with some relatively small exceptions in the case of municipal and provincial service, has been fully maintained. The annual average of external remittances for the three-year period, October 1, 1927-October 1, 1930, covering imports, private debt service, immigrant remittances, and tourist expenditures was roughly one billion gold pesos. For the calendar years 1933 and 1934 these payments for which exchange permits were granted totaled 384 and 466 million gold pesos, respectively. If private external debt service remittances are counted in terms of foreign currencies in which received, the above totals would be curtailed still further, by perhaps some 25 to 50 million gold pesos annually.[35]

For the calendar year 1935 the export surplus, including exporters' profits, approximated that for 1934, equaling 265 million gold pesos. As shown in Table XIV, the value of exports and imports increased 36 and 40 million pesos each, respectively. The export surplus exceeded estimated total external service

[34] *Ibid.*

[35] Statistics published by the Exchange Control Commission of exchange sales do not show total private debt service remittances separately, so that it is impossible to tell the exact total of these remittances.

remittances by five million gold pesos. With gold exports equivalent to seven million gold pesos, the result was an estimated decrease in net foreign indebtedness of 12 million gold pesos. This situation in the international accounts of Argentina is corroborated in the foreign exchange rates, since, as shown in Chart I, the trend in prices of foreign currencies in the free market during 1935 was downward.

We turn now to a more detailed analysis of the mechanism through which this equilibrium was restored, and its effects upon the Argentine internal price structure. In general, three methods may be distinguished under which a readjustment of a country's balance of payments may be effected:

1. Maintenance of gold standard
2. Inconvertible or free currency
3. Exchange control

1. *Gold standard mechanism*

There is little unanimity of opinion as to the exact nature of the mechanism under which equilibrium in a country's balance of payments is maintained, or even that there is any automatic tendency to equilibrium. Granted, however, that such a tendency does exist,[36] any ordinary disturbance in the balance of payments, under a gold standard, according to the classical theory, is supposedly corrected through the operation of monetary factors reacting on relative price levels. A deficit in the balance of payments leads to gold exports. Bank reserves decline with a consequent contraction in the supply of money and credit. This restriction of the means of payment decreases the buying power of the population, which is reflected in lessened imports. The curtailment of purchasing power brings about a tendency to lower prices, at least relatively to other countries. Lower prices stimulate exports, aided by the opposite tendencies in other countries of increased gold reserves, expanding means of payments, and

[36] E.g., Gifford states that (*op. cit.*, p. 11) ". . . there is a tendency towards an equal balance of payments without gold movements, or movements of short loans, apart from purely seasonal movements of capital, and apart from gold or capital movements carried out for reasons unconnected with the state of the balance of payments."

increased purchasing power. Thus, an expanding export surplus eliminates the deficit in the balance of payments, further gold exports are unnecessary, and equilibrium is restored.[37]

Such a mechanism of restoration of equilibrium, however, may require a drastic price decline, particularly if world prices are declining simultaneously, and the demand for the country's exports is inelastic; a situation which existed in Argentina after 1928.[38]

2. *Inconvertible currency mechanism*

If the gold standard mechanism does not restore equilibrium promptly, excessive gold exports may lead to suspension of gold payments and the adoption of an inconvertible, or free currency. Such a policy frees the domestic price level from the restraining influence of gold, and may lead to inflationary tendencies.[39] In fact, such is precisely the mechanism whereby equilibrium in the balance of payments is restored. With the balance of payments "unfavorable," the external or foreign exchange value of the free currency declines, and the price level tends to rise in accordance with the premium on gold. Increases in exporters' costs, however, tend to lag behind the higher prices received for exports, and thus exports are stimulated. At the same time imports

[37] The above is a very brief description of a highly complex mechanism, the operation of which may be affected by many other factors. The restoration of equilibrium may be fostered or retarded by other balance of payments items, e.g., short-term ("equalizing") capital movements, which in turn may have been affected by central bank policies, government fiscal policies, etc.

[38] Several recent writers on the theory of international trade contend that changes, even in relative price levels, need not *necessarily* occur, in order to restore equilibrium. According to this "modern" school it is held that, as a result of differing demand schedules for export, domestic, and import commodities in the countries concerned, the shifts in purchasing power may work out their effect without a shift in relative price levels. See B. Ohlin, *Interregional and International Trade*, Harvard University Press, 1933, for a comprehensive expression of this viewpoint. Also Carl Iverson, *Aspects of the Theory of International Capital Movements*, Copenhagen, 1935, and G. Haberler, *The Theory of International Trade*, London, 1936.

[39] The writer recognizes, but is not here concerned with, the implications of the theoretical controversies over what is a proper or exact definition of "inflation." The above use of the term "inflation" connotes a rise in paper money prices, relative to gold prices.

are discouraged, because of higher costs of foreign goods resulting from the appreciation of foreign currencies in terms of the domestic paper currency. As equilibrium is restored, the continued decline in the exchange value of the currency is halted, and the lags in the domestic price structure are eliminated.

The above mechanism of adjustment, however, does not require necessarily an absolute increase in the domestic price level, but only a relative increase; that is, with falling world gold prices, domestic paper prices might also continue to fall, but relatively less rapidly than gold prices.[40]

3. *Exchange Control*

Between a mechanism of adjustment based upon the gold standard and one based upon an inconvertible or entirely free currency, there has been introduced into the monetary structures of many countries, during recent years, a monetary mechanism based upon some form of exchange control which may be properly considered as a hybrid variation midway between a gold currency and a free currency, at least with respect to external payments.

Such exchange controls have frequently been the sequel to a period of a fluctuating inconvertible or free currency, following upon the abandonment of the gold standard. Under a system of exchange control, the domestic currency may be pegged rigidly to some foreign currency, which may be either a gold or a free currency. Where a country's currency is thus pegged, the price levels of its exports and imports are presumably also linked to those of the other country, and equilibrium in its balance of payments must be achieved in some other way, frequently by the rationing of foreign currencies. Under such a mechanism, presumably the degree of deflation or inflation depends upon the dual factors of the peg ratio and the trend of prices in the country upon which the peg is established.

A modification of such a rigid system of control may be effected whereby, although the purchase price of foreign currencies

[40] Peters, in his recent study, in discussing the late Argentine experience, apparently misses this point, i.e., that it is *relative*, and not *absolute*, changes in price levels which are significant. See H. E. Peters, *op. cit.*, pp. 169-70.

remains fixed, competitive factors are permitted to operate in the sale of such currencies. Under such a system, export prices are still linked to the foreign price level, but import prices may rise, because of the higher prices of the foreign currencies as a result of competitive bidding. These higher prices may thus promote restoration of equilibrium.

Since 1928, Argentina has experienced each of these three types of mechanisms for the adjustment of its international balance of payments. As an aid to reviewing this experience, the country's net balance of payments on current items for each year since 1928, as well as net gold exports, is repeated:

(in millions of gold pesos)

	1927/28	1928/29	1929/30	1930/31	Oct.-Dec. 1931	1932	1933	1934	1935
Balance of Payments	—36	—129	—340	—134	+14	—60	—109	0	+5
Gold Exports		125	64	171	24	8	19	7	7
Gold Imports	150								

(1) *Deflation: 1928-30*

For the "economic" year 1927-28 (October 1-September 30), Argentina's balance of payments was in approximate equilibrium, with an estimated "adverse" balance on current items of only 36 million gold pesos. Notwithstanding, there was a net import of gold totaling 150 million pesos, the result, it will be recalled, of large foreign borrowing. The succeeding "economic" year, however, brought an "adverse" current balance of 129 million gold pesos, which was due both to lessened exports and increased imports. The gold standard was maintained, nevertheless, leading to gold exports approximating the amount of the "adverse" balance, since during 1929 foreign loans had practically ceased.

The effect of these gold exports upon the Argentine price level, however, was apparently very slight, since, as shown in Chart II-A, the index of wholesale prices of all commodities declined only from 98.5 to 96.4. Furthermore, as the indices in Charts II-A and II-B indicate, this decline was confined almost entirely to agricultural or export commodities. The index of non-agricultural products remained practically constant, the

CHART II. ARGENTINE WHOLESALE PRICES, 1926-34
INDEX 1926 = 100

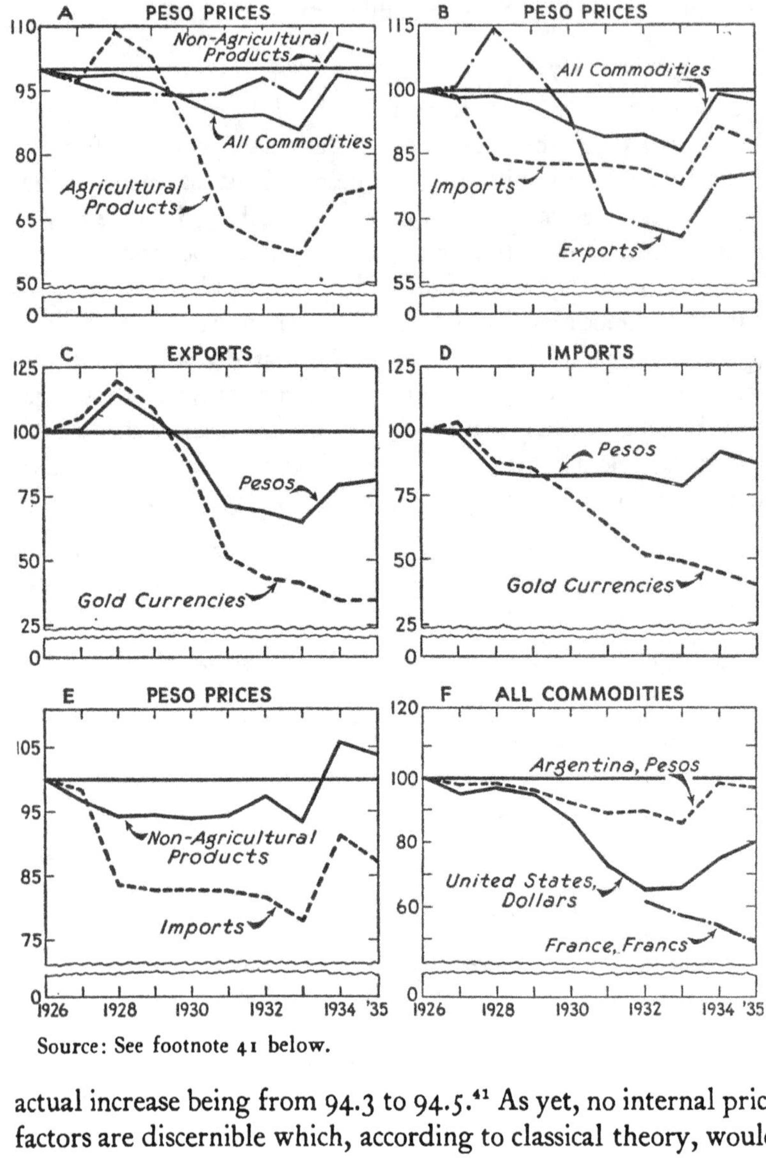

Source: See footnote 41 below.

actual increase being from 94.3 to 94.5.[41] As yet, no internal price factors are discernible which, according to classical theory, would

[41] The indices of prices of "all commodities," "agricultural products," and "non-agricultural" products are those compiled by the Banco de la Nación and,

promote restoration of equilibrium in the balance of payments. In fact, the general world decline in prices of Argentine exports was only accentuating the disequilibrium.

(2) *Free Currency: 1930-31*

This situation was confirmed in the following "economic" year (1929-30), when Argentina's "adverse" balance of payments totaled 340 million gold pesos. Gold payments were suspended in December 1929, it will be recalled, followed by a rapid depreciation of the peso. Export prices continued to decline as a result of the continued drop in world prices of agricultural commodities. Peso prices for Argentina's exports during 1930 failed to decline, however, as rapidly as gold prices (see Chart II-C), thus reflecting the external depreciation of the peso; in other words, there was a relatively smaller decline in paper peso prices, which was in accord with theoretical expectations as outlined above (p. 77). Nevertheless, the total value

---

since its organization early in 1935, the Banco Central de la República Argentina. The index of agricultural products is composed of 23 articles; the index of non-agricultural products is composed of 22 "national" articles and 57 "foreign" articles. These individual series for a total of 105 articles are combined in the general wholesale price index. It is only since the beginning of 1933, however, that separate indices have been compiled covering prices of "national" and "foreign" articles, and these indices have not been published (to the writer's knowledge) since February 1934. For a complete list of the individual items composing the indices, see Banco de la Nación, *Economic Review,* Jan.-Mar., 1934, pp. 29-33.

Annual indices of export and import prices are compiled by the Dirección General de Estadística de la Nación, and published in the *Anuario del Comercio Exterior de la República Argentina.* These indices are also published by the League of Nations in its annual *Review of World Trade,* both in pesos and their gold currency equivalent.

The data used in Chart II were compiled from the following sources:

Argentina:

Banco de la Nación, *op. cit.,* Jan. 1932, p. 9; Jan.-Mar. 1934, p. 30; Oct.-Dec. 1934, pp. 166, 170; League of Nations, *Review of World Trade,* 1934, p. 77; 1935, p. 73; League of Nations, *Monthly Bulletin of Statistics,* Sept. 1936, p. 74.

United States:

United States Bureau of Labor Statistics, *Wholesale Prices,* Feb. 1936, p. 9.

France:

League of Nations, *Monthly Bulletin of Statistics,* Sept. 1936, p. 74.

of Argentina's exports was only 661 million pesos, or approximately 34 per cent under the previous year. The decline amounted to 340 million gold pesos, or exactly the estimated deficit on current items in the balance of payments for the year.

The peso value of imports contracted, however, only some ten per cent, or by 103 million pesos. Non-agricultural peso prices (including imports) remained practically constant (see Charts II-D and II-E). With world gold prices declining, however, this was equivalent to a relative increase.[42] During 1930 inflation was beginning, then; that is, inflation relative to gold prices. A comparison of the indices of the general price level in Argentina and the United States (Chart II-F) shows that in Argentina the decline from 1929 to 1930 was only from 96.4 to 92.2, or 4.2 per cent, whereas in the United States the decline was from 95.3 in 1929 to 86.4 in 1930, a drop of 8.9 per cent.

For the following "economic" year, 1930-31, the estimated "adverse" balance of payments was reduced to 134 million gold pesos. Crops were excellent, and the *volume* of exports increased by approximately 67 per cent. With world prices for agricultural products continuing to fall, however, the total value of exports was 606 million pesos, or 55 million pesos less than the previous year. The continued disequilibrium in the balance of payments was reflected in a further marked depreciation of the peso.[43] As indicated in Chart II-C, this continued depreciation was reflected in a further increase in the spread between peso prices for exports and gold currency prices; that is, peso prices of exports increased relative to gold prices. Both export peso prices and export gold prices continued to decline rapidly, however, because of non-monetary world supply and demand factors, the former index dropping to an annual average of 64.4 for the calendar year 1931 and the latter to 46.3. The price index for non-agricultural commodities remained practically constant at 94.4, and the import price index in pesos was 82.6 for 1931, compared with 82.8 for the previous year. With world

[42] The failure of the means of payment to contract during 1930 (as a result of government fiscal and banking policy) as a factor in maintaining imports has already been considered. See pp. 57-58.

[43] See Charts III and IV, pp. 83 and 86.

gold prices continuing to decline, this was equivalent again to a relative increase; its effect was shown in sharply curtailed imports which dropped in value from 779 million pesos in 1929-30 to 547 million pesos in 1930-31, or a decline of approximately 30 per cent.[44] Thus, a tendency toward a state of equilibrium in current items was developing, in accordance with theoretical expectations under an inconvertible currency,[45] which, during the succeeding nine months (October 1931-June 1932), was to restore approximate equilibrium in Argentina's international accounts.

For the fourth quarter of 1931, as stated previously, there was an estimated surplus of 14 million pesos on current account. During the calendar year 1932, the estimated deficit was 60 million pesos. It was not until the third quarter of 1932, however, that the forces of disequilibrium (evidenced by a decreasing export surplus) reappeared, so that for the "economic" year, October 1, 1931-September 30, 1932, there was presumably approximate equilibrium in Argentina's balance of payments. Chart III, showing quarterly figures, illustrates more clearly the reappearance of the forces of disequilibrium; that is, the declining export surplus during 1932.

(3) *Exchange Control: 1931-34*

Following the suspension of gold payments by the United Kingdom, the peso depreciated rapidly in terms of the dollar, reaching a peak in October 1931, when the dollar was quoted at 180 per cent of par.[46] Thereupon, it will be recalled, the system of exchange control was inaugurated and the peso was arbitrarily pegged to the dollar at the rate of $.584 (U. S. gold dollars) per gold peso, or approximately 165 per cent of its former parity. The significance of this pegging of the peso in the reappearance of a deficit in Argentina's balance of payments, at what appeared later to have been an artificially low rate, has already been discussed.[47] Its effect upon Argentina's price levels

[44] Tariff increases were also a factor in this decline.

[45] As summarized above, p. 77.

[46] See Charts I and IV, pp. 31 and 86.

[47] See pp. 65-66; also Chart III, p. 83.

CHART III. CHANGES IN ARGENTINE FOREIGN TRADE, 1929-35, BY QUARTERS, COMPARED WITH PESO DEPRECIATION

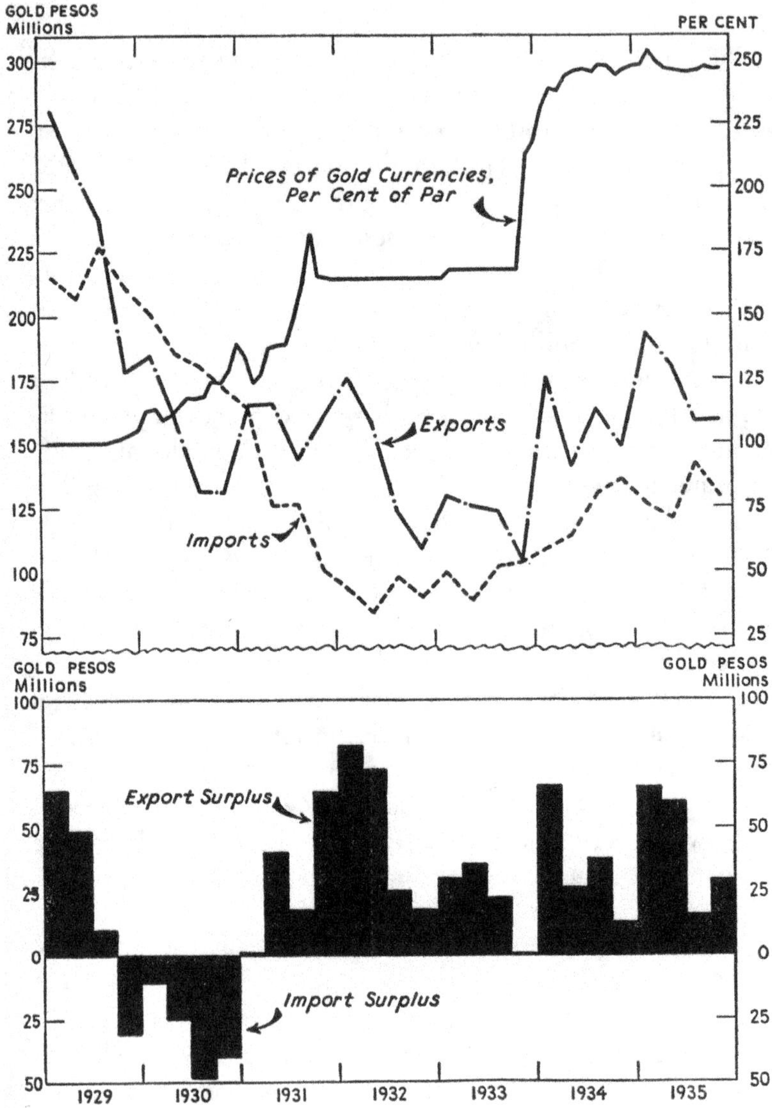

Source: República Argentina, Dirección General de Estadística de la Nación, *El Comercio Exterior Argentino*, Boletín No. 217.

is not shown clearly in the annual indices in Chart II, but is reflected in Chart IV showing the average monthly prices of gold currencies in Argentina, compared with monthly indices of wholesale prices.

The rapid depreciation of the peso late in 1931 was accompanied by a sharp rise in the price of both non-agricultural and agricultural prices. Following the pegging of the peso, however, non-agricultural prices (including imports) declined gradually, in sympathy with declining prices in the United States and other gold currency countries. The result was a gradual increase in imports from the middle of 1932 which led to an increase in total imports for 1933 over 1932 of 27 million gold pesos, or from 368 to 395 million gold pesos.

Agricultural prices, although showing a similar sharp rise late in 1931, were subsequently dominated more completely by world market prices, and fluctuated rather widely, although with a continued downward trend. For example, the sharp rise during the middle of 1933 was the result of the drouth in the northern hemisphere, accentuated by dollar depreciation in the United States and the speculative "pre-NRA" boom. The drouth in the northern hemisphere during the following year, 1934, had a similar effect.

The continued net decline in agricultural prices during 1933, however, accompanied by a decrease in total export volume of approximately two million tons, resulted in total export values declining from 574 million pesos in 1932 to 500 millions in 1933, which left Argentina again with an "adverse" balance of payments on current items for 1933 estimated at 109 million gold pesos.

As previously related, this reappearance of disequilibrium, resulting in part at least from the artificial pegging of the peso at too low a level, led to drastic reorganization of the exchange control mechanism in November 1933, with the introduction of the prior permit and auction system, accompanied by a further depreciation of the peso of 20 per cent. This resulted in a sharp rise in the peso prices of both agricultural (export) and foreign

(import) articles (see Chart IV), with the former showing an increase from November 1933 to February 1934, of 20.7 per cent, and the latter of 16.5 per cent.[48] This difference in the rate of increase was the result, in part, of the following factors:[49] (1) Export prices, being more closely linked with world markets, immediately reflected the higher price of foreign currencies. Furthermore, as already stated, world prices of agricultural and pastoral products increased during 1934 because of non-monetary factors of both restricted supplies (drouth in the northern hemisphere), as well as an improved demand as economic recovery became more imminent; (2) on the other hand, at least half of the c.i.f. price of imports is absorbed by internal charges and profits (including customs duties) which are not directly affected by variations in the exchange rate. Furthermore, particularly in times of economic strain, it is difficult to pass on to customers the burden of increased prices. In certain cases, foreign manufacturers may have preferred to lower their prices in order to hold their position in the Argentine markets.

Following the rapid rise in prices from November 1933 to February 1934, the non-agricultural price index remained relatively constant until the third quarter of the year, when it increased slightly in sympathy with the sharp increase in agricultural prices resulting from the drouth in the northern hemisphere, although declining by the end of the year to approximately the level obtaining during the early months of the year (see Chart IV). Agricultural prices increased rapidly during the middle of 1934, in sympathy with world market conditions, declining by the end of the year, however, to within two per cent of the previous December-February level.

Thus, for the calendar year 1934, through the medium of currency depreciation (aided also, it is true, by fortuitous world conditions affecting its export prices) and its resultant effect upon internal prices, Argentina was enabled to achieve again

[48] Indices of import and "national" prices since February 1934, are not available.

[49] See *Economic Review*, January-March 1934, pp. 30-31.

CHART IV. INDICES OF WHOLESALE PRICES AND PRICES OF GOLD CURRENCIES IN ARGENTINA, MONTHLY AVERAGES, 1929-36

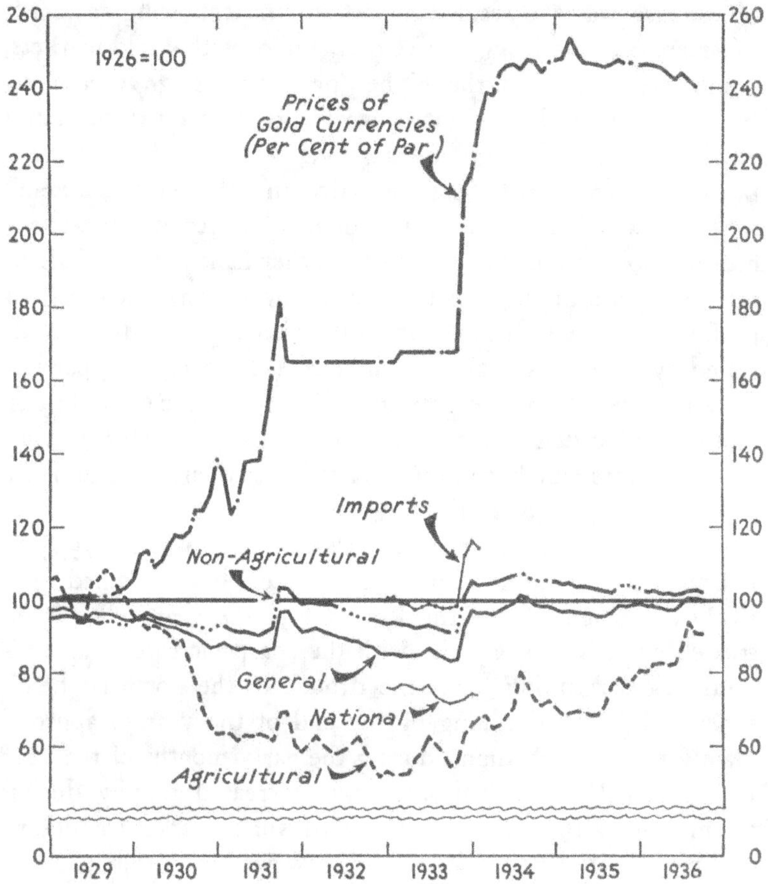

Sources: Jan., 1929-May, 1935: Banco de la Nación, *Economic Review*, Jan.-Mar., 1934, p. 30; Oct.-Dec., 1934, pp. 166, 170. June, 1935-Oct., 1936: Banco Central de la República Argentina.

approximate equilibrium in its international balance of payments.

As indicated in Chart IV, the index of non-agricultural products remained relatively constant throughout 1935 and 1936.

The index of agricultural prices, on the other hand, largely as a result of further crop shortages in other countries plus increasing demand, rose sharply during 1935 and 1936, averaging slightly over 90 per cent of the 1926 level during the latter part of 1936. By April of 1937 the index of agricultural prices had increased to 107.1 per cent of the 1926 level. The result was an increasingly "favorable" balance of payments during 1936 and the early months of 1937.

There remains to be considered, first, the question of whether the suspension of gold payments in December 1929 was necessary, i.e., could equilibrium have been restored in Argentina's balance of payments under a gold standard mechanism; and, secondly, what might have been the probable effect upon the Argentine economy had gold payments been maintained.

Was the suspension of gold payments by Argentina in December 1929, or subsequently, necessary? From the standpoint of maintaining external gold payments, that is, covering the current deficits in Argentina's international accounts, the abandonment of gold payments might have been avoided, at least until the fall of 1931, had Argentina been willing to pay the price. This statement is based upon the following analysis:

The total estimated deficit on current items in Argentina's balance of payments for the period October 1, 1928 to October 1, 1931, was approximately 600 million gold pesos, of which 340 million pesos was incurred in the "economic" year, 1929-30. Of this total sum, 360 millions was covered by gold exports, and the remainder of 240 millions by net new foreign borrowings. If the economic and fiscal policies initiated late in 1930 and 1931, which resulted in drastically reduced imports, had been inaugurated a year earlier, it is possible that this deficit might have been reduced by some 350 million gold pesos, or to about 250 million gold pesos. This figure of 350 million gold pesos was obtained by advancing by one year each the figures for imports and service items in the balance of payments beginning with 1930-31; that is, applying the figures for 1930-31 to 1929-30, etc., as follows, in round figures:

(in millions of gold pesos)

	1928-29	*1929-30*	*1930-31*	*Total*
Exports	1,001	661	606	
Imports	881	547	400	
Export Surplus	120	114	206	
Service Items	248	193	250	
Estimated Balance of Payments	—128	—79	—44	—251

If this entire deficit of 251 million gold pesos had been covered by gold exports, the sum required would still have been 100 million pesos less than was actually exported during this period. Total visible stocks of gold in Argentina October 1, 1928, were approximately 655 million gold pesos,[50] of which 151 million pesos were held by the banks, and 504 millions by the Conversion Office. Assuming that the stocks held by the banks had been utilized first (as actually occurred from 1928 to 1932)[51] there would have been required 100 million pesos from the reserves in the Conversion Office.

With England's suspension, presumably Argentina would have had no other alternative but to follow suit, as did many other nations with similar close economic relations with the former country; provided, of course, that the severe internal deflation which maintenance of the gold standard would have necessitated by the end of 1931 had not already provoked a severe domestic crisis, if not financial collapse.[52]

In order to show what effect the continued withdrawal of gold for export from the Conversion Office would have had upon the

[50] *Economic Review*, January 1932, p. 16.

[51] See Appendix III, p. 263.

[52] During the early months of 1931 (autumn in Argentina), a record corn crop was harvested in Argentina, but very low prices prevailed, that is, current peso prices. Had gold prices been maintained, the price paid to growers would have been so low that presumably a large portion of the crop would not have been harvested. The peak in bankruptcy figures, even under the partial relief of a depreciated currency, was reached in 1931. The opinion expressed to the writer by the Argentine economist, Dr. Carlos Garcia-Mata, was that with gold prices still operative in 1931 the situation would have meant a collapse of the internal monetary structure.

Argentine domestic economy (had the gold standard been retained), a brief description of the evolution of the Argentine monetary and banking structure is necessary. Any detailed analysis of Argentina's monetary and banking system is beyond the scope of this study; only its major features, particularly with reference to international transactions, will be summarized.

It will be recalled that following a period of currency depreciation between 1885 and 1889 a currency reform law was passed. Not only did this new currency law of 1889 provide that gold should be paid out in exchange for paper pesos at the rate of one gold peso for 2.27 paper pesos, but it also prohibited the issuance of paper money, except upon the deposit of an equivalent sum of gold in the Conversion Office at the stipulated ratio. This meant that any addition to the circulating medium had to have a one hundred per cent gold guarantee, and also that any gold withdrawals had to be offset by the retirement of an equivalent amount of paper currency.[53] The result was a highly inelastic system.

This inelasticity of the currency was accentuated by the character of the Argentine banking system. There was no central banking mechanism to provide for concentration of reserves and rediscount facilities; no provision for expansion, seasonal or otherwise, by the issuance of currency against commercial paper.[54]

Although the Banco de la Nación, which had been organized in 1891, was the official agent of the National Government, and occupied a dominant position in the banking system, it was not legally responsible for banking conditions. Doing a private banking business, and thus a competitor of other banks in Argentina, the Banco da la Nación was not primarily, however, a profit-making institution, and did perform certain functions of a central bank. Chief among these activities was the bank's policy of carrying large gold stocks in its own vaults which were used to stabilize the circulating medium by offsetting withdrawals from

[53] As a specie reserve for the paper already outstanding, totaling 293 million paper pesos, a fund of 30 million gold pesos, the equivalent of 68,100,000 paper pesos, or approximately 23.2 per cent, was subsequently established from the proceeds of special revenues.

[54] A situation thus somewhat similar to that which existed in the United States prior to the inauguration of the Federal Reserve System.

the Conversion Office; that is, when gold was withdrawn by the other banks for shipment abroad, the Banco de la Nación would transfer gold to the Conversion Office in exchange for paper pesos, which it would use in the purchase of commercial paper; thus tending to reduce fluctuations in the currency circulation.[55]

Beginning in 1914 the Banco da la Nación also provided limited rediscount facilities for other banks. One of the emergency measures enacted at the time of the financial crisis following the outbreak of the War in 1914, it will be recalled, authorized the Banco de la Nación to rediscount commercial paper presented to it by other banks which it could in turn deposit, upon authorization by the president, at the Conversion Office in exchange for paper money; provided that the gold reserve against total paper issued never fell below 40 per cent. Although the bank frequently discounted or purchased commercial paper from other banks thereafter, until 1931 none of this paper was ever exchanged at the Conversion Office for paper currency. As already indicated, all paper currency issued by the Conversion Office during this period was backed 100 per cent by gold.

Another factor accentuating the rigidity in the volume of means of payment in Argentina has been the failure of the use of checks to develop on a wide scale. This greater use of currency rather than checks as a means of payment, coupled with a decentralized banking system, has also necessitated large cash reserves on the part of the banks.[56]

[55] Other banks followed a similar policy on a smaller scale.

[56] Following agitation dating back at least two decades, early in 1935 the Argentine banking system was completely reorganized, in an attempt to remedy, among other things, this inelasticity. On March 28, 1935, legislation was enacted creating the Central Bank of the Argentine Republic, a commercial bank law was enacted for the first time, an institution to liquidate frozen assets of the banks was established, the organic laws of the two official banks, the Bank of the Argentine Nation and the National Mortgage Bank, were amended, and measures for the inauguration of the entire system were authorized in an organization law.

In accordance with Article 3 of Law No. 12,155 of March 28, 1935, the objects of the new Central Bank shall be:

1. To concentrate sufficient reserves to moderate the consequences of fluctuations in exports and investments of foreign capital on currency, credit, and commercial activity, in order to maintain the value of the currency;

We return, after this digression, to our original theme, the suspension of gold payments by Argentina in December 1929, and the events prior and subsequent thereto.

Cessation of foreign loans in 1929, it will be recalled, accompanied by a declining export surplus, resulted in an "adverse" balance of payments, leading to heavy gold exports in contrast to the large volume of imports during the preceding two years. This reversal of the gold movement which began in the last half of 1928 was greatly accentuated during 1929. Gold imports during the first half of 1928 totaled 99.4 million pesos; gold exports during the second half of 1928 equaled 12.3 million pesos, and for the calendar year 1929, 174.4 million pesos.

During the period of large gold imports from 1926 to 1928, a large portion of these imports had been retained by the banks, so that the gold exports late in 1928 and in the early part of 1929 came from these bank stocks and not from the Conversion Office. By the end of 1929, these stocks were largely exhausted, however, so that additional exports would have required a marked contraction of the currency. In fact, the beginning of such a contraction was already apparent, since the reduction in the gold holdings of the Conversion Office during 1929 totaled 70 million gold pesos, and from June 30 to December 31, 1929, there was a decline in note circulation equivalent to 107 million gold pesos.[57] Nevertheless, the gold reserve of the Conversion

2. To regulate the volume of credit and the means of payment, adapting them to the real volume of trade;
3. To promote the liquidity and sound functioning of bank credit; and to apply the provisions of the banking law for the inspection, examination, and regulation of banks;
4. To act as financial agent and counselor of the Government in foreign or internal credit operations and in the issue and service of public loans. [Translation from Institute of International Finance, Bulletin No. 86, *Credit Position of Argentina,* June 1, 1936, p. 13. See also *Federal Reserve Bulletin,* Federal Reserve Board, Washington, D.C., July, 1935, pp. 449-458.]

[57] *Economic Review,* April-June 1934, p. 46. Gold movements during 1929 were as follows:

	(in millions of gold pesos)
Withdrawals from Conversion Office	70
Reduction in Bank Stocks	110
Net exports	174

Office still stood at the relatively high level of 76.5 per cent, and the country's total monetary gold stock was still nearly as great as at the time of resumption of gold payments in 1927. Notwithstanding, on December 16, President Irigoyen issued a decree closing the Conversion Office. Although gold exports were not prohibited, nearly all the country's monetary gold reserves were, by now, held by the Conversion Office.

The immediate reason for suspending gold payments, before any excessive withdrawal of gold from the Conversion Office, was, as previously stated, to prevent a further rapid contraction of currency and credit, which would have led presumably to a rapid decline of prices. With two lines of action available for restoring equilibrium in its international balance of payments, that is, deflation under a gold standard, or inflation under an inconvertible currency, the existing Argentine Government chose the latter;[58] that is, external instability of the currency, rather than internal instability in terms of purchasing power. Thus the necessity of further currency contraction and presumably rapidly falling prices was removed.[59] Instead of attempting to restore

[58] Approval of suspension was far from unanimous, the decree being widely criticized both in Argentina and abroad, there being considerable difference of opinion as to the real reasons for suspension. It was maintained by some that the decision was also influenced by the desire to obtain higher prices for the powerful agricultural interests of the Republic, yet the index of prices of agricultural and pastoral products of 1929 stood at 103.2 per cent of the 1926 average. This was a decline from the 1928 level of 109.6, however, of 6.4 per cent. It was not until after 1929 that the really drastic decline in agricultural prices occurred, which by 1932 reached a level of 37 per cent (of the 1926 level) in gold currencies, or 59.1 per cent in paper pesos. See discussion by Lawrence Smith, *op. cit.*, pp. 434-5. Smith reaches the conclusion that had Argentina had a more elastic monetary system, gold payments would not have been suspended at so early a date, but that events would have forced suspension some months later.

[59] In 1931 and 1932 additional emergency measures were also taken looking to an expansion of the currency, the more important of which were the following:
1. By a decree of April 8, 1931, the Conversion Office was authorized to issue notes against gold deposited with Argentine Legations abroad. As a result of this decree approximately 54 million gold pesos were deposited with Argentine Legations in Washington and London, and the circulation of notes in Argentina was increased by 122 million paper pesos. The primary purpose of this measure was to assist in financing the movement of the crops.
2. On April 25, 1931, a decree authorized the Banco de la Nación to redis-

equilibrium in the international accounts through an offensive policy of stimulating exports by permitting internal deflation, with lowered prices and costs, to occur, and thus place Argentine exports in a more favorable competitive position, the defensive policy of permitting the external value of the peso to decline was adopted. Presumably the cost of imports, in pesos, would thereby be increased, and their volume curtailed. Equilibrium would thus be restored by lessened imports rather than by increased exports, plus, at the same time, greater stability in the internal price level. What actually happened has already been described. The peso depreciated rapidly through 1930 and 1931, and by 1931 imports were severely curtailed (aided, it is true, by sharp increases in tariff duties); both export volume and prices dropped sharply in 1930, with a resultant drop in total value of exports from 954 million gold pesos in 1929 to 614 million in 1930. In 1931 export volume jumped, however, to the highest level since 1927. With export prices declining, the total value in pesos increased only slightly over that for 1930. With gold prices declining much more drastically, however, this was equivalent to an increase in peso prices, relative to gold prices.[60] Thus, by the end of 1931, Argentina achieved approximate equilibrium in its international accounts, with the peso depreciated, in terms of gold, by nearly 40 per cent.

---

count with the Conversion Office up to 200 million paper pesos of commercial paper in exchange for paper currency, provided that the gold reserve should be maintained at not less than 40 per cent.

3. On August 29, 1931, the limit of 200 million paper pesos was removed; by the end of the year 359 million paper pesos had been issued against such rediscounts.

4. In 1932 the Conversion Office was authorized to discount bonds issued under the internal 500 million paper peso "Patriotic" Loan of that year at 85 per cent of their par value. The gold reserve requirement of 40 per cent was, however, still maintained.

[60] That exports increased in 1931 cannot be ascribed entirely to theoretical expectations under a depreciated currency; on the contrary, it illustrates the fact that the course of Argentina's exports during the past decade has been dominated, not by Argentine monetary factors, but primarily by two totally independent forces, namely: (1) fortuitous climatic conditions; (2) inelasticity of both demand and supply which characterizes agricultural and pastoral products.

The question remains unanswered as to whether this divorcing of the Argentine peso from gold was a wise policy (assuming, of course, that it was voluntary rather than involuntary). Anyone wishing to justify the Argentine procedure might at once point out that it was the policy subsequently adopted by Great Britain in 1931, immediately followed by many other countries. The United States, after suffering from the effects of a rapidly falling gold price level, which brought in its wake a tremendous wave of mortgage foreclosures and other debtor defaults, culminating in an almost complete collapse of the banking structure, finally chose the same road in the spring of 1933.[61] Although Argentina might have restored equilibrium in its international economic position by the end of 1931 through the policy of maintaining gold payments, it is difficult to see how the drastic deflationary effect on the domestic economy which such a policy would have necessitated, could have been otherwise than disastrous. This domestic economy, it must be remembered, was primarily agricultural and pastoral in character (although to a less extensive degree in recent years); much more so than in the United States where deflation brought the agricultural sections to the verge of economic and social collapse.[62] With gold prices of Argentina's agricultural and pastoral products dropping to 46 per cent of the 1926 level in 1931 and 37 per cent in 1932, a complete internal collapse might have resulted, had the gold standard been retained. Abrupt changes in the purchasing power of money work great hardships upon the members of any modern economy so inextricably bound up with creditor-debtor relationships, and these creditor-debtor relationships are as much a part of Argentina's agricultural economy as elsewhere. Early in 1932 it was estimated that Argentina's mortgage indebtedness totaled nearly two billion gold pesos, or roughly 250 gold pesos per capita of rural population,[63] compared with a per capita

[61] At least the Administration then in power did so.

[62] Witness the farmers' strikes, prevention of mortgage foreclosures, etc., during the winter of 1932-33.

[63] *Economic Review*, February-March 1932, p. 41. Argentine rural population in 1932 was estimated at 4,800,000 or 40 per cent of the total population. *Revista de Economía Argentina*, Dec. 1934, p. 267.

figure of rural population for the United States of 306 dollars (U.S.).[64]

On the other hand, it must not be forgotten that currency depreciation increases the cost of imports, as well as other contractual external remittances in the form of financial service on foreign borrowings, etc., which are payable in foreign currencies. With respect to foreign borrowings, the additional cost to Argentina of meeting the external debt service on its public (i.e., governmental) borrowings abroad, as a result of currency depreciation, has averaged about 12 million gold pesos annually since 1933.[65]

The earnings on foreign investments in private undertakings in Argentina, however, the estimated value of which in 1931 was 3,366 million gold pesos, or 82 per cent of the estimated total of 4,100 million gold pesos, are measured in Argentine currency, so that the external depreciation of the peso has simply reduced the amount of these earnings in terms of foreign currencies. Furthermore, upon the institution of exchange control late in 1931, it became increasingly difficult to obtain exchange, even for the reduced remittances, in terms of foreign currencies, which might otherwise have been made.

The British were, of course, the largest sufferers, since about half of the total of private foreign investments in Argentina are British-owned.[66] The negotiation of the Roca-Runciman Agreement provided some relief,[67] yet the estimated return on British-owned railways in Argentina in 1934 was 1.6 per cent, contrasted with 5.5 per cent in 1929. The situation is clearly reflected in current prices of Argentine railway shares, some of

[64] United States Department of Agriculture, *Yearbook*, 1934, p. 62.

[65] Of the estimated total foreign investment in Argentina in 1931 of 4,100 million gold pesos (see Table XVII, p. 108), something over 700 million pesos was governmental (i.e., national, provincial, and municipal) borrowing, practically all of which was payable in foreign currencies. The total amount transferred from the Exchange Profits Fund to the Treasury to cover exchange losses on the public foreign debt service during the three years 1934-36 inclusive was approximately 37 million gold pesos (84.5 million paper pesos), or roughly 12 million gold pesos annually.

[66] Estimated at 53 per cent in 1931. See Table XVII, p. 108.

[67] See pp. 189, 191-92.

which have been quoted on the London Stock Exchange at about ten per cent of par.

The real burden of restoring equilibrium in Argentina's balance of payments fell largely, then, upon the holders of private foreign investments in Argentina and the recipients abroad of immigrant and other private remittances from Argentina, as well as the users of Argentine imports. Presumably, the reduction in these remittances far more than offset the increased cost of imports and public foreign debt service. In other words, a greater proportion of the decrease in the total Argentine national income since 1929 came from that portion formerly remitted abroad than it did from the share which was consumed within the country. Whether, on balance, the distribution of Argentina's national income has been more equitable under a depreciated currency and relative internal stability of prices than would have occurred under a gold standard and rapidly falling domestic prices, the writer does not presume to answer with any finality. The *total* income available for distribution, however, was probably greater than it would have been, had deflation been permitted to pursue its course.[68]

[68] "With the peso at par, and the price of wheat at $3.50 per 100 kilos [approximately $.40 U. S. per bushel], a considerable area of land would be left untilled. Land rents would fall even lower than they have done already. According to how one considers this possibility, it need not in itself of course be regarded with disfavour, but it stands to reason that its operation would have disastrous effects on mortgage and commercial credit which depends directly or indirectly on the value of land. The social consequences of such a fall in values would be extremely serious, not only in the country districts but also in the urban centres. The drop in industrial prices, held up thus far by the currency depreciation and the increase of import duties for fiscal reasons, would bring in its trail an industrial crisis and a serious unemployment situation.

"Prices in general would admittedly be lower but the people's means of payments for consumption purposes would also be smaller." *Economic Review*, February 1932, p. 42.

Peters, in his recent study *The Foreign Debt of the Argentine Republic*, *op. cit.*, p. 178, concludes: "More than likely, [a] central bank, had it existed from 1928 to the present, would have made vigorous efforts to keep the peso at par with the gold currencies. In the writer's opinion, this would have had much more disastrous effects than the policy actually followed. That Argentina suffered so little from the world depression, in spite of the fact that the country produces those commodities whose values were most seriously affected by price

Since 1929 Argentina has, then, maintained relative stability in its price level at the expense of external currency instability. In fact, throughout the period covered by this study, Argentina's

CHART V. INDICES OF WHOLESALE PRICES, ARGENTINA AND THE UNITED STATES, ANNUAL AVERAGES, 1913-35

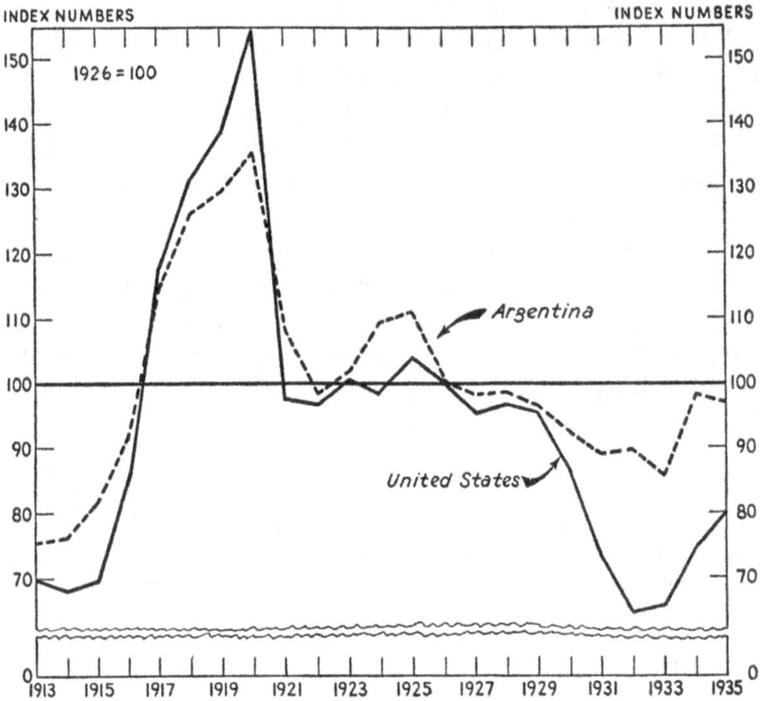

Sources: Argentina: *Revista de Economía Argentina*, June, 1930, p. 448; Banco de la Nación, *Economic Review*, Jan.-Mar., 1934, p. 30; Oct.-Dec., 1934, p. 166. United States: United States Bureau of Labor Statistics, *Wholesale Prices*, Feb., 1936, p. 9.

price level, as indicated in Chart V, has shown a relatively marked degree of stability, in contrast to wide fluctuations in the

declines, must be at least in part attributed to the behavior of the peso. Inelastic, rigid, uncontrolled, and subject to numerous other theoretical objections, the peso has sustained an extraordinarily constant level of prices. This is probably the greatest single advantage that a currency can possess. As such it deserves at the very least to be carefully weighed when the establishment of a new system is contemplated and when a currency policy is to be determined."

external value of her currency.[69] For Argentina, or any other country, whose economy is so dominated by external factors, to achieve both internal and external stability of purchasing power in its currency may well prove a difficult, if not insurmountable, task. In fact, it may be impossible to maintain external stability even at the expense of internal instability.[70]

With the major items in its balance of payments subject to such wide fluctuations, it appears that only by the maintenance of very large idle gold stocks or foreign exchange reserves, can a country such as Argentina hope to maintain both external and internal stability in its currency.[71] Whether the dual objective of relative internal and external stability may be achieved in Argentina through the retention of a free currency implemented by an exchange equalization fund remains to be seen. Certainly the maintenance of such stability under a restored international gold standard is difficult to conceive, unless the periodic world-wide economic crises and breakdowns which now characterize the world's economic system are eliminated.

[69] See Chart I, p. 31.

[70] Smith concludes (*op. cit.*, pp. 447-49), after a consideration of the recent experience of Argentina, Brazil, and Australia, that, in the event of a world-wide deflationary movement, the breakdown of the gold standard is inevitable in any country whose major exports are raw materials, and which is also an international debtor on a large scale. The "Macmillan Report" (Great Britain, Committee on Finance and Industry, Report Cmd. 3897, 1931, p. 80), in describing the process of international investment, emphasizes the fact that, due to the fluctuating character of all raw material production (e.g., bad harvests), if new capital loans are not forthcoming to offset reduced exports, gold reserves may soon be exhausted and "there may be no alternative except a departure for the time being from the gold standard."

[71] The debatable assumption is, of course, implied here that internal stability in purchasing power of a country's currency is desirable.

V

GROWTH OF FOREIGN INVESTMENTS IN ARGENTINA
1910-1934

THE INCREASE in total foreign capital invested in Argentina during the period 1910-34, as well as the growth by countries of origin, is summarized in Table XV.[1]

TABLE XV
ESTIMATED GROWTH OF FOREIGN CAPITAL INVESTED IN ARGENTINA, 1910-34
(in millions of gold pesos)

	1910	*1913*	*1917*	*1920*	*1923*	*1927*	*1931*	*1934*
Great Britain	1,475	1,928	1,950	1,825	1,975	2,075	2,100	2,285
United States	20	40	85	75	200	505	807	590
Germany	200	250	275	265	285	285	300	315
France	410	475	465	410	415	415	425	450
Others	150	557	575	575	325	320	468	660
Total	2,255	3,250	3,350	3,150	3,200	3,600	4,100	4,300

Note: For sources and details of the compilation of this table, see Appendix II.

[1] Most of the statistical data used in this chapter were compiled by the writer during the latter part of 1935. Presumably changes in the total volume, as well as the distribution and composition, of foreign investments in Argentina since 1934 have been relatively unimportant. According to the Balance of Payments statement of the Central Bank of Argentina, the amount of new foreign capital invested in Argentina during 1935 equaled 66 million gold pesos (150 million paper pesos). As indicated in the preceding chapter, however, the estimated change in Argentina's *net* foreign indebtedness in 1935 constituted a reduction of 12 million gold pesos. Although the Central Bank's statement of Argentina's balance of payments for 1936 is not yet available, it is probable that a substantial volume of new investments from abroad will be revealed. As a percentage of the total accumulated volume, however, the change cannot be significant. The apparent further marked decline in investments of United States capital in Argentina since 1934 is described briefly in succeeding pages.

The distribution of the foreign investments of other countries not itemized in the above table was estimated in 1924 as follows:[2]

	U. S. dollars	*Gold pesos*
Netherlands	150,000,000	155,400,000
Belgium	135,000,000	139,860,000
Spain	60,000,000	62,160,000
Sweden and Norway	25,000,000	25,900,000
Italy	25,000,000	25,900,000
Miscellaneous	15,000,000	15,540,000
Total	410,000,000	424,760,000

Analysis of Table XV reveals the following major trends:

(1) The increase of total foreign capital invested in Argentina from 1910 to 1913 of approximately 1,000 million gold pesos reflects the rapid rate at which new funds were flowing into Argentina in the years immediately preceding the outbreak of the World War.

(2) Not only was this flow of funds halted during the World War, but Argentina was enabled to reduce her foreign indebtedness, although relatively by a small amount.[3]

(3) Relatively little new foreign capital entered Argentina during the post-war period of liquidation, 1920-23, but in the ensuing eight years Argentina increased her foreign borrowing by nearly a billion gold pesos or, roughly, some 30 per cent. This growth in foreign capital invested in Argentina was, how-

[2] This is the estimate of the Argentine statistician, A. B. Martinez, referred to in Appendix II, p. 253, which is quoted by Dunn in *American Foreign Investments*, 1926, and by Winkler in *Investments of United States Capital in Latin America*, 1928, World Peace Foundation.

[3] The estimated reduction of 200 million gold pesos in total foreign investments in Argentina between 1917 and 1920 as given in Table XV, is considerably less than has been frequently stated. See Appendix II, p. 254. This reduction, it must be remembered, excludes consideration of Argentine loans to foreigners. The reduction in Argentina's *net* long-term foreign indebtedness (foreign borrowings minus foreign lending) from 1917 to 1920 was, according to Tornquist's balance of payments figures, some 376 million gold pesos. See Table II, "Estimated International Capital Transactions of Argentina, 1913-1934," Appendix II, pp. 240-41.

ever, still considerably below the pre-war rate. It has been estimated that during the thirty years preceding 1914, the investment of foreign capital totaled 2,640 million gold pesos, or an average of approximately twenty pesos per capita per year, whereas during the twelve years preceding 1928 the new foreign capital invested in Argentina averaged only slightly over three pesos per person per year.[4]

(4) The major portion of these new funds after 1923 came from the United States, the total investments of which increased from less than 100 million gold pesos in 1920 to over 800 millions at the end of the decade.[5] From 1914 to 1928 practically all of Argentina's public foreign financing (including national, provincial, and municipal) was done in the New York market.

(5) British, as well as other European investments remained relatively constant throughout the entire period, 1913-31, the estimated total increase between 1913 and 1931, of all other foreign capital excepting United States, being only 83 million pesos. Of the estimated increase from 1920 to 1931 of 950 million pesos, only 218 millions was European, the balance of 732 million pesos coming from the United States. Since 1931 the value of United States capital invested in Argentina has shown a marked decline relative to other foreign capital.

The growth of financial relations between the United States and Argentina during the twenty-year period 1914-34 may be divided into six distinct periods, as follows:

1. *1914-17: Public short-term borrowing*

During the early war years the Argentine National Government turned to the New York market for funds to cover budgetary deficits. The total of these short-term loans obtained in New York reached 80 million dollars in 1917.

[4] A. E. Bunge, *La Economía Argentina*, Buenos Aires, 1928, Vol. II, p. 19.

[5] The peak was presumably reached in 1930, since at the end of that year total United States investments in Argentina were estimated at 837 million pesos. Paul Dickens, A New Estimate of American Investments Abroad, *TIB* No. 767, United States Bureau of Foreign and Domestic Commerce, Washington, D.C., 1931.

2. *1917-20: Repayment of short-term borrowing*

By 1920 these short-term loans had all been repaid, due in part to official pressure on the part of the United States government.[6] Very little was accomplished, therefore, of a permanent nature in the use of the New York money market by Argentina during the War. Investments of United States capital in private undertakings during this period are estimated to have been increased some 35 million gold pesos.

3. *1920-23: Renewal of public short-term borrowing*

From 1921 to 1923 the Argentine National Government again entered the New York money market, but was successful only in obtaining short-term advances at relatively high interest rates. The high interest rates demanded, together with domestic political difficulties encountered by President Irigoyen in obtaining Congressional authorization for external funding loans which the bankers insisted upon, prevented the consummation of any long-term loans until 1924. Protracted negotiations were entered into, however, throughout the period.[7] By 1923 these short-term loans had reached a total of 95 million dollars.[8]

4. *1924-28: Public long-term borrowing*

These years were the hey-day of Argentine public borrowing in the United States. During 1924 70 million dollars in long-term bonds of the Argentine National Government were floated successfully in the United States. By the end of 1928 this sum had been increased to 289,900,000 dollars. This was not all new borrowing, however, since the floating debt of 95 million dollars was entirely extinguished during the period. In addition, municipal and provincial long-term loans were made totaling approximately 75 million dollars.[9] Except for refunding opera-

[6] H. E. Peters, *op. cit.*, p. 96.

[7] *Ibid.*, pp. 111-20.

[8] *Ibid.*, p. 127.

[9] The net increase in Argentine public indebtedness in the United States during this period was, of course, considerably less, due to refunding, commissions paid, etc. According to the estimates given in Table XVII below, p. 108, the net increase in Argentine public borrowing from the United States from 1923 to the end of 1927 was 120 million gold pesos. During 1928 new public issues

tions, no public long-term issues have been floated by Argentina in the United States since 1928.

During this period there was also a less spectacular, but nevertheless considerable, increase in United States investments in private undertakings in Argentina, the estimated total of which was 185 million gold pesos. Practically all of these took the form of "direct" investments, however, since the total volume of publicly offered corporate securities was negligible during the period.[10]

5. 1928-30: Private investments

The cessation of Argentine public long-term borrowing in the United States in 1928 was in decided contrast to private investments, which continued to expand rapidly until 1931. During the three years, 1928-30 inclusive, the total of net new corporate issues publicly offered in the United States (the proceeds of which were destined for use in Argentina) was as follows:

1928	$62,640,000
1929	3,185,000
1930	16,638,000

These figures do not include the "direct" investments made by American companies for which no public issue of securities was made; that is, the large investments in branch plants, etc., which were made directly from funds of the parent corporation. That these "direct" private investments were considerable during these years is borne out by the fact that the estimated net increase in total United States private investments in Argentina from 1927 to 1931, as given in Table XVII (p. 108), was 228 million gold pesos.[11] During 1930 there was a renewal of public

(excluding refunding issues) totaled 26 million dollars, of which 20 million dollars represented borrowing by the National Government.

[10] According to the United States Bureau of Foreign and Domestic Commerce, only one small issue, that of the Central Argentine Railway for $350,000, was offered between 1924 and 1928. Handbook of American Underwriting of Foreign Securities, 1914-1929, *Trade Promotion Series* No. 104, Washington, D.C., 1930.

[11] The total "direct" investments of the capital of the United States at the end of 1930 was estimated at 369 million gold pesos (358 million dollars). Dickens, *op. cit.*

short-term borrowing by Argentina from the United States which totaled approximately 85 million dollars.[12]

6. *1930-34: Decline in United States investments*

The period from 1930 to 1934 was characterized by a marked decline in United States investments in Argentina, both public and private, as shown in Table XVII. To a considerable degree this decline took the form of foreign purchases (including Argentine repatriation) of Argentine securities previously held in the United States, as a result of the bargain "panic" prices prevailing, particularly in the period 1931-33. Presumably the "direct" investments of American concerns remained at approximately the 1930 level, relatively small amounts of new capital having been invested during the depression. Between 1930 and 1934 eight new manufacturing branch plants operated by United States firms were established in Argentina, with an estimated total capital investment of approximately ten million dollars.[13] In recent months there have been indications of further renewed activity in this field; for example, in the textile industry, which has recently been witnessing rapid expansion in Argentina.[14]

On the other hand, the retirement since November 1936 of nearly 120 millions of the long-term dollar debt of the Argentine National Government out of the cash resources of the Argentine Treasury has resulted in a further marked reduction in the existing volume of United States investments in Argentina. Including amortization payments on that portion of Argentina's dollar obligations still outstanding, as well as the large volume of repatriations mentioned above, it is probable that the total volume of United States investments in all Argentine public securities (i.e., national, provincial, and municipal), is now (May

[12] *Ibid.* Fifty million dollars of this was by the National Government, the balance being municipal and provincial borrowing.

[13] D. M. Phelps, *Migration of Industry to South America*, McGraw-Hill Book Company, 1936, pp. 13 and 19.

[14] The Du Pont organization recently announced that it would invest some five million dollars of new capital in plant expansion in Argentina for the manufacture of rayon.

1937) not greatly in excess of 150 million gold pesos (340 million paper pesos). Assuming that the value of "direct" investments approximates 400 million gold pesos,[15] the total United States investment in Argentina at present may be estimated to approximate 550 million gold pesos (1,250 million paper pesos), compared with the figure of 590 millions in Table XVII as of 1934. This is equivalent to a decline of roughly one-third from the estimate of 807 million gold pesos in 1931.

Thus the growth and composition of United States investments in Argentina during the past twenty-five years may be summarized by pointing out that it has taken the same form as the previous expansion of English investment during the nineteenth century; that is, the first investments were government loans, which were later largely overshadowed by private investments. Again, with respect to the United States, growing familiarity with the country has resulted in a gradual shift from public loans to private investments, a trend which is likely to continue in the future.

The problem of valuation involved in estimating the foreign capital invested in a country is, at best, an exceedingly complex and difficult one; but under conditions of inconvertible currencies, exchange control, and blocked funds which have existed during recent years, together with several exchange rates effective simultaneously, the problem becomes almost insuperable. At least, the results obtained are of doubtful utility. In the first place, there is the problem of what should constitute the unit of value. Having decided this question, how should the existing data (at best inadequate and unsatisfactory) be converted into terms of this common denominator?

In attempting to meet this question of valuation, the writer has compiled estimates of the value of foreign investments in Argentina as of 1934, using three different bases of calculation. These estimates are contained in the accompanying table (Table XVI).

[15] See below, p. 112.

TABLE XVI

ESTIMATED VALUE OF FOREIGN INVESTMENTS IN ARGENTINA, END OF 1934, BY COUNTRIES (in millions of pesos)

	I[a] gold pesos	II[b] gold pesos	III[c] A gold pesos	III[c] B paper pesos
Great Britain	2,285	3,426	2,990	6,796
United States	590	856	758	1,727
Germany	315	630	630	1,830
France	450	1,103	1,072	2,433
Others	660	1,320	1,320	2,996
Total	4,300	7,335	6,770	15,782

[a] Column I gives the figures for each country converted at the old par of exchange prior to 1930. This was done in an attempt to make the data comparable with those for the preceding years, and this column is the one used in Table XV above for 1934.

[b] Column II contains the figures given in Column I corrected for the percentage deviation of the Argentine official selling rate of exchange at the end of 1934, relative to the old par of exchange prior to 1930. Since presumably none of the countries concerned will return to the old parity, these figures carry little significance, except for comparative purposes.

[c] Columns IIIA and IIIB show the figures for each country converted at the Argentine official buying rate of exchange at the end of 1934 for the respective for eign currencies (paper pesos having been converted to gold pesos at the old ratio of 2.27 to 1).[16]

To the extent that Argentina's foreign obligations are payable in foreign currencies, and subject to gradual amortization, the figures in Columns III^{A} and III^{B} carry some significance, and indicate in a rough way the additional burden involved in their repayment, following the depreciation and ultimate devaluation of the currency. Of the total public external debt as of December 31, 1934, all but 76 million gold pesos of a total of 1,040 million pesos was in foreign currencies, as the following figures indicate:[17]

[16] The percentage deviation for countries other than Great Britain, United States, and France was placed arbitrarily at 200 per cent; that is, midway between sterling and the franc, on the assumption that the total of other foreign investments in Argentina was divided equally between countries in the sterling group, and those which have maintained the gold standard.

[17] This total does not allow for repatriations, which are estimated at 73 million gold pesos.

ARGENTINE PUBLIC EXTERNAL DEBT, DECEMBER 31, 1934
(in millions)

	Sterling	*French francs*	*Dollars*	*Gold pesos*	*Total*
National	44	382	283	65	
Provincial	15	82	79	11	
Municipal	3	—	21	—	
	—	—	—	—	
Totals	62	464	383	76	
Equivalent in[a]					
paper pesos	931	93	1,164	173	2,361
gold pesos	410	41	513	76	1,040

[a] Converted at official buying rate as of December 24, 1934.
Source: United States Bureau of Foreign and Domestic Commerce, Washington, D.C.

With respect to private investments in Argentina, however, presumably the major portion is sunk permanently, and therefore the important factor with respect to its value is its income-producing capacity, plus the ability to transfer these earnings to foreign owners. This transfer problem has, of course, been acute in Argentina in recent years. As pointed out elsewhere in this study, the low returns transferred abroad on private investments has reduced their current market value to a fraction of their par value.

The character of the foreign investments in Argentina during the period of this study, as well as their distribution by country of origin, is summarized in Table XVII.[18]

[18] The distribution of the capital invested in Argentina by type of investment for the years 1909, 1911, and 1917 is given in considerable detail in Appendix II, Tables III, IV, and V. As of the end of 1927, Sr. Bunge classified foreign investments in Argentina as follows:

	Gold pesos
Loans (Public)	770,000,000
Railways	1,367,080,000
Mortgages	315,920,000
Banks	91,520,000
Miscellaneous	546,480,000
Total	3,091,000,000

See *Review of the River Plate,* Jan. 21, 1928, p. 25. The discrepancy in Bunge's total figure compared with that given in Table XVII is discussed in Appendix II, p. 258.

TABLE XVII
ESTIMATED GROWTH OF FOREIGN INVESTMENTS IN ARGENTINA, BY TYPES OF INVESTMENT, 1910–34
(in millions of gold pesos)

	1910	*1913*	*1917*	*1923*	*1927*	*1931*	*1934*	
							Gold pesos	*Paper pesos*
Total	2,255	3,250	3,350	3,200	3,600	4,100	4,300	9,761
Public: (total)	692	675	657	580	770	734	900	2,043
Great Britain		475	450	400	375	280	400	908
United States			25	110	230	304	217	492
Others		200	182	70	165	150	283	643
Railways: (total)	804	1,175	1,200	1,275	1,367	1,500	1,550	3,519
Great Britain		1,075	1,100	1,175	1,230	1,360	1,400	3,178
Others		100	100	100	137	140	150	341
Other Private: (total)	759	1,400	1,493	1,345	1,463	1,866	1,850	4,200
Great Britain		378	400	400	470	460	485	1,101
United States		40	60	90	275	503	373	847
Others		982	1,033	855	718	903	992	2,252
Great Britain: (total)		1,928	1,950	1,975	2,075	2,100	2,285	5,187
Public		475	450	400	375	280	400	908
Railways		1,075	1,100	1,115	1,230	1,360	1,400	3,178
Other Private		378	400	400	470	460	485	1,101
United States: (total)		40	85	200	505	807	590	1,339
Public			25	110	230	304	217	492
Private		40	60	90	275	503	373	847
Others: (total)		1,282	1,315	1,025	1,020	1,193	1,425	3,236
Public		200	182	70	165	150	283	643
Private								
Railways		100	100	100	137	140	150	341
Others		982	1,033	855	718	903	992	2,252
Others: (total)		1,282	1,315	1,025	1,020	1,193	1,425	3,236
France		475	465	415	415	425	450	1,497
Germany		250	275	285	285	300	315	1,021
Others		557	575	325	320	468	660	718

Source: See Appendix II, p. 262.

Analysis of the above table reveals that by far the greater part of the foreign capital has been invested in private undertakings rather than in public securities, the percentage of the total which was invested in public loans being 21, 18, and 18 per cent,

as of 1913, 1923, and 1931 respectively. Notwithstanding the fact that public loans increased rapidly from 1923 to 1931 (from 580 million to 734 million gold pesos, or an increase of 27 per cent), private investments grew at a parallel rate.

This growth in public loans was due, as indicated, to the rapid expansion of foreign lending by the United States. In fact, public borrowings in the United States (i.e., borrowing by Argentine governmental units) from 1923 to 1931 exceeded the total increase in public borrowing abroad during the same period by 40 million pesos, increasing by 194 million pesos as compared with a total increase of 154 million pesos. In contrast to this increase in United States loans to Argentine governmental units, British capital invested in Argentine public loans during the same period declined by 120 million gold pesos. Of this 120 millions, 40 millions, as just pointed out, may be assigned to the United States; the balance of 80 million pesos was attributable to increases in the purchase of Argentine public securities by other nations. Since 1931, however, the trend in public (governmental) loans to Argentina has been reversed, as previously indicated; that is, United States loans have declined not only relatively, but absolutely. This decline in United States holdings of Argentine public securities between 1931 and 1934 is estimated at 87 million pesos, or over 25 per cent.[19]

With the exception of Great Britain and the United States, the data available regarding type of investment by nationality are rather meager. French capital has been invested, in addition to government loans, largely in banks, railways, and port development. German investments are mostly in agricultural activities (large estates and cattle concerns), and also in banks and commercial enterprises. Extensive German investments in public utilities were sold after the War to Spanish interests. Dutch capital has been invested in government bonds, banks, steamship lines, and oil fields. Belgian capital is invested in banking institutions and land holdings. Italian and Spanish capital is mostly in banks.[20]

[19] See Appendix II, pp. 261-62 for details.

[20] F. M. Halsey, Investments in Latin America, I. Argentina, United States Bureau of Foreign and Domestic Commerce, *TIB* No. 362; Winkler, *op. cit.*, p. 67; Dunn, *op. cit.*

Considerable attention has been given to the composition of United States investments in Argentina. The most comprehensive studies are those of Dr. Paul Dickens of the Finance Division, United States Bureau of Foreign and Domestic Commerce.[21]

Following is Dr. Dickens' estimate of direct investments of United States capital in Argentina as of December 31, 1929, classified by type of investment:

(in thousands of dollars)

	Number of establishments	*Value of Investments*
Manufacturing	27	82,008
Selling	37	52,908
Petroleum	8	29,811
Mining and Smelting (included with Petroleum)		
Communication and Transportation (none in railways)	7	147,836
Miscellaneous	20	19,256
Total	99	331,819

The above figures show that United States private investments in Argentina cover a wide field.[22] Most of the public utility

[21] American Direct Investments in Foreign Countries, *TIB* No. 731, 1930, Washington, D.C.; A New Estimate of American Investments Abroad, *TIB* No. 767, 1931, Washington, D.C. A revised estimate of Dr. Dickens as of the end of 1933 was contained in The Balance of International Payments of the United States in 1933, *TIB* No. 819; his figures for the end of 1934 were furnished the writer by Dr. Dickens. See also Dr. Max Winkler's estimates published by the Foreign Policy Association. Earlier important studies which should be mentioned are Frederic M. Halsey, Investments in Latin America, United States Bureau of Foreign and Domestic Commerce, *Special Agents Series* No. 169, 1918, and Investments in Latin America, I. Argentina, *TIB* No. 362, 1925, a revision of the 1918 study; also the studies by Dunn and Winkler referred to previously. D. M. Phelps's recent study, *Migration of Industry to South America*, contains valuable data covering direct investments of United States capital in Argentina, particularly with reference to manufacturing operations in branch plants.

[22] According to Dr. Dickens' classification, total "direct" investments are not

properties, which constitute nearly half of the total, were acquired since the middle of 1928. The large investment in selling organizations is due not only to the importance of the Argentine market, but also to the fact that many American corporations make Buenos Aires their headquarters for the lower part of South America. Of the manufacturing interests, meat packing is the most important. The industry was one of the first to attract American capital, the first investment having been made by Swift and Company in 1907. In addition, the Armour, Morris, and Wilson companies all have important plants in Argentina. Other important industrial investments are in automobiles (assembly plants), cement, glass, agricultural and industrial machinery, and chemicals. Petroleum investments include not only distribution, but production and refining as well.[23]

D. M. Phelps's estimate of the total of United States investments in Argentina (presumably as of 1935), exclusive of "investments in purely merchandising activities, financial institutions, or governmental or other securities," places the figure as "between 400 and 425 million dollars," divided as follows:[24]

	No. of plants	*Investment*
I. *Branch plants:*		
1. Mineral products	3	$ 55,498,000
2. Others	28	105,280,000
Total	31	160,778,000
II. *Merchandising concerns engaging in minor assembly and service activities:*		26,559,000
III. *Public utilities:*	3	215,000,000
Total	34	$402,337,000

exactly synonymous with total private investments, since he includes under portfolio investments private corporate securities publicly offered. In the case of Argentina this is not a large sum, totaling, at the end of 1934, 17 million dollars.

[23] Dunn, *op. cit.*, gives greater details as of 1926.

[24] *Op. cit.*, pp. 19-20.

Another estimate in 1935 placed the total of *all* United States direct investments in Argentina at 400 million dollars.[25] It will be noted that these estimates are some 50 million dollars higher than those of Dr. Dickens which are used by the writer. As of Dec. 31, 1934, Dr. Dickens estimated that total United States direct investments in Argentina equaled 341 million dollars.

Portfolio investments, that is, securities publicly offered, were divided as follows at the end of 1934:

	(in millions of dollars)
Public:	
National	283
Provincial	81
Municipal	21
Total Public	385
Private:	
Corporate	17
Total	402

Of this sum, however, it was estimated that some 175 millions had been repatriated.[26]

Presumably, the trend toward private or "direct" investments, particularly in evidence since 1928, will be continued in the future. Argentina's present program of increasing economic self-sufficiency will no doubt promote the investment of industrial capital within the country.[27] Since such investments are more apt to be in the nature of equities than fixed income obligations, such a trend, particularly for a raw material and food producing country such as Argentina, so susceptible to international economic influence, is probably desirable. Such equities would, in times of

[25] Lansing Wilcox, Manager of the Buenos Aires branch of the First National Bank of Boston, and President of the Chamber of Commerce of the United States in Argentina, in an address delivered September 20, 1935 (see *Comments on Argentine Trade,* Vol. XV, No. 2).

[26] See Appendix II, p. 262.

[27] On the other hand, it is interesting to note that many firms which opened branch plants abroad since 1929 to avoid trade barriers report that such branch activities are uneconomical, and would be closed, provided the trade barriers were removed.

CHART VI. ESTIMATED ARGENTINE FOREIGN DEBT SERVICE REMITTANCES, 1914-35

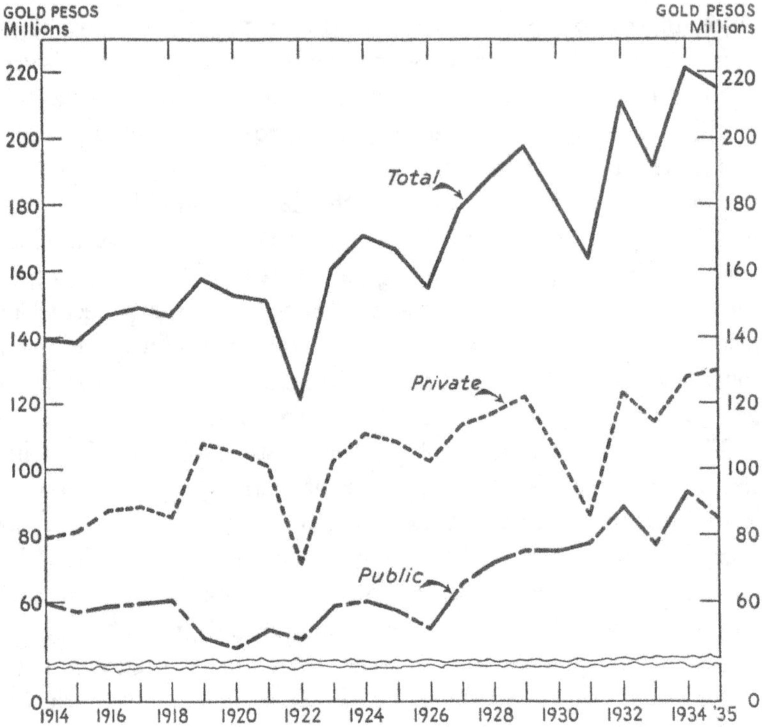

Source: Table I, Appendix I, opposite p. 238.

prosperity, earn relatively high returns which presumably could be remitted without difficulty, but during periods of depression would require no fixed external remittances, thus relieving the strain at such times on the country's international balance of payments.

The accompanying chart (Chart VI), showing the distribution of Argentina's estimated foreign debt service between private and public remittances for the period of this study, is illustrative of the point just made.[28] As the chart indicates, private remittances have fluctuated much more (in accordance with fluctua-

[28] These are net remittances; that is, gross remittances less income from Argentine capital invested abroad. They also include amortization payments.

tions in Argentina's general economic prosperity) than have public remittances, which have been, generally speaking, of a fixed character.[29] Furthermore, the decline in private remittances in 1921-22 and 1930-31 was due in part to the unwillingness of foreign concerns to assume the exchange losses involved in the purchase of foreign currencies. Earnings were frequently held in Argentina in anticipation of improved exchange rates.

The chart also reflects the war-time prosperity of private investments in Argentina, as well as the decline in public indebtedness during the same period. The rapid increase in investments, both public and private, during the decade of the twenties, is shown in the upward trend of remittances. The sharp decline in private remittances in 1930 and 1931, whereas public remittances continued to increase, perhaps best illustrates the point made regarding fixed income investments vs. equities.

The wide fluctuations in Argentina's estimated annual net increase (or decrease) in its international debtor position is graphically illustrated in Chart VII, which shows also the relationship between the volume of new borrowings and the debt service payable abroad on previous loans. During the war and post-war period of prosperity Argentina not only met its external debt service payments from current items in the balance of payments (i.e., commodity export surpluses, primarily) but reduced its external debtor position by some 235 million pesos. During the twenties, however, a considerable portion of the external debt service payments was offset by new borrowings. When these new funds from abroad were suddenly curtailed in 1929, large gold exports resulted which led to suspension of gold payments (as described in the preceding chapter), late in 1929. Failure of imports to contract in 1930, it will be recalled, accompanied by

[29] I.e., in the absence of defaults, which have been relatively unimportant with respect to Argentine public securities during this period. According to data obtained from the United States Bureau of Foreign and Domestic Commerce, Washington, D.C., the total interest in default on the "American share" of Argentine municipal and provincial dollar bonds as of December 31, 1934, was less than four million dollars. No defaults have occurred on the dollar bond issues of the National Government.

CHART VII. ESTIMATED ARGENTINE ANNUAL FOREIGN DEBT SERVICE REMITTANCES COMPARED WITH ESTIMATED NET CHANGE IN INTERNATIONAL DEBTOR POSITION, 1914-35

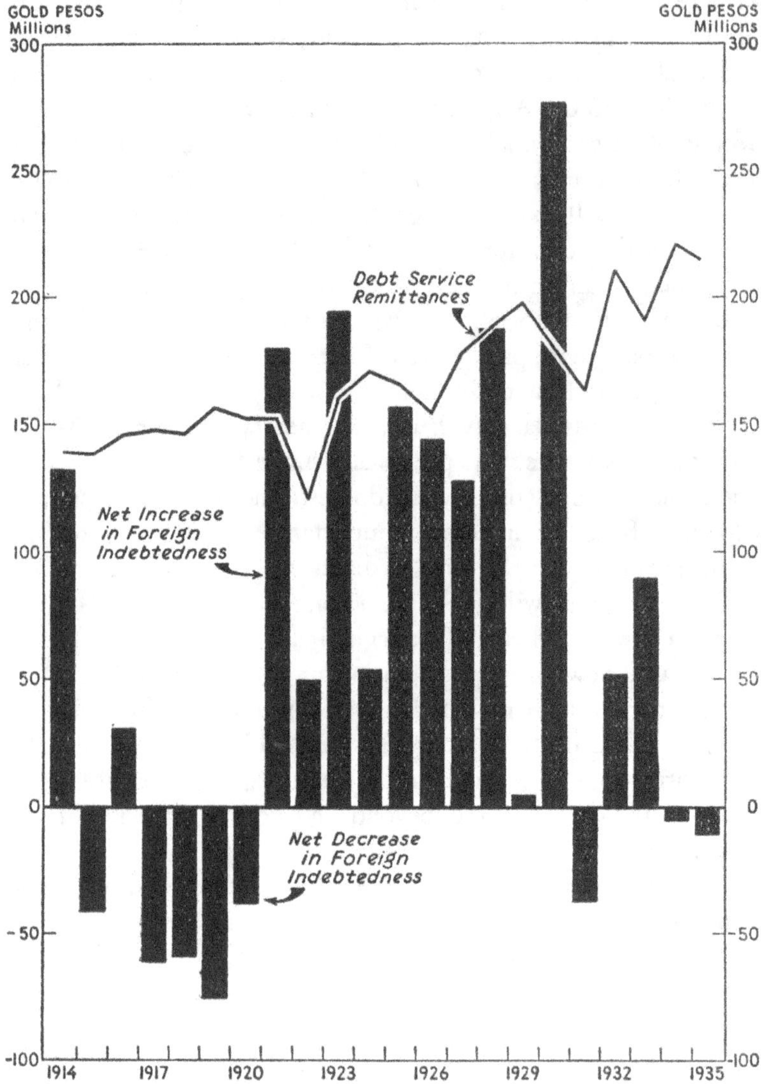

Source: Table I, Appendix I, opposite p. 238.

rapidly declining exports, necessitated foreign borrowings totaling approximately 275 million pesos, in order to effect a balance in the international accounts. The restoration of equilibrium by 1931, the reappearance of disequilibrium in 1932 and 1933 with renewed borrowing again necessary, and the achieving of equilibrium again in 1934, have already been described.

The abrupt cessation of foreign capital imports in 1929 was a severe shock to the Argentine economy, as was the similar sharp decline of large annual foreign borrowings fifteen years earlier, upon the outbreak of the World War. Opportunities for foreign capital still exist in Argentina, however, and it does not seem probable that foreign capital will fail to seek profitable investment again in this rich young country, as soon as evidence of economic recovery and the restoration of international confidence become more pronounced. In fact, all reports indicate that during 1936 and the early months of 1937 an increasing volume of foreign funds, largely European, has been entering Argentina for investments.[30] As previously suggested, the new Argentine economic policy of fostering domestic industrial development will be a factor of increasing importance in attracting foreign capital, primarily in the form of direct investments. Presumably, the United States will again participate to an increasing degree in this movement of capital to Argentina.

We turn now to a consideration of the trend of Argentine foreign borrowing with respect to other indices of national development during the past twenty years. Have Argentina's foreign borrowings been excessive? Is the foreign debt service which these borrowings required beyond the normal capacity of the country to pay?

The growth of Argentine indebtedness compared with the estimated increase in population and national wealth is shown in Table XVIII. Table XIX gives a comparative analysis of the growth of Argentine debt service with respect to growth of population and national government revenues.[31]

[30] For example, in its issue of December 21, 1936, *The Times of Argentina* stated that the capital market boom was "probably" due to "millions of pesos having been sent to Argentina during the past few days."

[31] Paucity of data prevents comparisons of growth of debt service with na-

TABLE XVIII

ANALYSIS OF GROWTH OF ARGENTINE INDEBTEDNESS WITH RESPECT TO NATIONAL WEALTH AND POPULATION (in millions of gold pesos)[a]

Year	*National Wealth*[b]		*Total Foreign Debt*		*Total Public Debt*[c]				*Total Funded National Debt*[d]			
	Total[b]	*Per Capita*	*Total*	*Per Capita*	*Total*	*Per Capita*	*Total Held Abroad*		*Total*	*Per Capita*	*Total Held Abroad*	
							Total	*Per Capita*			*Total*	*Per Capita*
1914	13,000	1,760	3,250	415	710	89	675	85	545	69	475	60
1930	26,000	2,200	4,100	350	1,614	141	734	63	995	87	500	43
1934	26,000	2,125	4,300	350	2,486	204	900	74	1,247	102	583	48

[a] Except per capita figures.

[b] No recent estimates are available of the national wealth of Argentina. Sr. Bunge estimated the total national wealth at 14.5 billion gold pesos as of 1916, and 10.2 billions in 1908. *Riqueza y renta de la Argentina*, Buenos Aires, 1917. The estimate of 13 billions for 1914 is a rough approximation based upon Bunge's two estimates. In 1929 the total wealth was estimated at roughly 26.4 billion gold pesos. The assumption is made that there was little increase in national wealth between 1930 and 1934, due to the depressed economic conditions in the interim.

[c] National, Provincial, and Municipal.

[d] Including floating debt the per capita figures for total National Debt were, for the years given, 83, 133, and 135 gold pesos, respectively. The total floating debt Dec. 31, 1934, was 402 million gold pesos, making a total National Debt of 1,649 million gold pesos. The external floating debt was completely paid off by September, 1934.

Source: Complied from sources cited and data given in Appendix II.

Inspection of Table XVIII reveals the following trends:

(1) Although total foreign borrowing (public and private) increased about a billion dollars between 1914 and 1934, the total per capita foreign debt declined from 415 pesos in 1914 to 350 pesos in 1930 and 1934, compared with an increase in the estimated per capita wealth from 1,760 to 2,200 pesos between 1914 and 1930.

(2) The increasing importance of the Argentine domestic

tional income. Apparently only one authoritative estimate of Argentina's national income has been made. In 1916, Bunge estimated the total national income at 2,384 million gold pesos, or approximately 300 gold pesos per capita. *Riqueza y renta de la Argentina*, Buenos Aires, 1917.

capital market as a source of funds during the past twenty years is reflected in the trend of public borrowing. Although the major portion of the public debt was held abroad in 1914, by 1934 approximately two-thirds was held internally. This resulted in an actual decline in the per capita public debt held abroad from 85 gold pesos in 1914 to 63 and 74 pesos in 1930 and 1934, respectively. This decline in that portion of the public debt held abroad was paralleled, nevertheless, by a growth in the total public per capita debt from 89 gold pesos in 1914 to 141 and 204 pesos in 1930 and 1934, respectively.

(3) The total funded national debt was about doubled between 1914 and 1930. This increase, however, was paralleled by a similar expansion in estimated national wealth. On a per capita basis, the increase was about 25 per cent in each case. Presumably, the increase in the total funded national debt of approximately 25 per cent between 1930 and 1934, however, was not accompanied by a similar growth in national wealth, although no estimates of the latter are available. This rapid increase from 1930 to 1934 was due, in part, however, to funding operations which reduced the floating debt (see footnote (d), Table XVIII). The total national debt (funded and floating) increased between 1930 and 1934 from 1,517 to 1,649 million gold pesos. Comparative figures for the United States were as follows:

PER CAPITA NATIONAL DEBT

	Argentine gold pesos	*United States dollars*
1914	83	12
1930	133	131
1934	145	214

(4) In contrast to an increase in the total national funded debt between 1914 and 1930 of nearly 100 per cent, the sum which was held abroad was approximately the same in 1930 as in 1914. Although in 1914 about 85 per cent of the total national funded debt was estimated to have been held abroad, by 1930 only about one-half was held outside of Argentina. In other words, most of the net increase in the debt from 1914 to 1930

came from domestic sources. This increasing reliance upon the local capital market has continued since 1930 for in 1934 (as shown in Table XVIII) slightly over 50 per cent of the total funded national debt was held internally. With an increase in population between 1914 and 1930 of about 44 per cent (from 7,950,000 in 1914 to 11,450,000 in 1930), the result has been a marked decline in the per capita funded national debt held abroad, the reduction having been from 60 to 43 gold pesos per capita. By 1934, however, the comparable figure had increased to 48 gold pesos per capita.

Table XIX

Analysis of Growth of Argentine Debt Service with Respect to National Revenues
(in millions of gold pesos)[a]

Year	Total Debt Service Payable Abroad	Private Debt Service Payable Abroad	Total Public Debt Service Payable Abroad[b]		National Debt Service				
					Total		Payable Abroad		
			Total	Per Capita	Total	Per cent of national revenue	Total	Per cent of total	Per cent of national revenue
1914	139	79	60	7.5	41	25.1	37	90	23
1930	180	105	75	6.6	102	31.0	52	51	16
1934	221	128	93	7.6	126	28.0	70	56	21

[a] Except per capita figures.
[b] National, Provincial, and Municipal.

The proportion of the total funded national debt held internally has continued to increase since 1934. As of June 30, 1936, the total funded national debt had increased to 1,644 million gold pesos (3,736 million paper pesos), or approximately 132 gold pesos per capita, although the total amount held abroad was probably somewhat less than in 1934.[32]

Of greater significance than the actual volume of a country's indebtedness, relative to its wealth and population, is its income-producing capacity to meet the interest and amortization charges resulting from such indebtedness. These data are presented in Table XIX, and may be summarized as follows:

[32] See footnote 26, p. 122 below.

Argentina's estimated total annual debt service payable abroad increased from 139 million to 180 million gold pesos in 1914 and 1930, respectively, or an increase of approximately 30 per cent, or two per cent annually. From 1930 to 1934, however, total debt service payable abroad increased by the same amount as in the previous fifteen years, or at an annual rate of about five per cent (of the 1930 figure). Total foreign investments in Argentina during the same period, however, are estimated to have increased only five per cent. The increase in debt service remittances between 1930 and 1934 totaled 41 million gold pesos, of which 23 millions was for private remittances, and 18 millions for public. A considerable part of the increase on governmental obligations was due to the higher cost of foreign currencies.[38] As indicated above (p. 72), the exchange differential in the servicing of the Government's external debt in 1934 which was covered by a transfer of exchange profits to the Treasury equaled ten million gold pesos (22.8 million paper pesos).

The estimated total external public debt service increased from 60 million gold pesos in 1914 to 75 million gold pesos in 1930. On a per capita basis, however, this was a decrease from 7.5 pesos to 6.6 pesos. By 1934 the per capita cost of total external public debt service remittances was again approximately what it was in 1914.

The data with respect to the Argentine national debt service show that for 1914, 25.1 per cent of total cash revenues was required for total debt service, compared with 31 and 28 per cent in 1930 and 1934, respectively. Comparative figures for the United States were as follows:

	Argentina	*United States*[a]
1914	25.1	3.1
1930	31.0	33.6
1934	28.0	36.0

[a] Annual Report of the Secretary of the Treasury, 1935, p. 322.

[38] Differences in methods of computation may have also affected the results. The 1930 figure is that compiled by Sr. Tornquist, whereas the 1934 figure is the estimate of the new Argentine Central Bank. Furthermore, amortization payments in the latter year may have constituted a larger percentage of the total.

Although that portion of the Argentine national debt service which was payable abroad increased from 37 to 52 million pesos in 1914 and 1930, respectively, yet in 1930 it required only 16 per cent of the total national revenues compared with 23 per cent in 1914. As already pointed out, this was due to the marked decline in the proportion of the national debt held abroad.

With respect to her internal economic development, the general conclusion seems warranted from the above analysis that Argentina's position as an international debtor was not less favorable in 1930 than it was in 1914—on the contrary, its position in 1930 was superior to what it had been fifteen years earlier. Although by 1934 Argentina's external debt burden had increased sharply over 1930, yet the country's position was still superior to that existing at the outbreak of the World War, which, it will be recalled, brought to an end an era of heavy foreign borrowing.

One important exception should be noted—the marked increase in total public borrowing. Although the external burden of public indebtedness was relatively less in 1930 and 1934 than in 1914, this was due, as already stated, not to a decline in total borrowing, but to a shift from foreign to domestic sources of funds. The increase in total national debt service in recent years to nearly one-third of the national revenues is probably excessive.

Although it is beyond the scope of this study to consider the details of other public borrowing (i.e., municipal and provincial), the history of many such loans since 1930 is probably sufficient evidence of their undesirability. Since these provincial and municipal bond issues during the middle twenties were sold to yield from 6.25 to over 7.5 per cent, however, the purchasers were duly warned (or should have been) of their speculative character.[34]

The capacity of a country to borrow abroad involves not only its internal income and revenue producing capacity, however, but also the external problem of transferring the debt service into foreign currencies. And here we come upon Argentina's major

[34] The highest yield was 7.61 per cent on the Province of Mendoza Secured Loan of 1926. See Peters, *op. cit.*, pp. 138-39, for details of these loans.

difficulty in recent years. As the above analysis has shown, Argentina's debt problem has not been one of raising the revenues, but of transferring them to her creditors abroad.[35] The explanation of this situation is found, as was described in the preceding chapter, in the wide fluctuations which have occurred in the income items in Argentina's balance of payments. In contrast to a fixed outgo item for debt service remittances approaching 200 million gold pesos, the country's export surplus has been frequently completely wiped out. During such periods, voluntary loans from abroad also decline, thus necessitating recourse to "forced" or involuntary borrowing in order to effect equilibrium in the country's balance of payments; that is, cessation of external debt service payments.

Since wide fluctations in the major income items in Argentina's international accounts are not apt to be eliminated in the future, the solution of such recurring deficits in her balance of payments appears to be in building up a short-term creditor position abroad which may serve as a reserve upon which to draw when her normal income items fail. That such is apparently the policy now being pursued by Argentina is evidenced by the fact that the Exchange Control Office is building up an exchange equilization fund in London, as indicated in the previous chapter.[36]

[35] Peters, *op. cit.*, reaches the opposite conclusion, namely, that the problem of raising the funds has been of much greater importance than their transfer. See p. 150.

[36] Since the above paragraph was written (May 1936), economic recovery in Argentina has continued apace, fostered during recent months by the marked increase in world prices of agricultural and livestock products. During the first quarter of 1937 the country's export surplus equaled 533 million paper pesos, compared with 536 millions for the entire year 1936. Thus an increasing quantity of foreign exchange has been made available for external remittances.

As a result of this situation, plus the relatively low interest rates prevailing in the domestic money market, it is reported (*New York Times*, May 1, 1937) that a banking consortium has been organized under the auspices of the Argentine Central Bank to float domestic loans with which the government will eventually purchase all of its outstanding foreign bonds.

In the opinion of Argentina's financial leaders, the country has progressed to the point where it is able to finance its public borrowing without further recourse to foreign financial markets. The fact is emphasized that Argentina

was forced to make heavy sacrifices during the recent depression in order to maintain payments on its external loans, and that therefore one of the strongest reasons in support of the new project is to avoid a repetition of such sacrifices in future economic depressions.

The consummation of such a program is contingent, it seems worth while repeating, upon two factors: (1) the absorption of the necessary new capital issues by the Argentine money market, plus (2) the existence of a continued surplus of foreign exchange making possible the transfer of these funds abroad for the retirement of the external bond issues. Granted the maintenance of favorable world prices for Argentina's major export products, plus a continuance of exchange control, presumably the necessary foreign exchange will be forthcoming. Whether the current level of export values will be continued, however, is of course impossible to predict; some recession from the recent high levels seems not unreasonable to anticipate.

VI

TRENDS IN THE FOREIGN TRADE OF ARGENTINA

I. THE BALANCE OF TRADE

THE DECADE prior to the outbreak of the World War was, it will be recalled, a period of rapid growth in Argentina's foreign trade; exports and imports each increased about fivefold, or roughly from 100 million to 500 million gold pesos. A major factor in this rapid development in exports was the expansion in the export of agricultural products. Agricultural and pastoral products have always dominated Argentina's export trade, accounting for over 90 per cent of the total.[1] Prior to 1900, however, pastoral or range products predominated over the products of the farm, accounting, as late as 1894, for 63 per cent of total exports, and consisting chiefly of wool and hides. Only one agricultural product—wheat and wheat flour—had assumed any importance, amounting to about one-fourth of the total exports at the end of the century.

Although Argentina's foreign trade dates back some three hundred years, its real development started about 1875. During the fifty-year period following 1875, Argentina's trade increased some eighteenfold, or from 100,000,000 gold pesos to 1,800,000,000 gold pesos, thus placing Argentina among the first ten commercial nations of the world.[2] This rapid growth in Argentina's foreign trade following 1875 may be divided into four distinct periods, as follows:

(1) The period 1875-1900 was marked by a steady growth of exports, chiefly pastoral products, as already stated. With respect to imports, there was a rather marked increase up to 1890,

[1] See Table XX below, p. 134.

[2] Clarence F. Jones, "Argentine Trade Developments," *Economic Geography*, July 1926, Vol. II, No. 3, p. 358.

with imports exceeding exports in every year of the decade 1880-90. This was the "immature debtor" stage in Argentina's economic development, during which capital was being imported in large quantities, primarily for railroad construction. Thus the commodity import surplus reflected the rapid influx of capital. The rapid opening of new territory which railroad construction made possible, accompanied by a high rate of immigration, paved the way for the expansion of agricultural exports which was to mark the closing years of the nineteenth century and which continued until 1929.

(2) The severe financial panic which shook the country in 1891 (the so-called Baring Crisis) was accompanied by a rapid decline in imports, so that by the end of the decade, imports were only slightly larger than during the seventies and eighties. This decline in imports brought an overturn in the trade balance; Argentina had reached, temporarily at least, the "mature debtor" stage, where debt service on previous borrowings exceeded new foreign loans, with the balance being covered by an export surplus.[3]

[3] According to Williams' computations, the interest and amortization payments on previous foreign borrowings exceeded new foreign borrowings in every year from 1890 to 1900 inclusive, the total excess for the eleven-year period being 199.3 million gold pesos, or an annual average of 18.1 millions. In contrast, during the preceding decade 1880-90, new borrowings from abroad exceeded interest and amortization charges each year, the total excess of borrowings for the decade being 516.4 million gold pesos, or an annual average of 57.4 millions. (John H. Williams, *Argentine International Trade Under Inconvertible Paper Money, 1880-1900*, pp. 45, 101, 136, 152.) The decade preceding the World War, however, brought a new wave of loans from abroad, so that for a number of years prior to 1914 Argentina presumably reverted again to the status of an "immature debtor," since from the available data it appears that new foreign borrowings again exceeded interest and amortization payments on previous borrowings by at least 40 million gold pesos annually, possibly by as much as 50-60 millions. (See Table V, p. 24 above; also Appendix I, p. 234 and Appendix II, pp. 242-43 below.) It has already been shown (Chapter V, and especially Chart VII, p. 115) that following the outbreak of the World War cessation of loans from abroad plus a large commodity export surplus enabled Argentina, for a time, to jump almost directly from the "immature debtor" stage to that of the "immature creditor"; i.e., she became a net creditor on international account. Revival of foreign borrowing during the twenties, however, again placed Argentina in the position of a "mature debtor," with estimated external interest and amortization pay-

(3) Beginning in 1897 exports increased rapidly, accompanied by a growing proportion of farm products, which increased from 37 per cent of the total in 1894 to 48 per cent in 1903, and 58 per cent in 1912.[4] With an increasing percentage of the exports based on crops, the fluctuations from year to year have been much greater since 1900 than in the earlier period. The marked fluctuation in the value of exports since 1910 is shown clearly

CHART VIII. VALUE OF ARGENTINE EXPORTS BY MAJOR GROUPS OF PRODUCTS, 1910-36

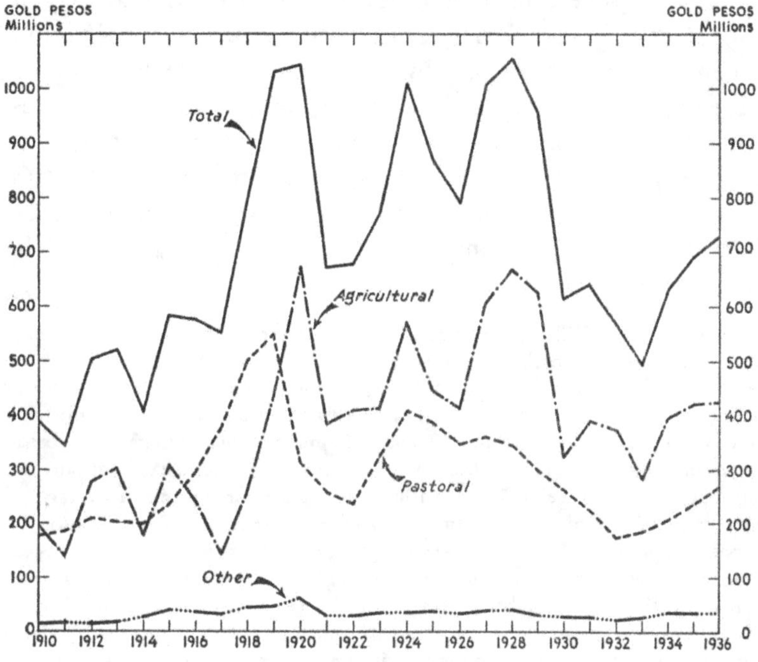

Source: *El Comercio Exterior Argentino.*

ments exceeding new foreign borrowings for the decade 1921-30 by 293.6 million gold pesos, or nearly 30 millions annually. From 1931 to 1935 inclusive, Argentina's estimated external debt service remittances payable abroad exceeded estimated net new foreign borrowings by roughly 180 million gold pesos annually, although a portion of these payments probably was not remitted, due to exchange restrictions.

[4] The composition of Argentina's foreign trade is discussed in greater detail in the next section of this chapter.

in Chart VIII.[5] After remaining relatively constant from 1897 to 1902, imports also increased rapidly until 1914, even exceeding exports in 1911, when the latter showed a considerable decline. The result was roughly a fivefold increase from 1897 to 1913.

(4) From 1913 to 1929 the same general trend of increase which began about 1900 was maintained, although the actual increase was only about twofold. Furthermore, the fluctuations became increasingly severe, because of rapid changes in demand as well as supply resulting from the abnormal conditions of the war and post-war periods. Subsequent to 1929, the value of Argentina's foreign trade declined so precipitously that by 1932 it was considerably below the 1913 level, although substantial recovery has occurred since that time.

We turn now to a more detailed analysis of the period since 1910, as reflected in the trends shown in Charts IX and X.[6] The World War produced marked changes not only in Argentina's total foreign trade, but in its composition and direction as well. We shall restrict our discussion in this section, however, to changes in the total trade balance. The factors brought about by the European War which had the greatest effect upon the Argentine trade have been enumerated as follows:

> (1) Increased demand for certain of its products, such as meats and wheat; (2) practical cessation of trade between Argentina and the Central Powers; (3) difficulties in obtaining certain imports usually purchased in countries then engaged in the War; (4) lack of shipping, which prevented its obtaining sufficient supplies of coal and distributing its corn crop; and, (5) the great reduction in immigration, which affected the labor supply.[7]

The rapid growth in the value of exports during the World War reflected the increased European demand for Argentine

[5] See also pp. 139-40 below.

[6] Some attention has already been given to the trade balance in the discussion of Argentina's balance of payments in Chapters II, III, and IV.

[7] United States Bureau of Foreign and Domestic Commerce, "The Economic Position of Argentina During the War," *Miscellaneous Series* No. 88, Washington, D.C., 1920, p. 85.

Chart IX. Argentine Foreign Trade, 1910-35: Index Numbers of Volume, Price, and Value

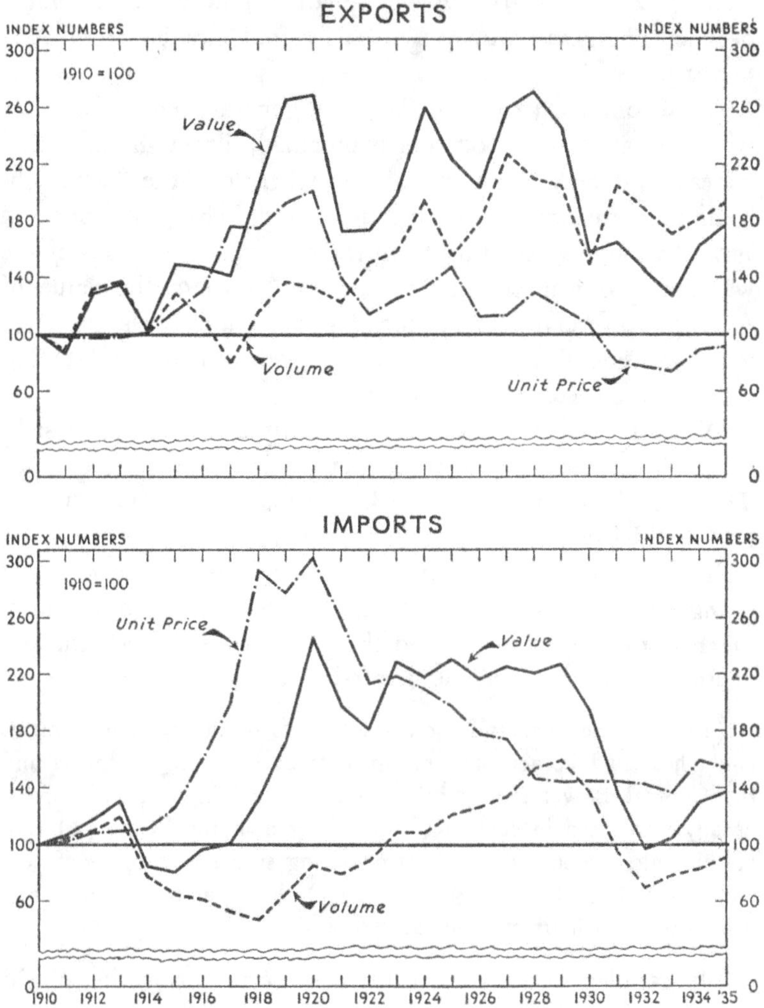

Source: *Anuario del Comercio Exterior de la República Argentina.*

food products. Chart IX shows clearly, however, that this was an increase in value only, and not in volume. In fact, the average of the quantity index of exports used in Chart IX for the four years, 1914-18, was less than the average of the three years

1910-13, by some 6 per cent.[8] The marked declines in the volume of exports in 1914 and 1917 were a result, in large part, of the crop failures in those years. Following a period of stable prices

CHART X. ARGENTINE FOREIGN TRADE, 1906-36: VALUE OF EXPORTS AND IMPORTS, AND TRADE BALANCE

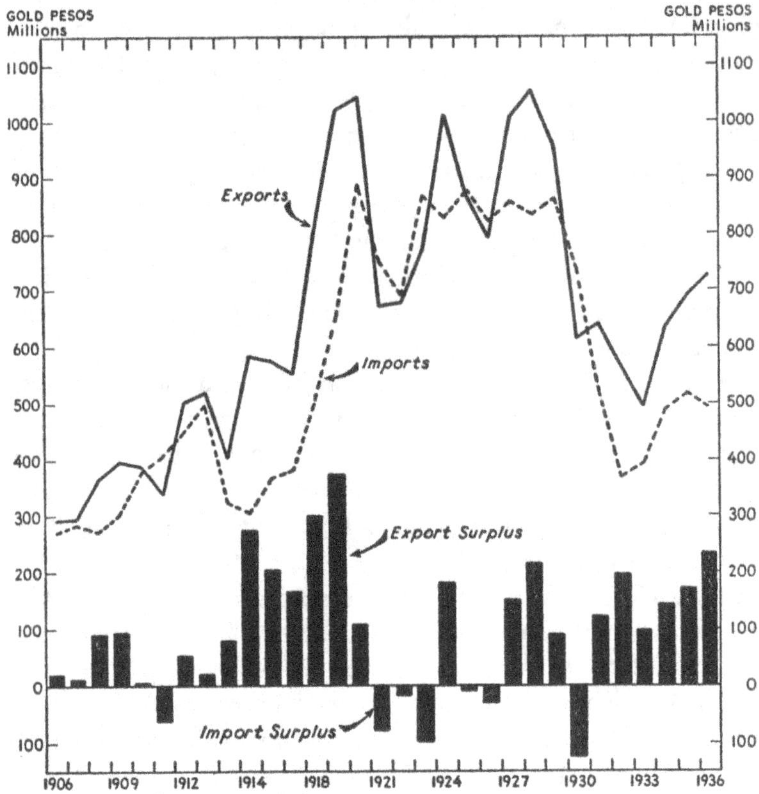

Source: *Anuario del Comercio Exterior de la República Argentina.*

from 1910 to 1914, export prices increased to a peak in 1920 of 200 per cent of the 1910 level, which was, in large degree, responsible for the increase in the value of exports in excess of 260 per cent for the same period. The large export surplus resulting is shown in Chart X. That this export surplus was not still greater was because of the fact that imports during the same period in-

[8] 108 and 114 per cent, respectively.

creased in price to a still greater degree, reaching a peak in 1920 300 per cent above the 1910 level. Following a marked decline in both value and volume of imports in 1914 and 1915, the value of imports increased rapidly, reaching a total value in 1920 of nearly 250 per cent of the 1910 figure. The volume of imports continued to decline throughout the war period, however, reaching a low point in 1918 of only 47 per cent of the 1910 figure. Even in the peak year of post-war prosperity, 1920, the index of quantity of imports stood at only 85.6 per cent of the 1910 level; it did not reach the 1913 level until 1925.

Chart IX shows also that the wide fluctuations in the value of exports from year to year, particularly since 1920, were caused more by the fluctuations in volume than by unit price changes. Furthermore, volume fluctuations from year to year, resulting primarily from climatic and crop conditions, were largely independent of price changes. This is in accordance with the general principle that the production of agricultural products, over short periods of time, is relatively insensitive to price changes. Particularly was this true after 1930; although prices continued to decline, the volume of Argentine exports in 1931 showed a marked increase, and only a relatively small decline in 1932 and 1933.

Chart IX also shows clearly the post-war trend as regards supply and price of pastoral and agricultural products, at least with respect to that portion supplied world markets by Argentina. Throughout the decade after the War the trend of volume indices was upward, accompanied by a constant downward trend in prices. This continued increase in supply was, no doubt, a factor in precipitating the collapse since 1929.[9]

The value of total Argentine imports remained relatively constant between 1922 and 1929, the increasing volume being offset by a marked decline in price. Between 1929 and 1933 the price index of imports remained fairly constant, the marked de-

[9] Granted that Argentina supplied a relatively small per cent of the world total of her major exports, nevertheless, the world supply of agricultural products during this period showed the same upward trend, as European countries restored their production.

cline in value being caused almost entirely by a sharp curtailment in the volume of imports.

The severity of the depression in its effect on Argentina's external purchasing power is perhaps best illustrated in terms of the country's per capita foreign trade. In Argentine currency total foreign trade in 1932 was roughly 130 million gold pesos less than in 1913. During this twenty-year period the population increased from 7,482,300 to 12,029,600, so that the annual per capita foreign trade declined from 136 to 74 gold pesos. Converted to gold currencies, the decline was, of course, much more severe.

The effect of these changes in the relative prices of Argentina's exports and imports upon the country's "real" terms of international commodity exchange; that is, the "net barter terms of trade," are shown in Chart XI. This index of Argentina's "terms of trade" is the ratio of the import price index to the export price index;[10] thus a decline in the index indicates a gain, or improvement, in the country's net terms of trade. Chart XI shows, therefore, that during the War and immediate post-war years (1915-22) the trend of Argentina's terms of trade was "unfavorable," whereas during the middle twenties (1922-28) the country's terms of trade were increasingly "favorable." Although the prices of Argentina's exports increased rapidly during the War, the decline in the terms of trade during these years reflects the still greater rate of increase in the cost of imports. During the post-war slump the prices of exports declined more rapidly than did imports, thus causing the terms of trade to become increasingly less favorable to Argentina.

The marked improvement in the terms of trade from 1922 to 1928 was the result of the declining cost of imports paralleled by relative stability in the prices received for Argentina's exports.

The collapse in world agricultural prices which began in 1928 is reflected in the increasingly "unfavorable" terms of trade from

[10] These indices are compiled annually by the Dirección General de Estadística de la Nación and are published in the *Anuario del Comercio Exterior de la República Argentina.*

CHART XI. ARGENTINA'S NET BARTER TERMS OF TRADE, 1913-35

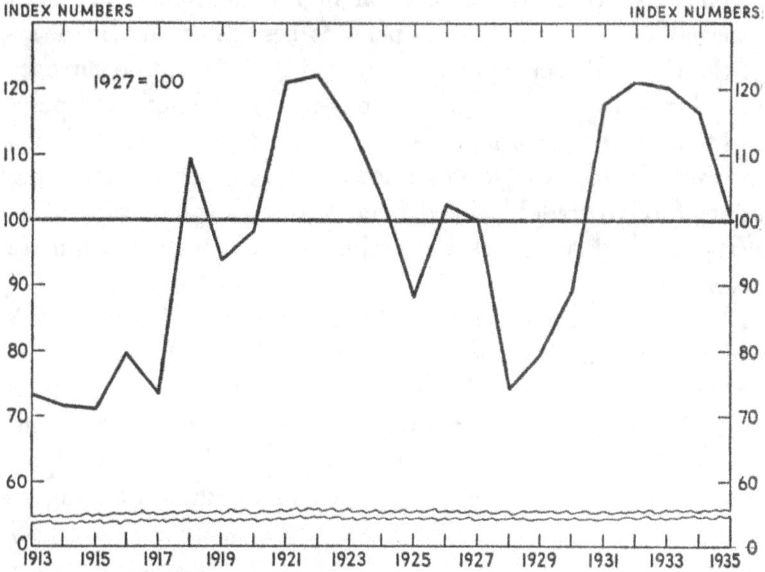

Source: Computed from data in *Anuario del Comercio Exterior de la República Argentina.*

1928 to 1932. For the years 1933, 1934, and 1935, however, a slight improvement occurred, as indicated in Chart XI.[11]

[11] Parenthetically, it may be pointed out that the changes in Argentina's net terms of trade during this period are generally in accord with the classical theory that the transfer of capital from abroad tends to improve the borrowing country's terms of trade. It will be recalled that during the War Argentina was reducing its indebtedness abroad; as indicated in Chart XI it was during this period that the terms of trade were "unfavorable" to Argentina. Also, the period of heavy borrowing from abroad during the twenties was again the period during which the terms of trade were increasingly "favorable" to Argentina. Following the cessation of these loans from abroad in 1929, the terms of trade again turned "unfavorable."

On the other hand, the years 1921, 1922, 1926, and 1930 were all years during which Argentina increased its net foreign indebtedness, yet the terms of trade in each of these years became less "favorable." It is probable, therefore, that the marked changes in world prices for its exports, as well as its imports, were more significant factors determining the net terms of trade than were capital movements.

II. COMPOSITION OF ARGENTINA'S FOREIGN TRADE

A. *Exports*

The dominant position of range and farm products in Argentina's export trade during the past twenty-five years is shown in Tables XX and XXI (see also Chart VIII, page 126), agricultural and pastoral products accounting for some 95 per cent of Argentina's total exports. This expansion in pastoral and agricultural pursuits was inevitable in a new country, rich in agricultural resources, but lacking the essentials for large manufacturing industries. In contrast, therefore, Argentina's imports have consisted almost entirely of a great variety of manufactured articles and fuel supplies.

Although products of the range and farm have predominated in Argentina's exports, their relative importance has changed, as well as the component parts in each group. Agricultural products account for an increasingly greater percentage of the total, having increased from 56 per cent of the total exports in the pre-war period 1911-13 to about 62 per cent in recent years. Correspondingly, pastoral products have declined from a pre-war average of 40 per cent to an average of 33 per cent in the three-year period 1932-34. This situation was simply a continuation of the trend, previously mentioned, which had existed for over a decade prior to the War, as the following percentage figures indicate:

	1894	*1903*
Pastoral Products	63	49
Agricultural Products	30	48
Miscellaneous Products	7	3
Total	100	100

During and immediately following the War there was a temporary reversal of this trend, a result of the heavy European demand for meat. Pastoral products averaged slightly over 47 per cent of total exports in the period 1918-20. Except for meat and dairy products, however, this was entirely a price increase, since, as shown in Table XXI, the volume of hides, wool, and by-products exported decreased.

The volume of meat exports continued to grow rapidly during the decade after the War. These meat exports consisted pri-

TABLE XX

VALUE OF ARGENTINE EXPORTS BY MAJOR CLASSES; ANNUAL AVERAGES FOR SELECTED PERIODS

(in millions of gold pesos)

	1911–13		*1918–20*		*1922–24*		*1927–29*		*1932–34*	
		Per Cent		*Per Cent*		*Per Cent*		*Per Cent*		*Per Cent*
I. *Pastoral Products:*										
1. Meats and Live Animals	56	13.0	221	23.1	130	15.9	144	14.2	87	15.4
2. Hides	47	11.0	66	6.6	74	9.1	75	7.4	33	5.9
3. Wool	51	11.8	114	12.0	64	7.9	77	7.6	42	7.5
4. Dairy Products	1[a]	[d]	21	2.2	24	2.9	16	1.6	10	1.8
5. By-Products	20	4.6	31	3.2	30	3.6	23	2.3	15	2.7
Total Pastoral Products	175	40.4	453	47.1	322	39.4	335	33.1	187	33.3
II. *Agricultural Products:*										
1. Cereals and Linseed	226	52.5	428	44.8	443	54.2	605	60.3	327	58.1
2. Wheat Flour and By-products	6	1.6	22	2.2	16	1.9	19	1.9	11	1.9
3. Miscellaneous	7	1.8	5	0.5	5	0.6	10	1.0	12	2.1
Total Agricultural Products	239	55.9	455	47.5	464	56.7	634	63.2	350	62.1
III. *Forest Products:*[b]	11	2.5	20	2.2	17	2.0	22	2.2	15	2.7
IV. *Other Products:*[c]	5	1.2	30	3.2	16	1.9	15	1.5	11	1.9
Total Exports:	430	100.0	958	100.0	819	100.0	1,006	100.0	563	100.0

[a] Includes butter only.
[b] Mostly quebracho.
[c] Includes mining, hunting and fishing products.
[d] Less than 0.1 percent.

Sources: Computed from data in *Anuario del Comercio Exterior*, 1932 and 1934; *El Comercio Exterior Argentino*, Boletíns Nos. 211 and 215.

marily of frozen and chilled beef, frozen mutton, and preserved meats.[12] Fresh meat exports date, of course, from the introduc-

[12] In addition to the above types of meat products, in 1934 Argentina exported 1,396 tons of frozen poultry valued at 458,545 gold pesos, and live

TABLE XXI

VOLUME OF ARGENTINE EXPORTS BY MAJOR CLASSES; ANNUAL AVERAGES FOR SELECTED PERIODS

(in thousands of tons)

	1911–13	*1918–20*	*1922–24*	*1927–29*	*1932–34*
I. *Pastoral Products:*					
1. Meat and Meat Products	452	691[a]	808[a]	845[a]	610[a]
2. Hides	133	111	196	174	146
3. Wool	139	125	153	137	134
4. Dairy Products	3[d]	35	46	36	37
5. By-Products	260	160	230	221	177
Total Pastoral Products:	987	1,122	1,433	1,413	1,104
II. *Agricultural Products:*					
1. Wheat and Wheat Flour	2,701	3,991	4,092	5,537	4,144
2. Corn	3,256	2,541	3,406	6,588	5,848
3. Linseed	649	769	1,110	1,819	1,598
4. Other Agricultural Products:					
a. oats	766	429	494	445	550
b. barley	20	32	93	258	422
c. rye	11	5	60	165	170
d. canary seed	3	6	7	9	25
e. raw cotton	—	2	7	17	26
f. miscellaneous	100	153	344	506	560
Total Agricultural Products:	7,506	7,928	9,613	15,344	13,343
III. *Forest Products*[b]	470	275	308	369	314
IV. *Other Products*[c]	243	286	443	364	190
Total Exports	9,206	9,611	11,797	17,490	14,951

[a] Includes live animals.
[b] Mostly quebracho.
[c] Includes mining, hunting, and fishing products.
[d] Butter only, 1911–13.

Source: See sources for Table XX.

tion of refrigeration about 1880, which revolutionized the whole future of the animal industries in Argentina. Exports of frozen beef increased rapidly after 1900, totaling approximately 300,000 tons annually by 1914. From this level the volume of

cattle and sheep valued at 3,180,408 gold pesos. Most of these latter went to Chile and Paraguay.

frozen beef exports, stimulated by war needs, jumped to nearly 500,000 tons in 1918, the highest figure ever attained. Dropping thereafter to a total of 160,000 tons in 1922, frozen beef has, since the War, been of decreasing importance in Argentina's beef exports. Beginning in 1922 exports of frozen beef were rapidly supplanted by chilled beef, a superior product, which now constitutes over 90 per cent of the fresh beef exports of Argentina. Practically all of this chilled beef is destined for the English market, as the following figures indicate:

	1934	*1935*
Total	349,644 tons	348,531 tons
United Kingdom	349,404 "	348,305 "

Exports of frozen beef in 1934 and 1935 were as follows:

	1934	*1935*
Total	31,584 tons	30,651 tons
United Kingdom	8,331 "	9,309 "
Continental Europe	21,725 "	19,955 "
Others	1,528 "	1,387 "

Exports of preserved meats expanded during the War to a total of nearly 200,000 tons in 1918, but declined rapidly thereafter, both because of cessation in foreign demand and rapid improvements in cattle breeding in Argentina to meet the demand for superior types of beef. During recent years exports of preserved beef have averaged roughly 50,000 tons. The percentage of "scrubs" or rough inferior cattle raised in Argentina has declined from over 75 per cent in 1900 to less than 20 per cent in recent years.[18]

This expansion of Argentina's beef exports since 1900 was paralleled by a corresponding decline in beef exports from the United States; in fact, by 1914, Argentina had replaced the United States as the chief source of Europe's beef supply. In recent years Argentina has furnished more than 50 per cent of the world's beef exports.

Prior to 1902 the volume of frozen mutton exports exceeded

[18] Clarence Jones, *op. cit.*, p. 367.

that of beef, averaging some 60,000 tons annually. Although continuing to increase in the succeeding decade, averaging some 75,000 tons annually, the much more rapid growth of beef exports far outstripped the increased volume of frozen mutton exports. During the War frozen mutton exports declined as a result of the rise in the price of wool and the greater emphasis on beef exports for war purposes. In the decade following 1912 exports averaged 52,000 tons. After the War, frozen mutton exports increased rapidly, reaching a peak of 92,000 tons in 1925, and fluctuating between 67,000 and 83,000 tons until 1933. In 1933, 1934, and 1935, exports totaled 63,000, 49,000, and 50,000 tons, respectively. Over 90 per cent of these mutton exports go to the United Kingdom.

Before 1900 wool exports led all other commodities, amounting to 23 per cent of the total value as late as 1903. A rapid decline occurred in the succeeding decade, however, as Argentina turned from a pioneer pastoral type of economic activity to more intensive agricultural pursuits; that is, this decline in the wool trade was chiefly the result of the decrease in the numbers of sheep in the expanding cereal belts of Argentina. In the period 1911-13, wool exports averaged 51 million gold pesos in value, slightly less than 12 per cent of total exports. During the War the volume of wool exports declined still further from an annual average in 1911-13 of 139,000 tons to 125,000 tons in the period 1918-20. The value of this decreased volume, however, increased from 51 million gold pesos to 114 million pesos.

Although exhibiting a marked decline in 1920, wool exports increased considerably in 1921 and 1922 (in contrast to most other exports) reaching an annual average of 153,000 tons in the three-year period 1922-24. This level was not maintained, however, so that since 1925 the volume, as well as the value, of wool exports has approximated the pre-war average. At the same time, because of marked increases in other exports, the relative position of wool exports has declined to nearly half the pre-war percentage, or from 11.8 to 7.5 per cent of the value of total exports. This maintenance of *relative* stability in wool

production has been due primarily to the expansion of sheep raising in the bleak frontier regions of southern Argentina, which has partially offset the decline in the pampas. These wool exports are quite widely distributed, as the following figures for "unwashed" wool, which constitutes over 90 per cent of the total, indicate:

ARGENTINE WOOL EXPORTS IN 1935

	(tons)
United Kingdom	29,748
Germany	19,093
France	18,703
Italy	13,283
United States	19,065
Belgium	5,842
Others	7,923
Total	113,657

The trend in the export of hides and skins parallels very largely that of wool just described (see Tables XX and XXI). During the War exports of hides and skins decreased slightly in volume over the pre-war average, but increased in value 40 per cent. Following the post-war drop in 1920, exports increased rapidly to an annual average of 196,000 tons for the period 1922-24. This volume was not maintained, however, the annual average dropping to 174,000 tons in 1927-29 and 146,000 tons in 1932-34, or slightly above the pre-war average. At the same time the value of exports of hides and skins declined from 11 per cent of the total exports to 7.4 per cent in the period 1927-29 and 5.9 per cent in the 1932-34 period. In 1935 the major exports of hides and skins were as follows:

	Volume (tons)	*Value* (thousand gold pesos)
Cattle	137,238	35,300
Sheep	19,780	5,574
Horse	3,094	626
Goat and Kid	2,716	1,425

Germany, the United States, and the United Kingdom are the leading buyers of Argentina's cattle hides, taking some 75

per cent of the total. France purchases 70 per cent of the sheep skins. The United States takes most of the goat and kid skins. Poland and Italy are the chief purchasers of horse hides.

The expansion of the meat industry in Argentina has been accompanied by the growth of dairying. Although as yet constituting a relatively small percentage of Argentina's total exports (1.8 per cent of the 1932-34 average), exports of dairy products have increased rapidly since 1915. Both butter and cheese exports expanded rapidly during the War, reaching a total of 20,000 and 10,000 tons, respectively, in 1919. By 1925 most of this market for cheese exports was lost, however, as European producers recovered from the effects of the War. Butter exports continued to increase in volume until 1923 when they totaled 33,000 tons. During the period 1924-32 inclusive the average annual volume recorded was 24,000 tons. In 1934, however, butter exports declined to only 8,000 tons, valued at 3,068,479 gold pesos.

Another important export of the dairy industry is casein, the annual exports of which increased from less than three thousand tons in 1915 to 15 thousand tons in 1925, and ranging from 14 to 23 thousand tons since that date. The greatest volume was recorded in 1933, when casein exports totaled slightly over 23,000 tons, valued at 3,437,209 gold pesos, as compared with 20,000 tons valued at 3,884,976 gold pesos in 1934, and 17,000 tons valued at 3,165,661 gold pesos in 1935. Germany takes about one-half of these casein exports and the United States approximately one-fourth.

As previously indicated, agricultural products have accounted for an increasing proportion of Argentina's total exports;[14] furthermore, in contrast to pastoral products those of the farm show more frequent and much wider fluctuations from year to year, the result of three major factors: (1) wide variations from year to year in rainfall in the cereal-growing belt of Argentina; (2) locust plagues which descend periodically from the subtropical areas in the north; (3) inadequate storage facilities,

[14] The decline in relative importance of pastoral products is due almost entirely to the decreased value of hides, skins, and wool exports. See Table XX.

plus the fact that many of the cereal farmers are immigrants operating on a small scale with limited resources, a condition which forces them to sell their crops immediately.[15] In contrast, most of the cattle and sheep raising is conducted on a large scale by men of ample means who are able, when prices are low, to store their wool and hides and postpone the slaughter of their herds until prices improve.

Although characteristic of all cereal exports, corn (maize) has exhibited the widest fluctuations from year to year, because of the fact that the average rainfall is sufficient for a good crop only when properly distributed. Corn needs plenty of moisture early in the growing season, with dry weather during the harvesting period. In the corn belt of Argentina, however, weather conditions are frequently the reverse, with relatively little rainfall in the spring, followed by wet weather during the harvest period. The dry spring weather favors the locusts, which come by the millions and eat the young green stalks to the ground. If the harvest season is wet, much of the corn either spoils in the fields or in the inadequate unsheltered cribs (*trojes*) in which it is stored.[16] From 1925 to 1931, the annual volume of corn exports fluctuated as much as 300 per cent, as the following figures indicate:

ARGENTINE CORN EXPORTS
(thousands of tons)

1925	2,936
1926	4,907
1927	8,343
1928	6,372
1929	5,048
1930	4,670
1931	9,767

In addition to corn (maize), the major cereal exports by value are wheat (and wheat flour) and linseed. Minor exports are

[15] Strenuous efforts are now being made to improve grain storage facilities in Argentina.

[16] Jones, *op. cit.*, p. 376.

oats, barley, rye, and canary seed. Wheat, the first cereal crop to become important in Argentina, held first rank until 1935, when the value of wheat and wheat flour was exceeded by corn, as the following figures show:

ARGENTINE EXPORTS OF CORN AND WHEAT
(INCLUDING WHEAT FLOUR)
(millions of gold pesos)

	1934	*1935*	*1936*
Wheat and wheat flour	134.5	124.4	79.1
Corn	132.7	141.5	195.5

Corn and wheat together account for about two-thirds of the total value of cereal exports, or about two-fifths of the value of all exports. The dominant position which Argentina came to occupy in the world's cereal markets during the first quarter of the present century is evidenced by the fact that by 1925 she held first rank in exports of corn, oats, and flaxseed, and second or third in wheat and flour; she supplied 66 per cent of the total world corn exports, 72 per cent of the linseed, 32 per cent of the oats, and 20 per cent of the wheat and wheat flour.[17]

The growth of the volume of cereal exports since 1910 is indicated in Table XXI. Exports of wheat and wheat flour expanded rapidly during the War, increasing from an annual average of 2,701 thousand tons in the period 1911-13 to 3,991 thousand tons in the period 1918-20.[18] The peak was reached in 1929 when 6,613 thousand tons were exported. The 1927-29 average was 5,537 thousand tons, but the decline since 1929 brought the annual average for the three-year period 1932-34 to 4,144 thousand tons, with a further decline in 1935 and 1936 to 3,860 and 1,610 thousand tons, respectively.

Corn exports declined to a marked degree during the War, because of the scarcity of tonnage and high freight rates, as well as the increased demand for wheat. The decline in the annual

[17] Jones, *op. cit.*, p. 372.

[18] A crop failure in 1917 reduced wheat exports to less than a million tons (936 thousand tons).

average of 3,256 thousand tons for the period 1911-13 to 2,541 thousand tons in the period 1918-20 does not indicate the severity of this decline, as the following annual figures show:

ARGENTINE CORN EXPORTS
(thousands of tons)

1916	2,874
1917	894
1918	665
1919	2,485
1920	4,475

After the War the trend of production and exports of corn was steadily upward, but with marked annual variations, as already stated. The inelasticity of Argentina's exports to price changes is nowhere better illustrated than in the case of corn exports since 1928. In 1929 exports totaled 5,048 thousand tons, whereas in 1931, with prices at some 40 per cent of the 1929 level, exports reached the all-time record of 9,767 thousand tons. The United Kingdom normally purchases about one-half of Argentina's corn exports, Belgium and the Netherlands about one-sixth each, with the remainder widely distributed, but practically all going to western Europe.

ARGENTINE LINSEED EXPORTS
(thousands of tons)

	1934	*1935*
Netherlands	438	439
United States	193	390
France	206	217
United Kingdom	66	184
Germany	139	146
Belgium	112	141
Italy	57	56
Others	163	205
Total	1,374	1,573

Linseed ranks fourth in value among Argentina's exports (meat being third), accounting, in recent years, for some 13 per cent of the total value of exports. These shipments from Argentina have constituted over 70 per cent of the world's exports of this commodity. Argentine linseed exports increased nearly threefold from the pre-war average of 650 thousand tons to an annual average of 1,819 thousand tons in the three-year period 1927-29. As with corn, notwithstanding rapidly falling prices, linseed exports increased from 1,170 thousand tons in 1930 to 2,028 thousand tons in 1932, the all-time record. Marked declines in 1933 and 1934, however, reduced the annual average for the three years 1932-34 to 1,598 thousand tons. In 1935 exports totaled 1,778 thousand tons. Exports are quite widely distributed, as indicated by the figures on the opposite page.

The exports of forest products consist almost exclusively of quebracho extract and quebracho logs, the world's most important source of tannin. Although declining from a pre-war annual

ARGENTINE QUEBRACHO EXPORTS

(thousands of tons)

	1934		*1935*	
	extract	*logs*	*extract*	*logs*
United States	40	40	38	20
Germany	45	—	22	11
United Kingdom	24	—	15	—
France	14	—	11	21
Netherlands	31	—	9	3
Italy	13	33	4	38
Others	66	36	77	12
Total	233	109	176	105

average of 470,000 tons to an annual average of 275,000 tons in the period 1918-20, the exports of forest products have since averaged between 300 and 400 thousand tons. In value, however, they have accounted for less than three per cent of Argentina's total exports. With respect to quebracho exports, since 1913 exports of quebracho extract have increased steadily relative to quebracho logs. Quebracho exports declined relatively slightly dur-

ing the depression, the annual averages for 1927-29 and 1932-34 periods being 369,000 and 314,000 tons respectively.

The quebracho export trade began about 1880.[19] Germany was at first the chief consumer, but in recent years exports have been widely distributed, as shown by the figures on page 143. These quebracho exports were valued as follows:

(gold pesos)

	1934	*1935*
Extract	16,184,127	16,692,380
Logs	2,060,560	2,118,468

B. *Imports*

In decided contrast to her exports, which consist of a relatively small number of foodstuffs and industrial raw materials, a large proportion of Argentina's imports are manufactured goods of a wide variety.

Official statistics of Argentine imports are classified in major commodity groups (14 groups since 1928).[20] Annual averages of these commodity groups for selected years are given in the accompanying table. As indicated in the footnote to Table XXII, the official classifications were changed in 1918 and 1928 so that any continuous comparison of all groups during the period of this study is impossible.

From 1913 to 1923 inclusive, Argentine imports were also classified in the official statistics according to their "economic significance." This classification into four major groups for selected years is shown in Table XXIII below (page 146).[21]

[19] Jones, *op. cit.*

[20] Argentine import statistics in terms of "real" or current market values are not published in detail by commodities. "Tariff" values as recorded in the official statistics are based upon the official valuations established for duty-levying purposes. Since the tariff valuations are changed infrequently, they do not represent current market values. Such current or "real" values are compiled and published annually, however, for total Argentine imports, as well as for major commodity groups (see Table XXII). In the period 1911-13 the annual average of "real" values for total imports was 15 per cent above "tariff" values, and in the period 1924-26, 30 per cent.

[21] Unfortunately this classification was discontinued after 1923. Since the figures are in "tariff values," they represent quantity rather than value changes.

Table XXII

Value of Argentine Imports by Major Commodity Groups; Annual Averages for Selected Periods
(in millions of gold pesos)

	1911–13[a]	*1918–20*	*1922–24*	*1928–30*	*1932–34*
1. Live animals	.83	2.05	.56	[c]	[c]
2. Foodstuffs	31.47	74.51	81.55	88.24	44.90
3. Tobacco and Manufactures	6.84	9.53	12.92	13.68	7.22
4. Beverages (alcoholic)	14.17	9.68	10.33	10.33	3.46
5. Textiles and manufactures	79.19	223.79	226.83	196.83	146.78
6. Oils, greases, etc.	19.37	36.72	46.98	[c]	[c]
7. Fuel and lubricants	[c]	[c]	[c]	77.67	41.99
8. Chemical & Pharmaceutical Products	13.88	40.04	27.87 }	38.40 (8–9)	29.33 (8–9)
9. Paints & Dyes	2.50	5.53	6.28 }		
10. Wood and manufactures	10.37	33.93	46.77	42.86	23.54
11. Paper, cardboard, & manufactures	9.48	19.87	22.00	22.01	15.75
12. Iron and steel and manufactures	46.38	82.06	125.81	72.81	30.95
13. Other metals and manufactures	14.70	29.09	30.82	28.50	15.46
14. Agricultural implements and Machinery	11.79	19.95	26.16 }	131.35 (14–15)	20.58 (14–15)
15. Locomotion: Railway cars, equipment, automobiles & carriages	35.63	[c]	[c] }		
16. Stones, earths, glass and ceramics	34.74[b]	64.79	63.58 }	31.51 (16–17)	11.44 (16–17)
17. Building materials	33.61	[c]	[c] }		
18. Electrical apparatus	8.70	9.86	14.43	[c]	[c]
19. Rubber and manufactures	[c]	[c]	[c]	12.11	4.85
20. Miscellaneous	13.56	34.68	48.42	46.67	20.78
Total Imports	387.21	696.08	791.31	812.97	417.03

[a] 1911–13 in tariff values; remainder in "real" values. "Real" values for total imports averaged approximately 15 per cent above tariff values for 1911–13 period.
[b] Includes coal.
[c] The official classifications were changed in 1918 and 1928, which explains the omissions of certain classes in certain years.
Source: *Anuario del Comercio Exterior de la República Argentina.*

As indicated in the table, not only did all imports decline during the War, but there were also marked changes in their relative importance. The marked decline in "Capital Goods" in 1918, relatively as well as absolutely, was the direct result of the contraction in new foreign capital investments in Argentina during this period. The relative increase in "Raw Materials and Supplies" was evidence of the increased importance of industrial activity in Argentina as a result of the shutting off of foreign

supplies during the War. By 1923 the pre-war situation was largely restored with respect to all groups excepting "Capital Goods" which continued some 40 per cent under the 1913 figure.

TABLE XXIII
VALUE OF ARGENTINE IMPORTS CLASSIFIED ACCORDING TO THEIR ECONOMIC SIGNIFICANCE
(tariff values in millions of gold pesos)

	1913		*1918*		*1923*	
	Pesos	*Per Cent*	*Pesos*	*Per Cent*	*Pesos*	*Per Cent*
I. *Consumption Goods*						
1. Necessities	165.68	39.3	86.20	51.9	164.20	42.9
2. Luxuries	31.53	7.6	11.76	7.0	25.90	6.8
II. *Heat, Light, and Power Materials*	42.86	10.3	13.37	8.4	49.01	12.8
III. *Raw Materials and Supplies*	72.38	17.3	38.30	23.0	76.27	19.9
IV. *Capital Goods*	108.90	25.5	16.19	9.7	67.89	17.6
Total Imports	421.35	100.0	165.82	100.0	383.27	100.0

Source: República Argentina, Dirección General de Estadística, *Noticia Sumaria del Comercio Exterior Argentino de 1910 hasta 1923*, Informe No. 11, Serie C, No. 6, 1924.

Supplementing the broad classification of Argentine imports in Table XXII, Table XXIV (pages 148-52) presents the annual averages of Argentina's major imports for selected years, including the chief countries of origin for each commodity.

Of major importance were (1) textiles, which accounted for approximately 20 per cent of total imports; (2) iron and steel products, which, including machinery and automobiles, equaled nearly one-third of the total prior to 1930; and (3) coal and petroleum products which accounted for about 15 per cent of the total.

Although Argentina's domestic textile industry, aided by high tariff duties, is of increasing importance, textile imports averaged 18.1 per cent of total imports during the three-year period 1932-34, and 19.3 per cent in 1935. At the same time, however, increasing imports of yarns, particularly artificial silk (rayon)

yarns, are witness to the increasing importance of local textile manufacture.

Cotton goods account for nearly half the textile imports, totaling over eight per cent of all imports. They include all types of cotton goods from heavy duck and unbleached sheetings to fancy voiles and cotton and silk mixtures in bright colors. Competition is exceedingly keen. The United Kingdom, prior to 1935, dominated the trade, providing about half the total. In 1935, however, Japan made rapid inroads in the Argentine market for cotton textiles, securing 28.4 per cent of the total business, while the share of the United Kingdom declined to 37.8 per cent. At the same time Italy, which formerly ranked second by furnishing nearly one-third of Argentina's imports of cotton textiles, was relegated to third position with only 16.1 per cent. During 1935 Belgium and Spain continued to hold their respective positions after Italy as suppliers of Argentina's textile imports. The shares of the United States and France, however, which during the decade of the twenties had equaled approximately ten and five per cent, respectively, have in recent years declined to negligible proportions, amounting in 1935 to only 0.5 and 1.0 per cent, respectively, of total imports.

Woolen goods were formerly about one-third as important as those of cotton in the import trade, but in recent years have declined in relative importance. This decline was the result, in part, of recent depressed economic conditions, particularly since nearly all the woolen imports are of the better grades. Domestic production supplies more of the cheaper fabrics. Specialization by countries is found in the fact that England supplies high grade men's suitings, whereas France dominates the market for ladies' woolen dress goods, fine fancy woolens, and mixed silk and woolen goods.[22]

Other textile manufactures consist to a large degree of jute bags and bagging, practically all of which comes originally from India. They are used for grain bags and also in the slaughtering plants to cover the frozen and chilled meat carcasses which are shipped to Europe. A large portion of Argentina's grain crops

[22] Clarence Jones, *op. cit.*, p. 382.

Table XXIV

Major Imports of Argentina Classified by Chief Countries of Origin

Annual Averages for Selected Periods

(Tariff values in thousands of gold pesos)[a]

Commodity and Country	1911–13			1924–26			1932–34			1935		
	I[b]	II[c]	III[d]	I	II	III	I	II	III	I	II	III
Fruit	2,698	0.7	100.0	5,192	0.9	100.0	9,220	2.2	100.0	9,081	1.8	100.0
Brazil			6.0			6.5			32.0			40.0
Paraguay			8.6			9.3			23.0			16.4
United States			4.8			26.0			13.4			14.0
Spain			25.9			17.2			7.5			13.8
Others			54.7			41.0			24.1			15.8
Non-alcoholic Beverages (coffee, cocoa, tea, yerba maté)	9,248	2.4	100.0	18,419	2.8	100.0	14,318	3.4	100.0	13,985	2.8	100.0
Brazil			75.3			77.8			82.0			80.7
Paraguay			4.6			7.6			3.4			3.5
Ceylon			3.7			5.5			6.4			3.4
India			(included	with Ceylon)					3.0			0.3
Tobacco and Manufactures	6,681	1.7	100.0	7,734	1.2	100.0	6,380	1.4	100.0	5,601	1.1	100.0
Brazil			24.3			45.9			53.0			51.5
Cuba			13.9			20.7			20.3			21.4
United States			7.8			12.9			10.6			12.2
Italy			13.4			13.4			5.4			4.7
United Kingdom			29.4			1.7			3.5			1.9
Cotton Yarn and Thread	3,609	0.9	100.0	7,021	1.1	100.0	7,876	1.9	100.0	7,297	1.5	100.0
United Kingdom			35.7			24.6			42.6			58.5
Italy			19.3			16.5			26.8			11.2
United States			2.2			43.5			13.2			0.8
Belgium			11.8			4.7			8.0			10.9

[a] "Real" values not available for individual commodities.

[b] Tariff value of total annual average imports of each commodity.

[c] Per cent of total imports.

[d] Percentage of imports of each Commodity from Specified Countries of Origin.

Commodity and Country	1911–13			1924–26			1932–34			1935		
	I[b]	II[c]	III[d]	I	II	III	I	II	III	I	II	III
Cotton Textiles	34,247	9.0	100.0	56,189	8.7	100.0	34,013	8.2	100.0	47,376	9.6	100.0
United Kingdom			47.1			40.4			51.0			37.8
Italy			18.9			27.1			29.7			16.1
Belgium			5.1			6.8			5.5			6.8
Spain			4.7			2.1			4.5			3.0
United States			1.0			9.7			4.2			0.5
France			7.9			5.6			1.8			1.0
Wool Textiles	13,943	3.6	100.0	20,743	3.2	100.0	9,569	2.3	100.0	11,172	2.3	100.0
United Kingdom			51.6			52.7			63.0			79.1
France			17.4			22.2			21.0			7.5
Italy			3.2			5.3			7.8			4.4
Germany			22.9			7.6			3.1			1.7
Spain			1.0			3.8			2.7			0.5
Silk Textiles	6,216	1.6	100.0	14,256	2.2	100.0	7,929	1.9	100.0	6,785	1.4	100.0
France			47.7			44.0			31.4			30.8
Japan			7.2			9.9			27.6			22.9
Italy			10.4			15.0			15.1			8.6
United Kingdom			9.6			10.9			5.6			7.6
Artificial Silk Yarn	—	—	—	2,402	0.4	100.0	11,720	2.9	100.0	16,527	3.3	100.0
France						1.0			31.0			26.6
Italy						24.7			16.0			25.1
Netherlands						11.4			24.0			17.2
United Kingdom						22.7			7.9			7.5
Germany						13.7			12.8			3.6
Switzerland						11.5			7.1			2.0

TABLE XXIV (*continued*)

Commodity and Country	*1911–13*			*1924–26*			*1932–34*			*1935*		
	I[b]	*II*[c]	*III*[d]	*I*	*II*	*III*	*I*	*II*	*III*	*I*	*II*	*III*
Other Textile Manufactures	19,362	5.0	100.0	34,121	5.3	100.0	23,961	5.7	100.0	29,415	6.0	100.0
India			22.2			45.9			83.9			65.5
United Kingdom			37.0			20.9			11.6			9.9
Others			40.8			33.2			4.5			24.6
Wood (lumber, etc.)	20,388	5.3	100.0	18,073	2.8	100.0	15,943	3.8	100.0	20,952	4.2	100.0
United States			64.8			53.2			37.0			38.0
Brazil			3.1			8.8			15.8			19.3
Russia			0.7			—			7.5			5.7
Paraguay			7.0			11.0			5.2			3.9
Others			24.4			27.0			34.5			33.1
Paper and Paper Manufactures	9,429	2.5	100.0	23,847	3.7	100.0	23,807	5.7	100.0	26,198	5.3	100.0
Canada			—			4.0			20.0			20.4
Sweden			—			4.5			14.4			17.6
Germany			43.1			45.8			17.3			15.7
Finland			—			5.4			13.0			12.8
United States			17.6			7.4			5.6			5.5
Others			39.3			34.0			29.8			28.0
Coal (including coke)	24,439	6.4	100.0	34,241	5.3	100.0	28,482	6.8	100.0	29,820	6.0	100.0
United Kingdom			96.0			75.5			85.0			81.6
Germany			1.0			6.4			10.0			7.1
United States			2.1			14.0			1.6			0.5
Petroleum Products	26,988	7.0	100.0	64,132	9.9	100.0	42,863	10.3	100.0	49,114	10.0	100.0
Dutch Guiana			—			—			14.2			30.1
Peru			2.8			31.3			19.2			29.8
United States			76.3			44.8			30.0			25.9
Mexico			1.6			22.1			9.7			2.0
Venezuela			—			0.4			7.9			—
Others			19.3			1.4			19.0			7.2

Commodity and Country	1911–13			1924–26			1932–34			1935		
	I[b]	II[c]	III[d]	I	II	III	I	II	III	I	II	III
Iron and Steel Products	81,222	21.1	100.0	135,566	20.9	100.0	38,054	9.0	100.0	53,913	10.9	100.0
Belgium			15.0			18.6			19.1			26.7
Germany			26.4			23.6			25.0			19.9
United Kingdom			39.6			28.6			18.4			18.7
United States			11.2			10.2			9.9			8.0
France			2.0			4.1			8.7			7.8
Others			5.8			14.9			18.9			18.9
Electrical Wire and Cable	2,448	0.6	100.0	6,123	0.9	100.0	1,435	0.3	100.0	2,368	0.5	100.0
United Kingdom			36.3			41.1			32.8			54.6
Germany			39.9			36.2			21.8			16.5
United States			4.9			8.2			5.8			10.7
Others			18.9			14.5			39.6			18.2
Tin Plate	1,235	0.3	100.0	2,247	0.3	100.0	6,398	1.4	100.0	6,089	1.2	100.0
United Kingdom			83.6			68.3			56.0			41.2
Germany			1.5			1.1			12.7			25.8
United States			8.7			30.6			22.8			20.8
Italy			—			—			6.6			2.1
Others			6.2			—			1.9			10.1
Machinery	26,415	6.9	100.0	45,765	7.1	100.0	11,813	2.9	100.0	4,851	1.0	100.0
United States			33.6			55.0			54.0			48.3
United Kingdom			18.6			13.2			20.7			17.0
Germany			29.7			17.2			20.6			13.0
Others			18.1			14.6			4.7			21.7
Electrical Machinery	5,687	1.5	100.0	8,839	1.4	100.0	602	[e]	100.0	10,220	2.1	100.0
Germany			58.0			34.7			28.2			28.5
United Kingdom			17.2			21.6			19.4			23.6
United States			6.8			25.0			7.5			19.5
Others			18.0			18.7			44.9			28.5

[e] Less than 0.1 per cent.

Table XXIV (*continued*)

Commodity and Country	1911–13			1924–26			1932–34			1935		
	I[b]	II[c]	III[d]	I	II	III	I	II	III	I	II	III
Agricultural Machinery	13,350	3.5	100.0	21,892	3.4	100.0	1,822	0.4	100.0	7,502	1.5	100.0
United States			56.8			73.9			60.0			66.2
Canada			1.9			9.2			20.2			21.4
Germany			10.6			2.7			11.4			5.9
France			12.9			2.8			3.8			2.1
United Kingdom			5.1			3.1			3.0			1.2
Others			12.7			8.3			1.6			3.2
Automobiles	5,245	1.4	100.0	32,766	5.1	100.0	3,330	0.8	100.0	12,441	2.4	100.0
United States			10.0			90.0			87.0			91.1
United Kingdom			12.8			1.8			5.1			3.8
Germany			17.7			1.0			1.7			2.7
Italy			11.1			2.8			4.6			1.4
France			39.2			2.5			0.6			0.2
Tires and Tubes	257	•	100.0	12,744	2.0	100.0	3,412	0.8	100.0	1,144	0.2	100.0
United Kingdom			47.6			10.8			47.0			66.9
United States			9.7			47.6			16.8			17.0
France			2.8			12.5			8.7			3.5
Italy			2.4			12.0			24.0			0.6
Others			37.5			17.1			3.5			12.0
Total Specified Imports	313,107	81.9		572,312	85.6		302,947	72.1		371,651	71.9	
Total Unspecified Imports	79,246	18.1		96,183	14.4		117,431	27.9		145,341	28.1	
Total Imports	382,353	100.0		668,495	100.0		420,378	100.0		516,922	100.0	

• Less than 0.1 per cent.

Sources: Figures for 1911–13 and 1924–26 adapted from National Industrial Conference Board, *Trends in the Foreign Trade of the United States*, New York, 1930, pp. 84–86; figures for 1932–34 and 1935 compiled from Argentine official statistics by the writer.

still move to market in sacks, although recently intensive efforts have been made to improve and expand elevator and other storage facilities.

Lacking iron ore and coal resources to any significant degree, Argentina has been forced to import most of her iron and steel products. These represent a wide diversity of articles ranging from pig iron, iron bars, plates, sheets, rails, etc., to all types of machinery, from sewing machines, typewriters, and cash registers to locomotives, mining machinery and agricultural implements, as well as tools, cutlery, and kitchen utensils. Under the protection of high tariffs, however, Argentina produces increasing quantities of certain types of iron and steel goods, such as structural steel, bolts, rivets, small machinery, and some farm vehicles.

Imports of iron and steel products declined from 20.9 per cent of total imports for the period 1924-26 to nine per cent for the period 1932-34, with a slight increase in 1935 to 10.9 per cent. In actual value, the decline was much greater; in the period 1924-26 iron and steel imports averaged 135,566,000 gold pesos annually compared with an annual average of 38,054,000 gold pesos in the period 1932-34, or a decline of 72 per cent. No doubt this decline was the result in large measure of the depression, and will not be permanent. Argentine railways, always large purchasers of iron and steel, were of course severely hit by the depression.

The five leading countries in Argentina's iron and steel trade in the three-year period 1932-34 were Germany, Belgium, United Kingdom, the United States, and France. Germany ranked first, not because of an increase in her percentage of total imports, but because of a decline in the percentage supplied by Great Britain. Table XXIV shows that prior to 1935 Germany supplied about one-fourth of Argentina's iron and steel imports. In 1935, however, Belgium achieved first rank, providing 26.7 per cent, while Germany's share was reduced to 19.9 per cent. The United Kingdom's share in Argentina's imports of iron and steel products has declined from 39.6 per cent in the pre-war period to an annual average of 18.5 per cent in the period 1932-

35. Again this may be traced to the situation of the railways, which, it will be recalled, are largely British owned and purchase a large portion of their equipment and supplies from Great Britain. The United States continues to supply about one-tenth of Argentina's imports of iron and steel products, thus maintaining its position as fourth in importance.

When it comes to highly fabricated products of iron and steel, such as machinery, however, the United States holds first rank by a wide margin. Even prior to the War, one-third of Argentina's machinery imports came from the United States. During recent years this percentage has been steadily increased, so that the United States now supplies about half of Argentina's machinery imports. This predominance of United States machinery is attributable primarily to two factors: (1) the United States occupies a superior competitive position in the manufacture of many types of machinery which are particularly susceptible to mass production—in other words, the United States occupies a favorable position with respect to supply; (2) because of similarities between certain aspects of the Argentine economy and that of the United States, Argentina offers a market with an effective demand for certain types of products which are produced on a large scale for domestic consumption in the United States.[23]

A relatively high and improving standard of living in Argentina has provided a market for an increasing number of comforts and luxuries, in the production of which the United States excels. In other words, the United States has not replaced European producers in the Argentine market during the past twenty years so much as she has promoted a dormant demand for many new products. Chief among these products are automobiles, including accessories, and office and household appliances. The United States also supplies large quantities of mining machinery, particularly oil-well equipment, and dominates the market for agricultural machinery. Prior to the War a large proportion of the machinery imports from the United States, which, as already indicated, made up one-third of Argentina's total machinery im-

[23] This point is elaborated further in Chapter VII.

ports, were agricultural implements. Conditions in Argentina have been especially favorable to the introduction and use of agricultural machinery. Among these favorable factors may be mentioned (1) level land and fertile soil free from rocks and boulders which facilitate the use of agricultural implements of all kinds; (2) small rural population fostering the use of all types of labor-saving machinery; (3) relatively dry harvesting season which permits the use of the large "combine" type of harvester-thresher; (4) small domestic production due to lack of raw materials and power, as well as labor and capital.[24]

Similarity of agricultural conditions in both the United States and Argentina has made it possible for the United States manufacturers to produce on a large scale, and thus undersell European manufacturers, whose domestic markets do not require the type of implements used in the extensive type of agriculture practised in Argentina and many parts of the United States. Including Canadian exports (which are largely the output of United States branch plants) United States manufacturers supply over 80 per cent of Argentina's agricultural machinery.

One of the most striking developments in the import trade of Argentina since the War has been the increase of automotive purchases. Automobile imports increased in value from an annual average in the pre-war period of slightly over 5,000,000 gold pesos to an annual average in the period 1924-26 of nearly 33,000,000 gold pesos, or 5.1 per cent of total imports. The total number of motor vehicles (including passenger cars, trucks, and chassis) imported into Argentina annually since 1920 was as follows:

(in thousands of units)

1920	13.8	1928	51.7
1921	9.6	1929	90.6
1922	15.8	1930	48.7
1923	30.8	1931	17.9
1924	38.0	1932	7.2
1925	56.9	1933	9.5
1926	49.9	1934	17.5
1927	42.7	1935	25.0

[24] Jones, *op. cit.*, p. 384.

The number of motor vehicles in use in Argentina increased between 1925 and 1930 from 182,000, of which 162,000 were private cars, to 454,000, of which 358,000 were private, and 96,000 commercial, vehicles.

The retrenchment in Argentine purchases abroad in recent years is well illustrated in the case of automobiles, the average annual value of automobile imports having dropped to 3,330,000 gold pesos in the period 1932-34 (see Table XXIV), or 0.8 per cent of total imports. As the above unit figures show, however, there was a marked recovery in 1934 and 1935; during the latter year imports of automobiles were valued at 12,441,000 gold pesos. This decline in imports has resulted in a net decline in the number of motor vehicles in circulation, the number in use having dropped to 241,000 vehicles in 1936.[25] It is estimated that 100,000 motor vehicles must be imported annually for several years to meet requirements.

Prior to the War, European makes of automobiles dominated the Argentine market, the United States supplying only ten per cent of the total. These European automobiles were primarily high-priced cars for use only in the larger cities, since no suitable highways existed in the rural areas. United States automobiles offered for sale in Argentina were, up to 1911, largely confined to light cheap makes for country use which were frequently unsatisfactory, and, in consequence, United States cars were much discredited. During the War, however, the demand for automobiles in the rural areas increased rapidly as a result of the prosperity ensuing from the higher prices for wheat and other food products. This demand was supplied very largely by American manufacturers, whose product had been improved meanwhile, plus the fact that they provided increasing service and repair facilities. By 1917, 80 to 90 per cent of the American automobiles sold in Argentina went to the wealthy farmers.[26] By 1918, the United States supplied 5,612 of the 5,668 passenger automobiles

[25] *Comments on Argentine Trade*, Jan. 1937, p. 30, which cites a report of the Argentine "Institute de Estudios Economicos del Transporte."

[26] The above description is taken from the writer's unpublished manuscript (a Master's thesis), *Argentina as a Market for Passenger Automobiles, 1910-1927*, 1929.

imported into the Argentine, or 99 per cent. In 1921 the percentage had declined to 93.5 per cent, but continued thereafter to average over 95 per cent throughout the decade of the twenties. Including trucks and busses, the United States supplied 90.9 per cent of the total value of automobile imports in the three-year period 1924-26. Subsequent to 1930 this percentage declined slightly, equaling 87.0 per cent during the three-year period 1932-34. In 1935, however, United States automobiles accounted for 91.1 per cent of the total value of motor car imports.

Argentina has ranked as one of the leading export markets for American motor cars, purchasing from forty to fifty thousand cars annually prior to 1930. In 1932 and 1933, however, total passenger car imports from the United States declined to 5,278 and 6,761 units, respectively, although increasing to 10,863 and 16,385 cars in 1934 and 1935. In value this was a decline during the 1932-34 period of nearly 90 per cent over the prosperous years preceding 1930.

With respect to tires and tubes, however, the United States does not occupy such a commanding position. Prior to the War the United Kingdom supplied nearly half of Argentina's imports of tires and tubes, which totaled approximately 257,000 gold pesos in value. During the three-year period 1924-26 imports averaged nearly 13 million gold pesos annually in value, equivalent to two per cent of total imports. Of this total, the United States supplied 47.6, France 12.5, Italy 12.0, and the United Kingdom 10.8 per cent, respectively. By 1932-34 a decided shift in relative positions had occurred, with the United Kingdom again furnishing nearly half of the total with 47.0 per cent, and Italy, the United States, and France ranking second, third, and fourth, with 24.0, 16.8, and 8.7 per cent, respectively. By 1935 the United Kingdom had increased its share to 66.9 per cent, whereas Italy's share was reduced to the negligible figure of 0.6 per cent, compared with 17.0 and 3.5 per cent, respectively, for the United States and France. Total imports of tires and tubes have continued to decline, however, amounting to only 1,144,000 gold pesos in 1935, compared with the depression average of 3,412,000 in 1932-34 and 12,744,000 gold pesos

in 1924-26. This decline has been the direct result of a marked increase in import duties since 1931, which encouraged the erection of several branch plants in Argentina for the production of tires and tubes.

A large portion of the gasoline and lubricants to operate these automobiles also comes from abroad. Furthermore, a large part of the fuel supplies for the merchant marine, railways, and manufacturing comes from foreign sources. Petroleum products and coal constitute roughly ten and five per cent, respectively, of the total value of Argentina's imports. Imports of these two products declined to a lesser degree during recent years than did many other commodities, accounting together for 17.1 per cent of the total value of imports during the three years 1932-34, and 16.0 per cent in 1935. The United Kingdom dominates the coal trade, whereas the United States, until recently, constituted the leading source of petroleum products. Germany is the only other important source of coal, providing roughly one-tenth of the total in recent years. British dominance of the coal trade is due to the fact that British vessels, which transport a large share of Argentina's farm and animal products to Europe, are able to bring coal as ballast at a very low freight rate. Furthermore, preference is shown to British coal by the British-owned railroads, factories, and meat-packing plants.

In the pre-war period 1911-13 slightly over 75.0 per cent of Argentina's imports of petroleum products came from the United States. Since then, however, its share in these imports has declined steadily, equaling 44.8 and 30.0 per cent in the periods 1924-26 and 1932-34, respectively. Since the World War, Peru, Dutch Guiana, Mexico, and Venezuela have become important as suppliers of Argentine imports of petroleum products. In 1935 Dutch Guiana and Peru ranked first and second, providing 35.1 and 29.8 per cent, respectively, compared with 25.9 per cent for the United States. Many of these other sources are owned by United States companies.

Wood products (including lumber) constitute another important type of imports into Argentina, averaging from 15 to 20 million gold pesos annually in value during the past twenty-

five years. Before the War the United States furnished about two-thirds of these lumber imports, but this percentage has steadily declined, so that in recent years only slightly more than one-third of the total comes from the United States. The balance is widely distributed; during 1932-34 Brazil, Russia, and Paraguay ranked second, third, and fourth, respectively, accounting for about another third of the total. In 1935 Poland ranked third with 7.9 per cent.

Paper and paper manufactures, although in a large degree products of the wood industries, constitute another important class of imports, averaging nearly 25 million gold pesos annually. Germany formerly dominated the paper trade, supplying nearly one-half of the total. In recent years, however, this proportion has been reduced to less than 20 per cent (see Table XXIV). In 1935 Germany ranked third after Canada and Sweden. The share of the United States has declined from an average of 17.6 per cent in the pre-war period 1911-13 to approximately five per cent during recent years.

Imports of food products account for roughly another ten per cent of Argentina's imports. Like most other classes of imports, these include a large number of items, coming from all parts of the world. Fruits and non-alcoholic beverages,[27] however, are of outstanding importance. The latter includes primarily coffee, tea, and yerba maté. The chief sources of supply are then, naturally, Brazil, Ceylon, Paraguay, and India, with Brazil supplying about four-fifths of the total. Imports of fruit during recent years have ranged in value from five to ten million gold pesos. In the pre-war period, Spain ranked first, providing slightly more than one-fourth of the total. During the decade of the twenties the United States came to occupy first place, supplying 26.0 per cent of the total in the three-year period 1924-26, consisting largely of fresh apples and pears, and dried fruits, mostly prunes and raisins. Since 1931, however, these imports have been severely restricted, so that, in the period 1932-34, the

[27] Alcoholic beverages equal about one per cent of total imports, the annual average for the periods 1928-30 and 1932-34 being 10.33 million gold pesos and 3.46 million gold pesos, respectively.

United States ranked third with only 13.4 per cent, compared with Brazil and Paraguay with 32.0 and 23.0 per cent, respectively. In 1935 Brazil increased its share to 40.0 per cent, compared with 16.4, 14.0, and 13.8 per cent, respectively, for Paraguay, the United States, and Spain.

Brazil has also supplied the greatest percentage of Argentina's tobacco imports in recent years, accounting for approximately one-half the total. Cuba supplies about 20 per cent with the United States and Italy providing most of the remainder.

III. DIRECTION OF ARGENTINA'S FOREIGN TRADE

Although Argentina's foreign trade is widely distributed, five countries—the United Kingdom, the United States, Germany, Belgium, and France—account for over two-thirds of the total. This is shown in Table XXV which gives, for selected periods, the average annual percentage of Argentina's exports and imports with the leading countries. As indicated in the table, the Netherlands in recent years has ranked among the first five in Argentine exports, but since her sales to Argentina are less than two per cent of the total, her position in the total foreign trade is below the first five. Similarly, Italy ranks fourth in supplying Argentina's imports, but in Argentina's export trade she ranks sixth or seventh.

The percentages in Table XXV are based upon Argentine official statistics. They are subject to the following important qualifications. A considerable portion of Argentina's exports are shipped "to order"; that is, their destination is not known at the time of departure. In 1932 these "to order" shipments constituted 41.6 per cent of Argentina's total exports. Since 1927, however, exporters have been required to provide information regarding the ultimate destination of "to order" shipments, so that beginning in 1927 these "to order" shipments have been allocated (except for a very small amount—usually not over one per cent) in the official statistics by countries. The percentage which these "to order" shipments bore to total exports in the years prior to 1927 is given in Table XXV. It is believed that the relative position of Argentina's export markets would not be greatly altered for the earlier years, could these "to order"

TABLE XXV

DISTRIBUTION BY LEADING COUNTRIES OF ARGENTINA'S FOREIGN TRADE

AVERAGE ANNUAL PERCENTAGES FOR SELECTED PERIODS

	1911–13	*1917–19*	*1922–24*	*1928–30*	*1932–34*	*1935*	*1936*
Exports							
United Kingdom	26.1	31.9	23.3	32.5	37.1	34.3	31.8
United States	6.3	22.8	10.2	9.3	5.5	12.0	10.5
Netherlands	3.3	2.2	4.1	10.0	11.2	8.9	6.7
Belgium	8.5	1.9	6.6	9.7	10.3	8.7	6.5
Brazil	5.0	4.0	3.4	4.6	3.4	4.8	6.2
Germany	12.2	0.3	8.8	10.8	8.2	6.9	5.7
France	9.2	12.8	6.7	6.6	7.0	4.8	5.1
Italy	4.2	4.8	3.7	6.3	4.5	4.0	2.0
To order	19.8	8.2	26.9				
Imports[a]							
United Kingdom	30.5	23.5	23.5	19.0	22.5	24.7	20.4
United States	14.8	35.2	21.7	23.9	13.4	13.6	14.6
Germany	17.2	0.1	12.2	11.6	9.7	8.5	9.2
Belgium	5.3	0.1	4.9	4.8	4.1	6.5	6.4
Italy	8.3	4.7	7.3	8.9	9.2	4.7	5.2
Brazil	2.7	9.1	5.6	3.9	6.1	5.9	4.8
France	9.7	5.0	6.1	6.4	5.3	4.3	4.2
Netherlands	2.3	—	1.2	1.4	1.4	1.4	2.8

[a] "Real" values, except 1936 which are provisional "tariff" values. In 1936 India ranked seventh after Brazil, and Japan and Dutch Guiana ninth and tenth with 3.6 and 3.3 per cent, respectively.

Source: Compiled from reports on Argentina in the *Foreign Trade Series* of the Pan-American Union and *Anuario del Comercio Exterior de la República Argentina*, except 1936, which are provisional figures as published in *El Comercio Exterior Argentino en 1936 y su comparacion con el de 1935, Informe No. 56, Serie C., No. 44*, 1937.

shipments be allocated for the years prior to 1927. The average annual percentage distribution of "to order" exports by leading countries for the six-year period 1927-32 was as follows:

	Per cent
United Kingdom	30.0
Belgium	12.7
Netherlands	10.0
Germany	9.1
Italy	7.4
France	6.8
Per cent of total "to order" shipments	76.0

Applying these percentages to the total "to order" shipments for the years 1922-24, and adding the results to the known exports to these countries, their percentage share in Argentina's exports, compared with their share excluding "to order" shipments, was as follows:

	Including "to order"	*Excluding "to order"*
	per cent	*per cent*
United Kingdom	31.4	23.3
Germany	11.2	8.8
United States	10.2[a]	10.2
Belgium	10.0	6.6
France	8.5	6.7
Netherlands	6.8	4.1
Italy	5.7	3.7

[a] Only 0.8 per cent of total "to order" exports went to the United States in the period 1927-32.

Including "to order" shipments, the United States ranked third instead of second, and Belgium was ahead of France.

A second important qualification respecting the final destination of Argentina's exports is the fact that many shipments are consigned to European seaboard countries (e.g., Netherlands, Germany, Belgium, etc.) but are later resold and transshipped to interior countries.[28]

Subject to the above qualifications, therefore, Table XXV shows that the United Kingdom is by far the leading purchaser of Argentine products, taking about three times as much as any other country. Her percentage share increased from an annual average of 32.5 per cent in the period 1928-30 to 37.1 per cent in the three years 1932-34, but declined thereafter to 34.3 and 31.8 per cent in 1935 and 1936, respectively. In recent years the Netherlands and Belgium have also increased their share to such an extent that they rank ahead of Germany, which formerly held second place, as purchasers of Argentine exports.

Argentina's exports of foodstuffs and raw materials have, until recently, found a ready market in the densely populated in-

[28] See *Anuario del Comercio Exterior*, 1932, p. LXXI.

dustrial countries of western Europe. The recent efforts toward greater national economic self-sufficiency have been, however, of serious concern to Argentina, and have forced her to give increasing attention to the domestic production of many industrial products which she formerly obtained abroad in exchange for her raw materials and foodstuffs. Whether this defeat of the principle of geographical specialization is but a temporary phase of the recent depression, or a permanent part of the world's increasing nationalism, cannot be foretold. The present situation does not present a very optimistic picture for increasing international specialization and exchange in the world's economic activity.

With respect to the United States, Argentina's exports have not generally held such a favorable position. Argentina's leading export commodities, it will be recalled, are wheat, corn, linseed, meats, wool, and hides. Since the United States is a large producer of all of these products, Argentina's exports do not normally find a ready market in this country, a condition which has been increasingly accentuated by the tariff policy of the United States since the War.[29] As a result, the United States has taken, until recently, a steadily decreasing share of Argentina's exports, as shown in Table XXV. Increasing from 6.3 per cent of Argentina's total exports in the years 1911-13, to 22.8 per cent in the three years 1917-19, United States purchases of Argentine exports declined to an annual average of 5.5 per cent of the total in the three years 1932-34. The marked increase in exports of grains to the United States during 1935 and 1936 has temporarily reversed this trend, since in these years the United States ranked second as a buyer of Argentine products, accounting for 12.0 and 10.5 per cent, respectively, of the total. Argentina's chief exports to the United States have been flaxseed, hides, skins, wool, and quebracho.

With respect to Argentina's import trade, however, the United States has occupied a much more dominant position, sharing with the United Kingdom the leadership in supplying Argentina with a wide diversity of manufactured products. As Table XXVI shows, these two countries have furnished upwards of

[29] See Chapters VII and IX.

half of Argentina's total imports during the past twenty-five years. In the pre-war period 1911-13 the United Kingdom provided 30.5 per cent and the United States 14.8 per cent of Argentina's total imports. Although Germany ranked second with 17.2 per cent of the total, the United States, in third place, already

TABLE XXVI

ARGENTINA'S FOREIGN TRADE WITH THE UNITED STATES AND THE UNITED KINGDOM; AVERAGE ANNUAL PERCENTAGES OF TOTAL TRADE FOR SELECTED PERIODS

	1911–13	*1917–19*	*1922–24*	*1928–30*	*1932–34*	*1935*	*1936*
Exports							
United Kingdom	26.1	31.9	23.3	32.5	37.1	34.3	31.8
United States	6.3	22.8	10.2	9.3	6.5	12.0	10.5
Total	32.4	54.7	33.5	41.8	43.6	46.3	42.3
Imports							
United Kingdom	30.5	23.5	23.5	19.0	22.5	24.7	20.4
United States	14.8	35.2	21.7	23.9	13.4	13.6	14.6
Total	44.3	58.7	45.2	42.9	35.9	38.3	34.9
Total Foreign Trade							
United Kingdom	28.4	27.7	23.4	25.8	29.8	28.8	27.1
United States	11.8	29.0	16.0	16.6	10.0	13.0	12.2
Total	40.2	56.7	39.4	42.4	39.8	41.8	39.3

Source: Data compiled from reports on Argentina in the *Foreign Trade Series* of the Pan-American Union and *Anuario del Comercio Exterior de la República Argentina*, excepting 1936, which are provisional figures as published in *El Comercio Exterior Argentino en 1936 y su comparacion con el de 1935*, *Informe No. 56, Serie C., No. 44*, 1937.

occupied a leading position. During the War the share of the United States increased rapidly. Averaging 35.2 per cent of the total in the three-year period 1917-19, the United States held undisputed first position, with the United Kingdom in second place with 23.5 per cent and Brazil third with 9.1 per cent. By 1922, however, the United Kingdom had regained first place, with an average annual percentage for the three years 1922-24 of 23.5 per cent, followed by the United States with 21.7 per cent and Germany in third place with 12.2 per cent. Germany

continued to hold third rank until 1932,[30] but in 1925 the United States again regained first position, which she held until 1931. The annual averages for the United States and the United Kingdom for the three years 1928-30 were 23.9 and 19.0 per cent, respectively. Following 1929, however, the share of the United States in the import trade of Argentina declined rapidly, reaching a low point in 1933 of 12.0 per cent, compared with an increase to 23.4 per cent for the United Kingdom. For the three-year period 1932-34 the annual average share of the United Kingdom and the United States equaled 22.5 and 13.4 per cent, respectively. For the United States this was slightly less than its pre-war average of 14.8 per cent. The other leading countries which obtained a greater share of Argentina's import trade during the period 1932-34 were Italy and Brazil.[31]

Largely as a result of Argentina's new bilateral foreign commercial policy, the share of the United Kingdom in the import trade of the former country increased in 1935 to 24.7 per cent. Beginning with the Roca-Runciman agreement signed with the United Kingdom in May 1933, Argentina during 1934 negotiated trade agreements with Belgium, the Netherlands, Switzerland, Germany, and Spain.[32] According to figures published in the 1935 annual report of the Argentine Ministry of Finance, the total imports for 1935 from countries with which trade agreements were in effect were 47.5 per cent greater than the total imports for 1933 from those countries, compared with an increase in imports from countries without trade agreements of 19.8 per cent.

Preliminary percentage figures for Argentine imports for 1936 contained in Table XXV show, however, a decline in the United Kingdom's share of the Argentine import trade to only 20.4 per

[30] During 1932 and 1933 Italy ranked third and Germany fourth. In 1934 imports from Italy declined sharply, however, so that the annual average for the three-year period 1932-34 shows Germany remaining in third place (see Table XXV).

[31] See Table XXV.

[32] See Chapter IX, pp. 206-9 for more detailed description, as well as subsequent additions to the list.

cent of the total, which was in large part offset by an increase in the shares of the United States, Germany, and Italy. This decline in the United Kingdom's share has continued in the early months of 1937, during which the United Kingdom supplied 19 per cent of total imports, compared with 17 per cent furnished by the United States.

As previously described in considering the composition of Argentina's foreign trade, the United Kingdom sells Argentina coal, textiles, general iron and steel goods, jute, railway equipment, and other miscellaneous manufactures. The United States dominates the trade in agricultural machinery, automobiles, wood and petroleum products, as well as sharing largely in the trade in fruits, tobacco products, general iron and steel manufactures, and numerous other types of machinery, particularly mining equipment and office and household appliances. Germany furnishes a great variety of manufactured goods to Argentina. Of particular importance are cheaper grades of hardware, machine tools, kitchen utensils, toys, and school supplies. Many of these articles are of the cheap "five and ten cent store" variety. Germany also provides a large share of Argentina's purchases of electrical wire and cable, and electrical machinery.

Italy specializes in cheap grades of cotton and woolen goods and artificial silk. The large Italian population in Argentina also fosters the sale of Italian products, especially certain types of foodstuffs (e.g., olives and olive oil) and tobacco products.

Belgium also furnishes considerable quantities of the cheaper grades of cotton yarns and textiles, as well as some 20 per cent of Argentina's imports of iron and steel manufactures.

French exports are primarily luxury goods, such as high grade silks and woolens, novelties, perfumery, fine leather goods, and ladies' notions. The urban population of Argentina, especially of Buenos Aires, looks largely to France for these types of goods, and Paris is the style center of the southern hemisphere as it is of the northern. France also obtains from five to ten per cent of the trade in tires and tubes and iron and steel products, and a considerable proportion of the trade in patent medicines.[33]

[33] Clarence Jones, *op. cit.*

VII

COMPETITIVE FACTORS IN THE IMPORT TRADE OF ARGENTINA

IN THE preceding chapter, our discussion of the direction of Argentina's foreign trade was primarily descriptive. We turn now to a more detailed analysis of the causal factors determining the competitive position of the various nations in the import trade of Argentina. Since the United States and Great Britain are the two chief competitors in the Argentine import trade, our analysis will concern primarily these two countries.

Great Britain's failure to regain her pre-war supremacy in the Argentine trade during the decade following the War resulted in growing concern on the part of the British, as evidenced by the increasing attention given to the problem of restoring their old position.

At the same time, in the United States the importance of the Argentine market was increasingly emphasized, and much consideration was given to the problem of how the United States might retain, or even further improve, its position.

The problem of evaluating the competitive position, even of two nations, in the trade of any third country is an extremely complex one. Various studies have been made of international competition in the trade of Argentina.[1]

The major factors affecting international competition in the Argentine trade prior to 1931 may be grouped as follows:[2]

[1] One of the most comprehensive of these was that sponsored by the Carnegie Endowment in 1929 and published in 1931 as "Studies in World Economy No. IV, International Competition in the Trade of Argentina," in *International Conciliation*, No. 271, June, 1931. This study was in two parts as follows:

(1) Roswell C. McCrea, and Thurman W. VanMetre, *The Export Trade of the United States and the United Kingdom with Argentina, a Statistical Essay with Explanatory Comments*; (2) George Jackson Eder, *Current Trends in the International Trade of Argentina*. This monograph has been drawn upon heavily in the following analysis, particularly Eder's study.

[2] This classification is adapted, with some modifications, from Eder, *op. cit.*

1. Racial Factors
2. Commodity Specialization
3. Cost and Quality
4. Marketing Methods and Advertising
5. Trade Promotion
6. Propaganda
7. Investments

The above factors were of primary significance and operative under conditions of a relatively free economy and equal treatment which characterized Argentina's foreign commercial policy prior to 1931. Since 1931, however, they have become of secondary importance, as Argentina has instituted increasingly severe governmental control covering the country's foreign trade, in fact, all of its international economic transactions. These controls have taken the dual form of exchange control coupled with the negotiation of bilateral treaties granting special treatment to individual countries. For example, of what avail is a skillful advertising campaign, or a superior product adapted to the needs and wants of the Argentine consumer, when the government imposes a surcharge of 20 per cent on the purchase of dollar exchange to cover remittances on goods imported from the United States?

Nevertheless the competitive factors listed above, in addition to being of historical significance, are still of some importance in affecting trade trends, and may again become primary, provided Argentina's present restrictive measures are but a temporary phase of the severe economic depression from which she has recently emerged. They warrant, therefore, brief consideration at this point.

1. *Racial Factors*

Because of the large number of immigrants resident in Argentina, racial influences have been an important factor in the determination of many classes of imports. Although the leading position of the United States and Great Britain in the Argentine market is based largely upon other factors, many of the imports of Argentina from certain other countries (particularly Italy,

Spain, and Germany) are to fill wants of the large numbers of Italians, Spaniards, and Germans and others who desire certain luxuries or necessities familiar to them in their own countries. A considerable portion of Italy's share of Argentina's total imports is attributable to this factor.

This influence of home ties soon wears off, however, as the new residents from abroad become "Argentinized," and purchases become more affected by their adaptability to Argentine conditions. If the rapid decline in immigration characteristic of recent years continues, the racial factor will be of decreasing significance in Argentina's import trade.

2. *Commodity Specialization*

The most important factor in determining the direction of the international movement of commodities under conditions of relatively free competition is that of commodity specialization. Each country tends to produce those products for which it is best fitted, either by reason of natural or acquired advantages. For many products these advantages may be so pronounced as to greatly reduce, if not practically eliminate, the possibilities of competition from another country. Furthermore, each country produces primarily what its own home markets demand. If a large home market exists for a product which may also be sold abroad, an important natural advantage exists. Illustrative of this point is the automobile in the United States, and numerous other products adapted to mass production and mass consumption in this country.

Recognizing the importance of commodity specialization, Eder, after making detailed analyses of the Argentine import trade for the year 1927, reached the conclusion that, with respect to competition among the five leading countries in the Argentine market, namely, United States, United Kingdom, Germany, Italy, and France, only about one-third of Argentina's total import trade could be considered strictly competitive, because of commodity specialization by countries.[3]

[3] For details see Eder, *op. cit.*, pp. 403-5.

With respect to United States exports to Argentina, Eder concluded that for the year 1929 not over one-fourth were competitive products; that one-fourth were non-competitive by reason of natural advantages, and one-half by reason of production advantages.[4]

Another important feature of United States exports to Argentina which characterizes the majority of these non-competitive products is the fact that they are generally new products—in other words, as suggested earlier in this study, the gains made by the United States in Argentine markets have not been made at the expense of Great Britain, in those products which Great Britain furnished Argentina, but in new types of goods for which an increasing purchasing power in Argentina has created a demand; for example, such products as automobiles, office and household equipment, radios, films, and machinery for new industries. Great Britain lost ground during the twenties only relatively and not absolutely to the United States.[5] Furthermore, the gains made by the United States during the War were in lines taken from continental competitors, particularly Austria, Italy, Belgium, and Germany rather than from Great Britain.[6]

[4] Eder, *op. cit.*, p. 408. The statistical study of the competitive position of the United States and Great Britain in Argentine trade which was made independently of Eder's study by McCrea and VanMetre showed that for 1927 about half of Great Britain's exports to Argentina were of those type of goods in which she supplied over 65 per cent of the total furnished by both countries (i.e., United States and United Kingdom but excluding similar products supplied by other countries), and for the greater portion of these items, the United Kingdom furnished in excess of 90 per cent of the joint trade of the two countries.

[5] The study by McCrea and VanMetre just referred to showed that two-thirds of the total value of exports from the United States to Argentina in 1927 were in this "new business" group.

[6] A study prepared in 1921 by Dr. Julius Klein showed that, comparing 1917 with 1913, the gains made by the United States in the Argentine market in such widely diversified products as cleaned rice, refined sugar, newsprint, cotton stockings, lead ingots and sheets, steel in bars and sheets, iron wheels and axles, steel fish plates, electroplated ware, iron in pigs and sheets, were all in items formerly supplied very largely by the continental countries mentioned above. There was only one clear case of the United States supplanting the United Kingdom, namely, tin plate. Julius Klein, "The Competitive Situation in South American Trade," *Harvard Review of Economic Statistics*, 1921, Vol. III, p. 12.

3. *Cost and Quality*

Too much emphasis, however, must not be placed on the non-competitive character of Argentina's imports. Competition does exist, in fact it is extremely keen, not only between products of different nations, but between products of the same national origin. Pursuit of the consumer's dollar is just as intense and effective in Buenos Aires as it is in Chicago, London, or New York City.

In Argentina, as elsewhere, cost, relative to quality, is generally the determining factor in the purchase and sale of merchandise. In this respect, criticism has been leveled at British manufacturing and merchandising policy. British goods have sometimes been of too high quality for the purpose for which they were intended. This factor of high quality, coupled with higher cost, has in certain cases resulted in the elimination of British goods from the Argentine market.

A member of the British Economic Mission to South America in 1929 emphasized this point in a paper read before the Royal Society of Arts (England) when he said,

> Argentina is increasingly a price market. . . . Price is everything; durability in a country changing and developing at such an astonishing rate is naturally a secondary consideration. The result has been a steady drift toward standards deemed by the buyers to be good enough for the time being, although admittedly not so good as the high standards which we in this country seek to maintain. . . . I regard this question of standards as of paramount importance and one deserving the most earnest consideration of all trade associations.[7]

This does not imply, however, that Argentina is necessarily a cheap market. In fact, in many instances, success in the sale of American goods has been the result of superior quality, but superior quality at lower costs than for British-made goods. On the other hand, for certain types of goods, we find that British prices have been progressively lowered, relative to prices of United States manufacturers for similar products.[8]

Apparently, therefore, no general conclusions may be drawn

[7] William Clare Lees, "Some Aspects of Trade with South America," *Journal of Royal Society of Arts*, Vol. 78, 1930, pp. 461-2.

[8] Eder, *op. cit.*, p. 410.

respecting cost and quality as between countries. As suggested in discussing commodity specialization, in certain lines one country has superior advantages, while in other types of commodities another country excels.

4. *Marketing Methods and Advertising*

The manufacture and sale of commodities is no longer primarily a production problem, but a dual problem of production and distribution. The factors of cost and quality just considered are primarily production problems. Even in those cases where one producer fails to have a definite superiority in cost or quality with respect to his product, he may nevertheless dominate the market because of superior merchandising technique. A considerable portion of the success of United States manufacturers in the Argentine market during the period covered by this study must be attributed to improvements achieved in the art of export merchandising. Marketing methods in the Argentine trade have been revolutionized during the past twenty years, the result, largely, of the changes introduced by United States firms. Although these changes in merchandising technique cannot be discussed in detail here, the most significant developments may be summarized as follows:

(a) *Growth of direct dealing between manufacturer and importer*

An important factor in promoting this tendency has been the increased sale of those types of products by the United States which require servicing, the automobile being perhaps the best-known example, although numerous other types of machinery fall in the same category. As a result, the old system of placing orders annually with commission houses or general export merchants has been superseded by the practice of utilizing either the services of a local agent or distributor or by employing a full-time representative on the ground, or, if the volume of business warrants, the establishment of a branch distributing organization. The result has been the speeding up of the merchandising process, with smaller orders, prompt deliveries, lower unit profits, and more rapid turnover.

(b) *Market analysis*

Although the English manufacturers have been slow to adopt the new technique in merchandising, perhaps their greatest handicap has been their apparent unwillingness to ascertain what the Argentine purchaser really wanted, and then go about providing it. This failure to adapt English goods to Argentine needs was recognized both by Argentinians and many Englishmen even during the War. For example, Sr. Mitre, editor and proprietor of *La Nación*, Buenos Aires, one of the outstanding newspapers of Argentina, in an address in London in February 1919, emphasized the fact that Great Britain had neglected to study market conditions in Argentina, and therefore held an inferior position.[9]

As recently as 1929, an English writer concluded that the United States would win out over Europe, and emphasized that one of the important facts favorable to the United States was the greater adaptability to Argentine needs.[10]

The Statist (London) of September 27, 1930, in discussing Argentine trade prospects stated that "British producers have always enjoyed a high reputation in Argentina. But friendly Argentinians will tell the inquiring reader that we have two serious defects in improving our trade with that country—(1) we will not learn the language and (2) we insist upon offering goods highly prized in this country." Since 1930 Great Britain has been showing marked improvement along these lines, and is giving special attention to the South American and especially the Argentine market, largely stimulated by the excellent reports of special investigating committees which have studied the problem.[11]

[9] Reproduced in the *South American Journal*, February 22, 1919, Vol. 86, p. 136. In numerous editorials as early as 1916, this English journal was urging British manufacturers and exporters to "wake up," to modernize their technique in order to meet the intense competition which was certain to ensue after the War.

[10] H. Hallan Hipwell, correspondent of *The Economist* (London), in discussing trade rivalries in Argentina. See "Trade Rivalries in Argentina," *Foreign Affairs*, October 1929, p. 150.

[11] E.g., the report of the Sheffield Industrial Mission to Argentina.

(c) *Changes in credit terms*

(1) In the wholesale trade, the tendency of United States exporters has been to reduce the length of credit terms, thus discouraging over-buying on the part of import houses and wholesalers; (2) on the other hand, the United States has increased the use of credit in consumer purchasing by the introduction of installment selling.

(d) *Advertising in Argentine trade*

Finally, advertising by United States companies has played an important part in building up a demand for their goods, although statements that the gains made by the United States in Argentine trade have been due largely to the sums spent on advertising are probably considerably exaggerated. Furthermore, this advertising has been of special importance in creating a market for new products; that is, where educational, rather than competitive, advertising was necessary and, as previously suggested, these lines were generally just those in which European manufacturers were not in a position to offer any effectual competition.

One of the most recent of the monographs published by the United States Bureau of Foreign and Domestic Commerce on Argentina,[12] in considering the present position of the United States in the Argentine market, stresses the fact that it is primarily by intensive modern advertising that the competitive position of the United States may be strengthened. Present-day competition is exceedingly keen, yet the possibility of an increasing market in Argentina during the next few years points to the commercial importance of good merchandising methods.[13]

5. *Trade Promotion*

In addition to the advertising and other merchandising activi-

[12] "Advertising Methods in Argentina," *Trade Information Bulletin* No. 828, 1935, Washington, D.C.

[13] Eder concluded, however, *op. cit.*, that "on the whole it may be said that while advertising, and American advertising in particular, has been invaluable as a means of opening up new markets and creating new desires amongst Argentine customers, its importance as a determining factor in international competition has probably been greatly overestimated."

ties of individual firms to promote sales in Argentina, mention should be made of the official and semiofficial trade promoting activities of organized groups. Under the heading of official trade promotion we have the activities of the permanent representatives of the various governments in Buenos Aires which have been a factor of importance in influencing trade. Here again, the activities of the British and American representatives have been outstanding. The reports on economic conditions which have been compiled annually since 1919 by the British commercial counseler in Buenos Aires are perhaps the outstanding accomplishment of the British governmental trade promotion staff. The United States Bureau of Foreign and Domestic Commerce has also published numerous monographs on the potentialities of the Argentine market.[14] Much current information

[14] The following list of such monographs is indicative of their scope and significance:

1. "Report on Trade Conditions in Argentina," United States Department of Commerce and Labor, *Special Agents Series* No. 8, 1906.
2. "Trade Developments in Argentina," United States Bureau of Manufactures, *Special Agents Series* No. 43, 1911.
3. "Economic Developments in Argentina Since 1921," United States Bureau of Foreign and Domestic Commerce, *Trade Information Bulletin* No. 156, 1923.
4. "Paper, Paper Products and Printing Machinery in Argentina, Uruguay, and Paraguay," United States Bureau of Foreign and Domestic Commerce, *Special Agents Series* No. 163, 1918.
5. "Wearing Apparel in Argentina," United States Bureau of Foreign and Domestic Commerce, *Miscellaneous Series* No. 68, 1918.
6. "Boots and Shoes, Leather and Supplies in Argentina, Uruguay, and Paraguay," United States Bureau of Foreign and Domestic Commerce, *Special Agents Series* No. 177, 1919.
7. "Electrical Goods in Argentina, Uruguay, and Brazil," United States Bureau of Foreign and Domestic Commerce, *Special Agents Series* No. 184, 1919.
8. "Jewelry and Silverware in Argentina, Uruguay, and Brazil," United States Bureau of Foreign and Domestic Commerce, *Special Agents Series* No. 214, 1922.
9. "Argentine Market for United States Goods," United States Bureau of Foreign and Domestic Commerce, *Trade Information Bulletin* No. 384, 1926.
10. "Markets for Agricultural Implements and Farm Machinery in Argentina and Uruguay," United States Bureau of Foreign and Domestic Commerce, *Trade Information Bulletin* No. 366, 1925.
11. "Electrical Equipment Market in Argentina," United States Bureau of

has also been made available either in weekly *Commerce Reports* or in mimeographed reports.[15] Prior to 1933, the American field staff in Argentina operated along different lines from the British efforts, since, in addition to the preparation of commercial reports, it devoted considerable energy to direct trade promotion, even to assistance in securing distributors for American products.[16]

This governmental interest in the Argentine market, it should be pointed out, is not solely a post-war development. As the list of monographs in footnote 14 indicates, official efforts to encourage interest on the part of the United States exporters in the possibilities of the Argentine market were active for a decade or more before the outbreak of the World War. These government activities were simply the reflection of an increasing public interest in Latin America. This increasing interest on the part of the United States in the Argentine and other South American markets was simply one aspect of a widely growing interest in the expansion of foreign trade throughout the world. This new interest in foreign markets led to the formation of several

---

of Foreign and Domestic Commerce, *Trade Information Bulletin* No. 536, 1928.

12. "Motion Pictures in Argentina and Brazil," United States Bureau of Foreign and Domestic Commerce, *Trade Information Bulletin* No. 630, 1929.
13. "Cattle Raising in Argentina," United States Bureau of Foreign and Domestic Commerce, *Trade Information Bulletin* No. 647, 1929.
14. "Legal Aspects in Collection of Accounts in Argentina," United States Bureau of Foreign and Domestic Commerce, *Trade Information Bulletin* No. 748, 1931.
15. "The Argentine Iron and Steel Industry and Trade," United States Bureau of Foreign and Domestic Commerce, *Trade Information Bulletin* No. 776, 1931.
16. "Manufacturing Developments in Argentina," United States Bureau of Foreign and Domestic Commerce, *Trade Information Bulletin* No. 820, 1934.
17. "Advertising Methods in Argentina," United States Bureau of Foreign and Domestic Commerce, *Trade Information Bulletin* No. 828, 1935.

[15] For example, *Latin American Financial Notes*, prepared under the supervision of Mr. J. C. Corliss of the Finance Division, contains much useful information regarding current financial developments in Argentina.

[16] Eder, *op. cit.*, p. 436. Since 1933, these direct trade promotion efforts have been abandoned.

organizations having for their objective the facilitation and promotion of American foreign commerce. These included the Philadelphia Commercial Museum, which was founded in 1894; the American Exporters and Importers Association, 1907; the American Manufacturers Export Association, 1911; the Chamber of Commerce of the United States in 1912; and the National Foreign Trade Council in 1914. Recently the American Manufacturers Export Association and the National Foreign Trade Council were merged to form the National Foreign Trade Association.

The creation of the Bureau of Foreign and Domestic Commerce in 1912, as an outgrowth of the Bureau of Manufactures which dated from 1906, with its commercial attachés and special trade commissioners, was a step of great importance in the expansion of governmental trade promotion.

Another important semi-public trade promoting agency requiring mention is the Pan-American Union, which was, in fact, one of the first organizations to promote interest not only in the Argentine market, but in all of Latin America. Even as early as 1893 we find this organization (at that time known as the Bureau of the American Republics) publishing a monograph entitled, *How the Latin-American Markets May Be Reached by the Manufacturers of the United States.*[17] This report contained an analysis of the Argentine market, including statistics of Argentine foreign trade.[18] The monthly *Bulletin of the Pan-American Union* has, since its inception, also contained frequent articles on the possibilities of trade with the Latin-American countries.

Great Britain also realized the importance of studying the potentialities of the Argentine at an early date. One of these

[17] Bureau of the American Republics, Bulletin No. 63, 1893, Washington, D.C.

[18] The annual foreign trade series published by the Pan-American Union contains an excellent digest of Argentine official foreign trade statistics. The Union also maintains a permanent staff of foreign trade advisers and financial counselors at its headquarters in Washington, D.C. One of its most recent activities has been the publication of a monthly bulletin, *Commercial Pan-America*, which first appeared in 1932.

earlier studies was published in 1898, and contained a detailed commodity analysis of trade prospects.[19]

Another important trade and good-will promoting agency in many foreign countries has been the Chamber of Commerce. Outstanding in Argentina have been the British and American organizations. The Chamber of Commerce of the United States in Argentina was organized in December 1918,[20] and has done much to promote friendly feeling between the two nations. One of its most important achievements has been in the field of arbitration of commercial disputes. Its monthly journal, *Comments on Argentine Trade,* is a valuable secondary source of statistical and current information regarding the Argentine. The British Chamber of Commerce in Argentina was established in 1913.[21]

(6) *Propaganda*

In addition to private merchandising activities and group trade promotion, the direction of a country's foreign purchases may be also considerably influenced by those activities which may be grouped under the general heading of propaganda.[22]

[19] Great Britain, *Commercial Mission to South America. Reports received from Mr. T. Worthington, the special commissioner appointed by the Board of Trade to inquire into and report upon the conditions and prospects in certain South American countries. Third report. The Argentine Republic, 1898* (Cmd. 9101). The opportunity which the Argentine market presented to neutral countries, and to Spain in particular, during the War, is reflected in a detailed study which was published in Madrid in 1916 entitled *El Comercio Exterior Argentino y El Intercambio con España: Analisis detallado de nuestra importacion y exportacion en la Argentino-Medios de aumentarlos.*

[20] The Chamber was an outgrowth of the American Commercial Club. See *Comments on Argentine Trade,* May 1926, for description of original purposes, early history, etc.

[21] See *Commercial Encyclopedia,* British and Latin-American Chamber of Commerce, published by the Globe Encyclopedia Company, 30 Fleet Street, London, 1922, for a description of the British organization.

[22] Eder defined propaganda in international trade as "those factors which bear on competition in foreign trade by exerting an influence on public opinion in general for or against the merchandise of a particular origin, aside from the direct, paid announcements of individual manufacturers or sellers which have been discussed under the heading of advertising." *Op. cit.,* p. 424. This definition thus includes the various forms of group trade promotion already considered, which in this writer's opinion it is preferable to place in a separate category.

A detailed discussion of the influence of propaganda in affecting the competitive position of countries trading with Argentina, particularly the United States and Great Britain, is outside the scope of this study. It is a subject to which a great deal of attention has been devoted, in the writings of the nationals of all three countries. Anti-American propaganda, however, may be summarized under two headings—first, that which has little direct connection with trade relations, but deals more with political relationships between the United States and all the countries of Latin America; and, second, that which finds its source and chief motivation in economic factors, and which originally had its origin in British sources, as much as in Argentina.

Throughout Latin America there has been, particularly since 1900, much opposition to the political and economic policy of the United States toward the rest of the American continent. The Monroe Doctrine as a unilateral declaration, and the fear of Yankee imperialism on the part of the "Colossus of the North" have been potent rallying cries for those anxious to discredit the United States in the eyes of the Latin peoples resident south of the Rio Grande; and Buenos Aires has been the focus of a great deal of this Latin-American antagonism to the United States.[23]

"Pan-Americanism makes no appeal in Argentina," said a British writer not many years ago.[24] These sentiments on the part of Britons (which might be claimed to have a bias) are corroborated by American students of Latin-American affairs.

> The rapprochement among the Latin-American peoples is not confined to intellectual or socialistic circles, although there the movement is most intense. It is apparent in commercial and journalistic, in military and diplomatic ranks as well. Prominent economists and industrial leaders of Brazil, Argentina, and Chile are advocating a closer economic union among the states of South America. . . . South Americans are alive to the desirability of inter-American co-

[23] C. H. Haring, "South America and Our Policy in the Caribbean," *Annals of the American Academy of Political and Social Science*, Vol. 132, July 1927, pp. 147-8.

[24] Sir Malcolm Robertson, *Journal of the Royal Institute of International Affairs*, Vol. IX, No. 2, London, March 1930, p. 223.

operation and solidarity; but many are also convinced that the disparity in wealth and power between the United States on the one hand, and all the other countries of the hemisphere on the other, makes equality between nations practically impossible and association with the United States dangerous . . . it is clear that what is needed is an intelligible declaration of American policy towards the Latin-American republics in general. . . .[25]

It may be that the recent much-publicized policy of the "good neighbor" will be the forerunner of a new era of greater inter-American good-will than has existed in the past thirty years. The results achieved at the recent "peace" conference at Buenos Aires appear to have furthered the accomplishments of the American delegation headed by Secretary Hull at the Montevideo Conference in 1933. Thus, perhaps, the Latin-American disease of "Yankeephobia" may be supplanted by a new era of coöperation among the states of the western hemisphere.

The Argentine revolution of September 1930 marked the beginning of a more friendly feeling on the part of that country toward the United States, since former President Irigoyen had been not only quite definitely pro-British but at times somewhat hostile to the United States.

We turn now to that type of propaganda which is more distinctly economic in character. "The most skillful, consistent and influential commercial propagandists in Argentina are beyond question the British statesmen, merchants, bankers, industrialists and others who for years have exercised an intelligent and well-directed influence in favor of British goods."[26]

Emphasis is placed by the British upon the fact that the friendly relations between Argentina and Great Britain date back as far as 1825; that Great Britain, in negotiating the famous Canning Treaty of "Amity, Commerce, and Navigation," was the first foreign nation to recognize the new republic. The centenary of this treaty in 1925 was widely celebrated, including a visit by the Prince of Wales to Argentina.[27] This early treaty

[25] Haring, *op. cit.*, pp. 150-52.

[26] Eder, *op. cit.*, p. 424.

[27] The *London Times* published a special Argentine Supplement celebrating the event.

greatly stimulated the commercial and financial relations between the two countries, although the first British loan to Argentina had already been made in July of the previous year (1824). This was a loan of one million pounds sterling negotiated through Baring Brothers, a name which ever since has been almost synonymous with Argentine foreign borrowing. Not only were British funds frequently made available to the Argentine Government, but (as was indicated in Chapter V), British capital was largely instrumental, prior to 1914, in developing this new country, particularly in the building of a vast network of railroads.

These investments of British capital have exerted a twofold effect upon Argentina's foreign trade: in the first place, as a balance-of-payments factor they provided a basis of settlement for British exports to Argentina (and contra, their amortization has taken the form of increasing exports from Argentina to Great Britain). In addition to this primary effect, there is what may be termed the secondary influence of these investments upon certain branches of Argentine trade; that is, subsequent purchases which are influenced by already existing investments in the country. The best example is without doubt the railroads.[28]

As suggested at the beginning of this chapter, recognition during the past decade, both by British business men and the British government, of the importance of regaining their pre-war position in the Argentine market is evidenced by the commercial and economic missions, trade expositions, etc., which have been sponsored and promoted by the British in recent years.

In 1927, partly as a gesture of good-will, the British diplomatic representation in Buenos Aires was raised to ambassadorial rank. In 1929, a British economic mission (known for its chairman as the D'Abernon Mission) was sent to Argentina to study "Anglo-Argentine . . . relations, industrial, commercial, and financial, with a view to their development to the mutual ad-

[28] After a careful study of this situation, Eder stated: "The conclusion is unescapable that the British railways in Argentina purchase their rails and locomotives in England regardless of price or quality . . . purchases in England by the British railways in Argentina are due to loyalty rather than to economic consideration."

vantage of the countries respectively concerned, and with full powers to investigate every aspect of trade and industry."[29] One of the objectives of this mission was to negotiate an agreement granting preferential treatment to British goods in the Argentine market. Such an agreement was signed by the representatives of the two governments on November 8, 1929, providing for the opening of reciprocal credits by each government for purchases of up to 100,000,000 paper pesos. The Argentine purchases were to consist of acquisitions directly by the Argentine government of supplies for the State Railways or other national departments. On the British side, however, the "purchases of cereals and other products of the Argentine Republic" although arranged by the British government, were to be made by private individuals. Since England was already purchasing each year far in excess of this amount of Argentine products, the agreement represented no increase in the volume of Argentine exports. Opposition developed to the agreement in Argentina; failing of ratification by the Argentine Senate, coupled with the downfall of the Irigoyen Government in September 1930, the agreement never became effective.

The attitude of the Mission which negotiated the agreement, however, was expressed by one of its members as follows:

> The agreement was based upon the recognition by both countries in their mutual dependence the one upon the other. It may well be that this agreement is the beginning of a new and enlightened economic policy which more widely adopted and wisely pursued, will prove a valuable method of increasing the trade of this country. As the largest buyer of foodstuffs and raw materials in the world, we are entitled to ask those from whom we buy to buy from us. . . . This is a much more fruitful method of increasing the trade of this country than any I can conceive of. It places no obstacle in the way of trade, creates no barriers and closes no doors. On the other hand, it ensures a square deal for this country.[30] [Meaning, of course, Great Britain.]

[29] *Report of the Mission*, p. 4.

[30] William Clare Lees, Member of the British Economic Mission to South America, "Some Aspects of Trade with South America," *Journal of Royal Society of Arts*, Vol. 78, 1930, p. 462. Although one may not agree with the statement, it is at least significant as a prediction of subsequent events.

A second method of obtaining preferential treatment for British goods, attributable to the efforts of the D'Abernon Mission, was the issuance of a decree signed by President Irigoyen on November 16, 1929, reducing the duties on artificial silk yarns and cloth from Great Britain and the North of Ireland. This plan also proved abortive, however, since the Argentine customs officials interpreted the decree to apply to rayon from the United States as well, under the provisions of the most-favored-nation commercial treaty with this country. It was, however, the forerunner of a successful attempt later to secure special privileges for British goods.[31]

The D'Abernon Mission was followed by the Sheffield Industrial Mission, the purpose of which was entirely different, in that its objective was to make a detailed investigation and analysis of the Argentine market in an attempt to discover what changes needed to be made in British production and merchandising methods to improve its competitive position in the Argentine trade.[32]

In 1931 an elaborate British Empire Trade Exposition was held in Buenos Aires, the purpose of which was to foster the sale of British goods in Argentina. At the same time the Prince of Wales made another good-will tour of South America, formally opening the Argentine exposition on March 14, 1931.

Eder nevertheless reached the following conclusion:

> Taken as a whole, propaganda can scarcely be considered a major influence in determining the trend of the usual run of trade, for it is difficult to visualize an Argentine customer entering a shop to make a purchase of a knife debating with himself as to whether he should buy the English knife in view of the visit of the Prince of Wales, the French knife in view of cultural affinity, or the Spanish knife because of racial ties. His probable decision would rest between a German knife because of its low price, and an American or British knife because of its high quality.[32a]

There is one type of anti-American propaganda in Argentina

[31] I.e., the Roca-Runciman Agreement of 1933.

[32] The Mission visited other South American countries besides Argentina.

[32a] *Op. cit.*, p. 436.

which has, however (since Eder wrote in 1931), borne fruit. This is the agitation centering around the slogan "Buy from those who buy from us" (*comprar a quien nos compra*). To whom is due the credit for originating this slogan is apparently open to dispute. Sir Malcolm Robertson, formerly British ambassador to Argentina, claims credit for it,[33] as does also the Argentine Rural Society.[34] Regardless of its origin, since 1931 it has played a significant rôle in the foreign commercial policy of Argentina, and is at present the major problem confronting the future trade relations between the United States and Argentina. The chief difficulty confronting American exporters in Argentina today is not in finding purchasers for their products, but in finding purchasers for the Argentine pesos which they receive in exchange for their products; in other words, the problem of creating dollar exchange. Since the institution of exchange control late in 1931, Argentina has to an increasing degree allocated foreign exchange on the basis of foreign currencies obtained from the sale of Argentine products abroad.

Whether this doctrine of bilateralism remains a permanent factor in Argentina's commercial policy, or is merely a temporary defensive device of the recent depression period, is difficult to predict. A conservative British source, in discussing this "Buy from those who buy from us" appeal in 1927, stated that "it would be unwise to count too much upon an emotional, and, in all probabilities, a transitory ground of appeal. For in the long run, the individuals who after all, compose any nation, will generally buy what they require from the seller who offers his wares most attractively from the points of view of price, quality, appearance, or prompt delivery."[35]

A similar view expressed by a United States writer in discussing the Argentine problem, was as follows:

After all, the trade relations between any two countries are not on a completely reciprocal and precisely balanced parity. . . . There are

[33] Eder, *op. cit.*, p. 228.

[34] An old and powerful group of wealthy landowners and agriculturalists. See Address by its former president, Luis Duhau, *Proceedings, Third Pan-American Commercial Conference*, Washington, D.C., 1927, p. 177.

[35] *The Times Book on Argentina, The Times*, London, 1927, p. 4.

no two nations . . . whose economic systems are so nicely correlated as to make traffic between them exactly equal in both directions. Nations buy from one another because they need their respective products and can buy them at reasonable prices. . . . International trade seeks its level of ultimate balance and adjustment along triangular or polyangular routes rather than on any idealized scheme of simple two-way traffic between nations whose respective industries are completely reciprocal.[36]

Much has been said and written, of course, about triangular settlements of United States export surpluses to Argentina: i.e., that Europe buy Argentine products and the United States receive payment from Europe; but the United States-Argentine trade and exchange problem is only a part of the problem which faces the United States in its total trade with all countries of the world. This problem was pointed out as early as 1927 in a frank expression by one of the Argentine delegates to the Third Pan-American Commercial Conference, Sr. Luis Duhau, President of the Argentine Rural Society, of the attitude of Argentina to the trade problem between the United States and herself. In discussing the question of "triangular compensation of commercial balances" Sr. Duhau pointed out that the United States tariff prevents even this by restricting imports from Europe, i.e., that the United States had a total export surplus. Sr. Duhau went on to say that Argentina could develop its own industries, but using the usual free-trade arguments, urged instead that each country should specialize and thus high-cost agriculture in the United States would be eliminated.[37]

The Argentine opposition to the United States tariff policy antedates by a great many years, of course, Sr. Duhau's pronouncement in 1927. The address of one of the Argentine delegates to the First Pan-American Commercial Conference in 1911, Sr. Jacinto L. Villegas, Argentine Chargé d'Affaires, stressed the importance of trade reciprocity; that is, increasing United States imports from Argentina. In fact, Argentine opposition to the tariff policy of the United States dates from the first serious

[36] Julius Klein, *op. cit.*, p. 310.

[37] *Proceedings, Third Pan-American Commercial Conference*, Pan-American Union, Washington, D.C., 1927, p. 177.

attempt to exclude Argentine products from the United States in the Tariff Act of 1867. This tariff placed a prohibitive duty upon unmanufactured wool, which was a major item in the Argentine export trade, and which practically excluded raw wool from the United States market. Manuel R. Garcia, Argentine Minister in Washington, at once set to work to obtain a modification of the restrictive clauses. By the use of newspaper articles, interviews with influential persons, and distribution of propaganda, he attempted to build up sentiment against the restrictions. An eighteen-page pamphlet entitled "Remarks Concerning the Means to Re-establish the Declining State of Commerce between the United States and the Argentine Republic by the Proper Reduction of the Present Tariffs" attempted to "show that the interests of industry, of commerce, of the consumer, and of the revenue require a reasonable modification of the duties which weigh so heavily upon the raw material imported by this country from the Argentine Republic."[38]

Sr. Garcia's campaign was climaxed by the suggestion of a treaty of commerce providing special rates upon the chief commodities in the Argentine-United States trade—lumber, breadstuffs, agricultural implements, wool, hides, and canned goods. Hamilton Fish, Secretary of State, informed Sr. Garcia, however, that such a treaty would not be considered, since it would make immediately operative the most-favored-nation clause in many existing United States treaties.[39]

Not only has the tariff policy of the United States created intense opposition in Argentina, but the practice of placing embargoes on certain Argentine products has perhaps aroused the greatest resentment. These embargoes have been three in number, affecting, respectively, grapes, alfalfa seed, and fresh and frozen meats.[40]

The embargo on fresh and frozen meat imports from Argentina has been perhaps the cause of the greatest misunderstanding.

[38] H. F. Peterson, *op. cit.*

[39] *Ibid.* This statement by Secretary Fish is difficult to understand, however, in view of the fact that the United States followed the conditional interpretation of the most-favored-nation clause prior to 1923.

[40] See Eder, *op. cit.*, pp. 426-28, for details of these embargoes.

The embargo was first imposed by the United States Department of Agriculture in January 1927, under Order 298, which authorized the prohibition of imported meats from any part of the world; the prohibition might cover an entire country or simply an infested area or region, while permitting imports from uninfested areas of the same country. The Smoot-Hawley Tariff Act of 1930, however, not only wrote this order into law, but enlarged it to require embargoes against every part of a country, even though well-defined areas of the country were known to be free from objectionable diseases. Foot-and-mouth disease, according to the experts of the United States Department of Agriculture, has never been known to occur in Patagonia, the southern frontier portion of Argentina which is entire isolated from the rest of the country by deserts, mountains, and the sea.

Argentina feels, therefore, that this embargo is a discriminatory cloak to prevent the entrance of fresh meats into the United States, and that it not only hurts Argentine trade with the United States but it has created suspicion and opposition among her European purchasers, especially the British. This latter objection is by far the more important, since Patagonia is almost exclusively a sheep-raising area, and under existing conditions, any considerable import of frozen or chilled mutton into the United States is unlikely. In May 1935 a sanitary convention was signed by the representatives of the two countries which would solve the difficulty by permitting entrance of fresh meats from areas unaffected by foot-and-mouth disease, thus restoring the provisions of the former order of the Department of Agriculture in effect prior to 1930. This convention has the approval and strong support of both the United States Departments of State and Agriculture, yet opposition on the part of the farm "bloc" has so far prevented its ratification by the United States Congress.

The problem of bilateral or bi-country balancing of a country's international accounts involves a consideration of the "invisible" items, as well as commodity movements. In the case of Argentina, capital items constitute the major "invisibles" in the country's balance of international payments. During the War and postwar period, it was frequently asserted that the expansion of

United States investments in Argentina made possible the continuation of an export surplus.[41] To what extent this has been true is considered in the next chapter, where an attempt is made to construct a rough estimate of the major items in the bilateral accounts of the Argentine with the United States and Great Britain since 1914. Such an attempt seems warranted in view of the present importance of the problem of "basis of settlement" for the future exports of the United States to Argentina; that is, does the experience of the past twenty years throw any light on the future possibilities of creating dollar exchange for renewed exports to Argentina?

[41] This statement was made also in connection with the total export surplus of the United States.

VIII

ARGENTINE BILATERAL INTERNATIONAL ACCOUNTS 1914-34

WITH A foreign commercial policy based upon the slogan "Buy from those who buy from us," the relative competitive positions of the United States and the United Kingdom in the future trade of Argentina, based upon their past record, are clearly unequal.

In order to make her new foreign commercial policy effective, Argentina has, since 1933, adopted the practice of negotiating bilateral agreements with the various nations with whom she has commercial relations, which, supplemented by a strict foreign exchange control, has aimed at effecting a closer balance in her transactions with individual countries.[1] In making effective her policy of bilateralism, Argentina has included "invisibles" as well as "visibles." In fact, "invisibles" are given precedence over "visibles." In the allocation of exchange, the Argentine public debt service payable abroad comes first, not only with respect to individual countries, but as regards total public service remittances. The Roca-Runciman agreement of May 1933 with Great Britain (which served as a model for subsequent agreements) provided for the deduction of a "reasonable sum"[2] annually towards the service of the Argentine public external debt payable in countries *other* than the United Kingdom. In other words, the allocation of sterling exchange for the payment of the Argentine public debt service in, say France, comes ahead of remittances for Argentine imports from Great Britain, or debt service remittances on private British investments in Argentina. Excepting this deduction for public debt service, however, the

[1] See Chapter IX.

[2] Which it was agreed should not exceed 3 million pounds.

TABLE XXVII

ESTIMATED MAJOR ITEMS IN ARGENTINA'S INTERNATIONAL BALANCE OF PAYMENTS WITH THE UNITED STATES, THE UNITED KINGDOM, AND OTHER COUNTRIES, 1914–34
(in millions of gold pesos)

	1914–1920			*1921–1930*			*1931–1934*		
	U.S.	*U.K.*	*Others*	*U.S.*	*U.K.*	*Others*	*U.S.*	*U.K.*	*Others*
Commodity Trade:									
Exports	933	1,733	2,375	769	3,009	4,644	131	1,161	1,041
Imports	1,077	885	1,504	1,826	1,618	4,253	249	409	1,111
Surplus Exports (+)		+848	+871		+1,391	+391		+752	
or Imports (−)	−144			−1,057			−115		− 70
Service Items:									
Immigrant Remittances	—	—	180	—	—	340	—	—	95
Tourist Expenditures	—	20	60	—	50	160	—	20	60
Interest and Dividends	35	560	416	221	1,021	414	160	400	223
Total Service Items	− 35	−580	−656	− 221	−1,071	−914	−160	−420	−378
Balance of Payments	−179	+268	+215	−1,278	+ 320	−523	−275	+332	−448
Covered by:									
Net Change in Foreign Indebtedness:									
Increase	+ 35			+ 750	+ 275			+185	+262
Decrease		−103	− 32			− 75	−247		
Gold Movements:									
Exports	2	18	12	128	53	59	160	20	26
Imports	208	31	29	143	11	42	—	—	—
Balance	−206	− 13	− 17	− 15	+ 42	+ 17	+160	+ 20	+ 26
Borrowings and gold (net change)	−171	−116	− 49	+ 735	+ 317	− 58	− 87	+205	+288
Residual covered by multangular payments, omissions, errors, etc.	−350	+152	+134	− 543	+ 637	−581	−362	+537	−160

Sources:

1. *Commodity Trade:* República Argentina, Dirección General de Estadística, *Anuario del Comercio Exterior*, 1934.

Argentine imports are valued C. I. F., so that official import statistics include ocean freights and marine insurance. These figures do not allow, however, in the imports from a particular country, for imports carried in vessels of other nationalities, nor for shipping earnings of that country in the imports from other countries. Rough estimates based upon the flag of carrier of tonnage of vessels cleared from the United States for Argentina, and flag of carrier of overseas vessels entered at Argentine ports during the period of this study show that, presumably, the earnings of United States and British vessels in non-national exports to Argentina roughly offset the earnings of vessels of other nationalities in the imports into Argentina of goods coming from these two countries. The assumption

balance derived from Argentine sales to Great Britain is reserved for meeting applications for remittances, both "visible" and "invisible," to Great Britain, with essential commodity imports generally having been given priority over "private remittances."[3]

has been made, therefore, that the Argentine C. I. F. values represent the payments due by Argentina to each of these two countries, inclusive of ocean freights and marine insurance. Furthermore, on a percentage basis, discrepancies in these items would not seriously alter the results of data which are admittedly subject to the wide margin of error that these are. For example, a study of British shipping earnings in the Argentine import trade showed that, for the year 1924, total earnings equaled approximately £3,000,000, or roughly 15,000,000 gold pesos, or less than 10 per cent of the average annual Argentine imports from United Kingdom. *The Times* (London), Argentine Supplement, Aug. 17, 1925, p. xiii. Estimates of the ocean shipping charges on exports from the United States to Argentina carried in U. S. vessels obtained by the writer from the files of the Finance Division of the Bureau of Foreign and Domestic Commerce showed that the average annual earnings for the period 1914–20 were $9,000,000; for the period 1921–30, $4,500,000; for the period 1931–34 $1,000,000.

Deductions from the official import statistics to allow for over-valuation, losses on bad debts, etc., based on the same percentages used in Appendix I for such deductions on total imports, were made as follows: 1921–22, 15 per cent; 1923, 10 per cent; 1923–25, 2 per cent; 1926, 12 per cent.

For years prior to 1927, 30 per cent of "to order" shipments were allocated to the United Kingdom. See Ch. VI, p. 161.

2. *Interest and Dividends:*

United States: Earnings on portfolio investments are rough estimates based upon data obtained from the files of the Finance Division, *op. cit.* Earnings on direct investments are, for the earlier years, estimates of the writer based upon the estimated annual average of such investments, and Tornquist's estimate of the rate of return on such investments. Tornquist estimated the earnings on such investments at rates varying from 6 to 12 per cent in the years from 1914 to 1920; for U. S. direct investments, however, the writer used rates varying from four to eight per cent. For the decade 1921–30 the rate of 5 per cent was used. Estimates of earnings on both portfolio and direct investments since 1930 are taken from the annual statements of the "Balance of International Payments of the United States" compiled by the Finance Division. For earnings on direct investments, however, the writer has applied to Argentina the same rate used for Latin America as a whole, which in 1930 was 4 per cent.

United Kingdom: Earnings on British investments are based upon figures contained in the *South American Journal*, March 30, 1935, p. 326. See Appendix II, p. 248.

Other countries: This residual figure is computed by deducting from the estimated total interest and dividend payments, as given in Appendix I, Table I, opposite p. 238, the earnings computed independently as above for the United States and the United Kingdom.

3. *Immigrant Remittances:*

These are totals taken from Appendix I, Table I, and the assumption is made that all of these payments went to countries other than the United Kingdom and the United States.

4. *Tourist Expenditures:*

One-fourth of total expenditures of tourists and Argentines resident abroad are allocated to Great Britain.

5. *Borrowings:*

Computed from data in Table XV, Chapter V, page 99. Figures are net, i.e., allowances have been made for sinking funds and repayments.

6. *Gold movements:*

Total gold exports and imports are taken from annual data in *El Comercio Exterior Argentino en 1934 y 1933*, excepting the years 1932, 1933, 1934, the figures for which are those contained in the estimates of the total Argentine Balance of Payments compiled by the Argentine Central Bank. Gold movements of the United States and the United Kingdom are based upon the official statistics of each country, converted at par of exchange.

[3] The Argentine and British Governments subsequently agreed that exchange was to be distributed in the following order of priority; (a) public debt; (b)

Since Argentina's new foreign commercial policy is based upon a bilateral or bi-country balance of payments, it is desirable, therefore, to consider what has been the history of such bilateral payments. Up to the present time, very little has been done in compiling such bilateral studies. Difficulties in obtaining the data with any degree of accuracy, even for a country's total balance of payments with the rest of the world, make the obstacles to the construction of any but very rough estimates of such bilateral balances of payments almost insuperable.

An attempt has been made in Table XXVII, however, to construct estimates of the major items in the balance of payments between Argentina and the United States and the United Kingdom, respectively (the two leading countries in her international economic transactions) for the period 1914-1934. Although stated precisely in figures, these data can be considered only as showing the general trend with respect to the economic position of the respective countries in Argentina's international payments. The figures are subject to a wide margin of error. Even with respect to the statistics of "visible" or commodity trade, no close approach to accuracy may be claimed.[4]

With these qualifications, however, the data in Table XXVII do present a picture clearly reflecting the contrasting positions held by the United Kingdom and the United States in the balance of payments of Argentina. With respect to the three periods reviewed, the following summary observations may be made:

1914-20

During the war years 1914-17 Argentina had an export sur-

importation of goods; (c) freights; (d) interest on debentures and other loans; (e) remittances of private individuals; (f) payment of dividends on preference and ordinary shares of British companies operating in Argentina. Summary of report issued by Argentine Minister of Finance, *South American Journal*, May 16, 1936.

[4] Anyone who has attempted to check the foreign trade statistics of two countries with each other needs no further proof of this statement. For example, in making such a comparison of the trade figures between the United States and Argentina, the writer found, with respect to Argentine export figures and United States import figures, discrepancies for certain earlier years in excess of 50 per cent. Even taking a long period of years, so that year-end lags cancel out, etc., a discrepancy of from 25 to 40 per cent still exists.

plus in her trade with the United States of approximately 60 million gold pesos. Purchases from the United States increased rapidly from 1918 to 1920, however, so that for the entire period 1914-20 the value of Argentine imports exceeded exports to the United States by 144 million gold pesos. Debt service remittances during this period were still relatively unimportant, and are estimated to have been practically offset by new loans to Argentina.[5] Notwithstanding this import surplus in commodity trade of 144 millions, Argentina also imported 206 million gold pesos (net) of gold from the United States during these seven years, which sum, added to the adverse trade balance, brought the total balance to be covered by triangular or multangular settlements through other countries (allowance being made always for unestimated items, errors, etc.) to 350 millions gold pesos. A partial explanation of these large gold exports from the United States to Argentina in the face of an "adverse" balance of payments is found in the fact that European countries, notably Great Britain, purchased gold in the United States for shipment to Argentina during the periods when gold was available for export in the United States but not in England; that is, 1914-17, and 1919-20.[6] Gold exports by calendar years from the United States to Argentina were as follows:

(in millions of gold pesos)

Year	
1916	7
1917	46
1918	3
1919	59
1920	93
Total	208

The heaviest shipments occurred, therefore, during the years when Argentina's trade with the United States showed a surplus of imports.

War-time shipments of food supplies to the United Kingdom,

[5] It will be recalled that at the outbreak of the War total United States investments in Argentina were estimated at only some 40 million gold pesos.

[6] Williams and Vanderlip, "The Future of Our Foreign Trade," *Harvard Review of Economic Statistics*, Supplement, April 1920, p. 12.

on the other hand, coupled with restricted imports, gave Argentina an export surplus to the former country for the period 1914-20 of 848 million gold pesos; she sold the United Kingdom nearly twice as much as she bought. Income from her heavy investments in Argentina enabled the United Kingdom, however, to reduce this "adverse" balance by some 560 million gold pesos, which coupled with an estimated expenditure of Argentinians in the United Kingdom of 20 million gold pesos, reduced the United Kingdom's estimated "adverse" balance on current account to 268 million gold pesos. An estimated reduction of 103 million gold pesos in British capital invested in Argentina, coupled with a net export of gold to Argentina of 13 million gold pesos, left a net balance in Argentina's favor of 152 million gold pesos. Deducting the sum of this balance and the estimated "favorable" balance with other countries of 134 million gold pesos from the "adverse" balance with the United States of 350 million gold pesos, leaves a net "adverse" balance unaccounted for of 64 million gold pesos, which presumably is covered by omissions, unestimated items, errors, etc.

1921-30

For the decade of the twenties Argentina's import surplus from the United States was approximately one billion gold pesos, with exports totaling 769 million gold pesos, and imports reaching the figure of 1,826 million gold pesos. From what source or sources was dollar exchange obtained to cover this adverse balance of some 100 million gold pesos annually?

Even before the outbreak of the World War, increasing emphasis was being given to the importance of foreign investments by the United States as a factor making possible increased "foreign trade," i.e., exports.[7] Between 1915 and 1930 this enthusiasm reached its full flower with the United States increasing its stake abroad to some 25 billion dollars. From 1915 to 1920 these investments took the form primarily of United States Government loans to the Allies. After 1920 private investment, both in the form of loans to foreign governments and "direct"

[7] Unfortunately, many Mercantilistically-minded people thought (and still think) of "foreign trade" as signifying, primarily at least, export trade.

investments in private enterprises abroad expanded rapidly. How much of this investment was destined for Argentina, and to what extent did it provide a basis of settlement for Argentina's import surplus from the United States?

Reference again to Table XXVII shows that the estimated increase in the net investment of United States capital in Argentina during the decade 1921-30 was 750 million gold pesos. As the volume of these investments increased, however, the debt service remittances in the other direction also increased, so that the estimated total of such debt service remittances due the United States for the decade was 221 million gold pesos. This left a net balance on capital account of 529 million gold pesos available to cover foreign exchange requirements for Argentina's import surplus of 1,057 million pesos.[8]

Although gold movements between Argentina and the United States in both directions were relatively important during the twenties, on balance there was a net import by Argentina of only 15 million gold pesos. The annual figures were as follows:

NET ANNUAL GOLD MOVEMENT
BETWEEN ARGENTINA AND THE UNITED STATES
1921-30[a]
(in millions of gold pesos)

	Imports[b]	*Exports*[b]		*Imports*	*Exports*
1921	—	1.0	1926	—	—
1922	—	—	1927	63.2	—
1923	—	5.2	1928	67.3	—
1924	—	22.8	1929	—	74.6
1925	8.8	—	1930	—	20.7

[a] U. S. statistics converted at par of exchange.
[b] Argentine imports and exports.

[8] The investment of capital by one country in another need not *necessarily* cause a transfer of purchasing power directly from the former to the latter. Transfer of ownership of existing investments in a particular country may not affect that country. Such was the case with certain types of United States investments in Argentina. For example, in 1928 the International Telephone and Telegraph Company purchased the United River Plate Telephone Company of Buenos Aires from its British owners. This transaction involved simply a transfer of cash and securities between Great Britain and the United States.

Although Argentina did not return to the gold standard until 1927, the exports in 1923 and 1924 represented authorized withdrawals by the Argentine Government to meet debt service payments in the United States. The heavy import from the United States in 1927 and 1928 paralleled the period of large borrowings by Argentina in the United States, a portion of which was taken by the Argentine Government in the form of gold to bolster its reserves upon the restoration of the gold standard in 1927. The reversal of this trend, which began in the second half of 1928, marked the decline in the volume of borrowing from the United States, and the turning against Argentina of its total balance of payments, as already described in Chapter III. The transfer of short-term funds to New York, attracted by high interest rates, was also an important factor.

The net result of these payments to and from the United States during the period 1921-30 was an estimated balance against Argentina of 543 million gold pesos, which was covered again (presumably) by multangular settlements through other countries.

The United Kingdom, again in decided contrast to the United States, had an estimated "favorable" balance of payments for the period of 637 million gold pesos; that is, the United Kingdom could have paid Argentina's obligations to the United States from its surplus, and still have a balance due of about 100 million gold pesos.

Argentina's exports to the United Kingdom were again nearly double her imports from that country during the decade 1921-30, exports totaling 3,009 million gold pesos and imports 1,618 million gold pesos. A major portion of this export surplus was offset, however, by interest and dividend payments due the United Kingdom on its large investments in Argentina. These payments are estimated at 1,021 million gold pesos, which, added to an estimated expenditure by Argentinians in the United

---

Except for the transfer of title to the properties, Argentina was not involved. Cited by Paul DeWitt, "The Commercial Relations Between the United States and Argentina," *The Southwestern Political and Social Science Quarterly*, Vol. XI, No. 2, September 1930, p. 14.

Kingdom of 50 million pesos, reduced Argentina's "favorable" balance on current items to 320 million gold pesos.

The estimated increase in the United Kingdom investments in Argentina during the decade was 275 million gold pesos, so that solely on capital account Argentina had *net* remittances due the United Kingdom of approximately 850 million gold pesos. Thus, during this period, the United States illustrated the situation of an immature creditor nation, with new foreign investments in Argentina exceeding debt service remittances on previous loans by some 500 million gold pesos, whereas the United Kingdom was representative of a mature creditor nation with earnings on previous investments exceeding new capital invested by some 850 million gold pesos.

Gold movements between the United Kingdom and Argentina were relatively unimportant during these ten years. Notwithstanding a decidedly "favorable" balance of payments, Argentina had an excess of gold exports over imports to the United Kingdom of 42 million gold pesos, which brought the estimated total balance of remittances due the United Kingdom to be covered by multangular settlements to the sum of 637 million gold pesos.

According to the data contained in Table XXVII, Argentina had a net "adverse" balance for the period 1921-30 with the rest of the world of 581 million gold pesos. Combining this sum with the balances due to and from the United States and the United Kingdom, there remains a net "adverse" balance or unaccounted-for figure of 487 million gold pesos.[9]

[9] This large residual figure is due, presumably, to errors and unaccounted-for items in the estimates of Argentina's total balance of payments used in Table I, "International Income Account of Argentina," 1914-35, Appendix I. As pointed out in the footnote to Table XXVII, the figures used in computing the balance with "Other Countries" were derived by subtracting from Argentina's estimated total balance of payments the independent estimates made for the balances between the United States and the United Kingdom and Argentina. The estimates of changes in capital investments in the bi-country data are taken from the "direct" estimates used in Chapter V, whereas for Argentina's total balance of payments, the volume of new capital invested in Argentina is derived "indirectly" from the difference between the current Income and Outgo items in the International Income Account. Furthermore, this difference between

During the period 1931-34 Argentina's "adverse" balance of payments with the United States continued. In sharp contrast to the decade of the twenties, however, this "adverse" balance resulted to a considerable degree from capital items; that is, from a net reduction in Argentina's borrowings from the United States.[10] Although the average annual "adverse" balance on commodity trade was reduced to some 30 million gold pesos annually, compared with an annual average of about 100 million gold pesos for the decade of the twenties, the reversal of the flow of capital resulted in an estimated average annual balance presumably covered by multangular remittances of 90 million gold pesos, compared with an annual average of 55 million pesos for the preceding decade.

With an "adverse" balance on commodity trade for the four years 1931-34 of 115 million gold pesos, coupled with estimated debt service remittances of 160 million pesos, there resulted a balance against Argentina on current items of 275 million gold pesos. This sum is further increased by the estimated net reduction in Argentine borrowing in the United States of 247 million gold pesos to a total of 522 million pesos. With net gold exports to the United States, however, of 160 million pesos, the balance to be covered by multangular settlements was reduced to 362

Income and Outgo items includes changes in Argentina's investments abroad, as well as foreign investments in Argentina. According to the data contained in Argentina's International Income Account, the estimated increase in Argentina's net foreign indebtedness for the period 1921-30 was 1,375 million gold pesos. Of this 1,375 millions, 75 millions represented the estimated decrease in Argentina's loans to foreigners, thus leaving a figure of 1,300 million gold pesos as covering the net increase in Argentina's borrowing from abroad. Of this 1,300 million pesos, 687 millions was long-term investment, and 613 millions estimated short-term investments by foreigners in Argentina. Included in the short-term figure, however, was the balancing, or residual unaccounted-for, item in Argentina's estimated total balance of payments, which, for the ten-year period, totaled approximately 500 million gold pesos, as compared with the residual of 487 millions in Table XXVII. Deducting this residual figure from 1,300 million pesos, we have a remainder of 800 million gold pesos as representing the "indirect" estimate of the increase in foreign investments in Argentina, as compared with our "direct" estimate of 950 million gold pesos.

[10] This reduction was due, in part, to purchase by Europeans of Argentine securities formerly held in the United States.

million gold pesos (allowance being made always for unestimated items, errors, etc.).

During the same period, Argentina's export surplus to the United Kingdom totaled 752 million gold pesos, or an annual average of nearly 190 million gold pesos, compared with an annual average of about 140 million pesos for the preceding decade. With debt service remittances estimated at 400 million gold pesos, plus estimated tourist expenditures of 20 million gold pesos, there remained a "favorable" balance on current account of 332 million gold pesos. Again in sharp contrast to the United States, there was an estimated net increase in Argentine borrowing from the United Kingdom of 185 million pesos. Adding a net gold export of 20 million pesos, there resulted an estimated "favorable" balance of 537 million gold pesos, presumably covered by the "adverse" balance with the United States and other countries.

Clearly, as long as the doctrine of bilateralism dominates the foreign commercial policy of Argentina, the United States is in a distinctly unfavorable position with respect to increased sales to Argentina, unless it is willing to increase its purchases of articles of Argentine production.

Renewed lending to Argentina by the United States would not increase the supply of dollars available to United States exporters in the official exchange market, under the existing system of exchange control, since foreign exchange derived from capital imports is sold in the free market where the cost of foreign currencies, including the surcharge effective since April 1935, cannot be less than 20 per cent above the official selling rate.

The recent retirement of a substantial portion, and the refunding of the balance, of the Argentine National Government dollar bonds which were outstanding has, of course, reduced the requirements for dollar exchange for debt service purposes, thus presumably leaving a larger portion of total dollar exchange available for purchases of commodities from the United States. The estimated reduction in the cost of the service of the dollar debt is approximately 15 million dollars in 1938 compared with 1936.

Although recent grain shortages in the United States have resulted in large increases in imports from Argentina since 1934, any marked permanent increase in United States purchases of Argentine products is probably contingent upon reduction in the United States tariff on articles imported from Argentina.

In the succeeding chapter, following a brief consideration of Argentina's foreign tariff and commercial policy, previous attempts to negotiate a reciprocity treaty between the United States and Argentina will be summarized, as well as the possibilities under the Trade Agreements Act of 1934.

IX

THE FOREIGN COMMERCIAL POLICY OF ARGENTINA

I. THE ARGENTINE TARIFF

As is true of most nations, Argentina's tariff policy has aimed neither exclusively at protection nor exclusively at revenue—the duties levied have brought both protection and revenue.

Different opinions have been expressed regarding the general character of Argentina's tariff policy. One writer described the Argentine tariff as follows:

> The manufacturing industries of the country have been developed under a high protective tariff because products of Argentine industries using foreign fuel cannot compete with cheaper and better imported commodities. In fact, the Argentine protective tariff goes beyond anything ever dreamed of in the United States by even the most partisan protectionist. It comes close to being the most unscientific tariff possible, and there seems to be no limit to the protective measures the government will adopt to foster infant industries.[1]

In criticizing Professor Jones' statement, however, Eder said:

> In his strictures on the tariff system, Professor Jones does Argentina an injustice. It is true that there has been little, if any, attempt to remodel the tariff and make it conform with present day needs, and that the whole is undoubtedly a patchwork and ill-adapted either for protection or for revenue purposes. . . . It must be remembered, however, in criticising the Argentine tariff, that its main function is not protection, but revenue, the *fostering of local industry being only incidental* (italics added).[2]

Eder concluded that "the Argentine tariff, despite its makeshift qualities, admirably accomplishes the purpose for which it is

[1] Clarence F. Jones, *op. cit.*, pp. 381-82.

[2] Eder, *op. cit.*, p. 463.

imposed, namely, the procuring of a maximum of revenues without too greatly impeding the flow of trade."[3]

Apparently no generalization can be made covering all commodities included in the Argentine tariff. The duties on certain items are decidedly protective, whereas on others they must be primarily revenue duties—otherwise they would not be imported to any extent and no revenue would ensue. That many of the duties on Argentine imports have been intended primarily for revenue, and only incidentally for protection, is evidenced by the fact that a considerable proportion of the national revenues

TABLE XXVIII

ANALYSIS OF ARGENTINE CUSTOMS DUTIES

	1913	*1918*	*1922*	*1928*	*1932*	*1934*
A. Per cent of total imports (tariff value)						
1. Subject to duty	70	78	73	68	77	72
2. Free of duty	30	22	27	32	23	28
B. Average ad valorem duties (real value)						
1. On total imports	18	8	12	17	29	22
2. On imports subject to duty	25	10	16	26	37	31

Source: Computed from data in *El Comercio Exterior Argentino* and *Anuario del Comercio Exterior* (annual).

is derived from this source, ranging from a low of 27 per cent in 1918 and 1919 to 46 per cent in 1925 and 1928.

The data presented in Table XXVIII further support the view that Argentina's tariff duties have been primarily revenue-producing levies. A relatively large percentage of total imports subject to duty is indicative of this fact. If the duties were highly protective, dutiable goods would be excluded to a greater degree, and thus the percentage of duty-free goods would be enlarged. Furthermore, the average rates of duty on dutiable imports (ranging from 10 to 37 per cent for selected years) do not indicate a high degree of protection, although, as previously pointed

[3] *Ibid.*, p. 465.

out, average rates are apt to be misleading, since it is the duty on specific commodities which is significant.[4]

The present Argentine tariff system was adopted in 1905,[5] when the practice of "official valuations" was inaugurated. The tariff law is complemented by schedules of officially fixed valuations upon which percentage rates of duty and percentage surtaxes are levied. Since these official valuations have not been consistently changed in accordance with market fluctuations, the ad valorem duties levied on these official valuations have resulted virtually in specific duties for the articles thus classified. There are also specific duties assessed without an indicated relationship to official valuations on commodities upon which it has been desired to grant a certain measure of protection; for example, foodstuffs, groceries, beverages, tobacco, and petroleum products. For articles not enumerated in the official classifications, ad valorem duties are levied on the basis of c.i.f. prices of goods in warehouses at Argentine ports. The basic rate is 25 per cent ad valorem. In addition, there are various surtaxes charged and added to the basic rates.

Although prices of Argentine imports increased rapidly during the War, no general increase in the official tariff valuations was made until 1920, when a 20 per cent increase was levied under Law No. 11,022. The one important change in Argentina's tariff between 1905 and 1931 came in 1923, at which time a general increase of 60 per cent was made in ten basic official tariff valuations. At the same time, specific duties were increased one-fourth.[6] These changes were made primarily for the purpose of increasing customs revenues.

Argentine tariff changes were relatively unimportant after 1923 until the installation of the Provisional Government following the Revolution in September 1930. During the succeed-

[4] In contrast, in the United States, the average ad valorem rate on dutiable imports, for selected years, has been as follows:

1913	40.08	1928	38.76
1918	23.65	1932	59.06
1922	38.07	1934	46.70

[5] Law No. 4933 of Dec. 20, 1905.

[6] Law No. 11,281, November 29, 1923.

ing year extensive revisions were effected by executive decree of the Provisional Government.

Most of these revisions were upward, although in December 1930 the official valuation on certain silk textiles, handkerchiefs, and stockings was reduced one-half, for the declared purpose of discouraging smuggling of these articles into Argentina. At the same time a duty on motor trucks, which had been allowed entry duty-free, was imposed.

In February 1931 import duties were established on all fresh fruits, vegetables, and fish, imported under refrigeration or otherwise preserved by artificial means.[7] Import duties were increased on numerous articles, including beverages and foodstuffs; cotton and woolen textiles, and cotton, woolen, and linen yarns; leather and certain leather goods; hats and caps; cement, motion picture films, typewriters and calculating machines. Surtaxes, from which the respective articles had previously been exempt, were imposed on rice, vetches, dried codfish, rubber, chestnuts, kerosene, sandals, certain tools of iron and steel, fine woods of all kinds, cotton fabrics and yarn or thread, needles for sewing, embroidering and sewing machines, writing pens and chalk. A surtax was imposed and the official valuation increased by 60 per cent on rough sawn and planed pine and fir lumber.[8] The duty was increased on both raw and refined sugar.

Not all changes were increases, however. In June 1931 the duty on crude fuel and Diesel oil was decreased (although the duty on gas oil was increased at the same time); and the duty on certain natural silk yarns for the loom was decreased, if imported for use in factories. These changes were intended, of course, to favor Argentine industry.

In September and October 1931 three series of changes were made, affecting about 1,500 tariff items. In many of these cases, official valuations were established (thus providing the equivalent of specific rates) for articles not theretofore specified in the tariff, and therefore dutiable ad valorem under a general pro-

[7] This affected particularly apples and pears from the United States.

[8] Another duty affecting an important United States export item to Argentina.

vision of the tariff law to that effect. Most of these changes resulted in higher duties, the purpose of which was apparently two-fold; to increase government revenues, and to effect a more "favorable" trade balance by reducing imports.

As a supplementary revenue measure, an additional duty of ten per cent on official valuations was decreed for most dutiable imports, as well as being extended to many imports which theretofore had been duty-free. Intended originally as a temporary measure, a graduated periodical reduction in this additional duty was to have begun late in 1933, and its complete extinction was contemplated by the end of 1934. The full ten per cent was restored in the 1934 budget law passed by the Argentine Congress in September 1933, however, and has since been reënacted and is still in force (May 1937).

Direct statutory prohibitions affecting specific imports or classes of imports have been used sparingly in Argentina, although sanitary restrictions of varying degrees of severity have been and are imposed. In 1931, severe sanitary as well as packing and wrapping regulations and seasonal import restrictions were applied to fresh fruits. In that year a high import duty was also enacted on apples and pears which had previously been duty-free. These measures contributed greatly to reduce American apple shipments to Argentina during the 1931-32 season, particularly from the Eastern states where shipments had previously been largely in the form of unwrapped barreled apples. In 1932, however, the wrapping requirements and seasonal import restrictions were removed, although the duty still remains in effect.

An anti-dumping law was decreed by the Argentine Government on August 28, 1931 (Executive Decree No. 1033), but so far has not been applied.

Import quota restrictions which have in recent years become such a popular trade weapon in Europe, have not thus far been utilized by Argentina as a method of restricting imports (except during a brief period for yerba maté). In fact, prior to 1931, Argentina's foreign commercial policy had always been characterized by opposition to preferential agreements; instead,

equality of treatment had been the cardinal principle of her trade relations with foreign countries.

Argentina's first commercial treaty, that with the United Kingdom in 1825, embodied the unconditional most-favored-nation clause. Argentina now has most-favored-nation treaties or agreements with fourteen countries; of these, however, eight are conditional and six unconditional. Unconditional treaties or agreements are in force with six countries—the Belgium-Luxembourg Union, France, Italy, the Netherlands, Switzerland, and the United Kingdom; conditional treaties are in force with the United States, Bolivia, Brazil, Germany, Norway, Sweden, Spain, and Japan. Unconditional treaties with Austria, Brazil, Finland, Rumania, and Spain have been signed but not yet reported as ratified. A commercial treaty with Chile, signed June 3, 1933, did not pledge most-favored-nation treatment.[9]

II. ARGENTINE RECIPROCITY AGREEMENTS

The Argentine tariff is single column, although since 1905 the tariff law has contained clauses authorizing the Executive to (1) impose penalty duties up to 50 per cent in case of discrimination by another country; or (2) to reduce the duties up to 50 per cent in exchange for "equivalent advantages" by other countries.[10] It was not until 1931, however, that advantage was taken of this latter reciprocity provision. In that year a preferential treaty was negotiated with Finland granting a concession of 50 per cent on birch plywood in return for free entry by Finland of bran, millards, and pollard. This agreement was abrogated by mutual consent, however, at the end of six months. Penalty duties have so far been applied in only one instance. In December 1935, apparently because Peruvian tariff concessions for imports of Chilean wheat were not extended to Ar-

[9] United States Tariff Commission, *Extent of Equal Tariff Treatment in Foreign Countries*, Washington, D.C., 1936.

[10] Article 74, Customs Law No. 4933, December 20, 1905, translation reproduced in Federal Trade Commission, *Report on Trade and Tariffs in Brazil, Uruguay, Argentina, Chile, Bolivia, and Peru*, Washington, D.C., 1916. Replaced in 1923 by Article 76, Customs Law No. 11,281.

gentina, penalty duties were imposed upon Peruvian crude petroleum.

The agreement with Finland was the forerunner of a series of bilateral preferential agreements since negotiated with a number of countries. With but one exception, however, (Chile) these agreements have been preferential exchange agreements rather than preferential tariff rate agreements.

The first, and by far the most important of these agreements, was the well-known Roca-Runciman Treaty signed in London on May 1, 1933. This was supplemented by a tariff agreement and a protocol signed September 26, 1933. The Treaty was ratified by the Argentine Congress on October 9, 1933, and became effective on November 7 of the same year. At the same time, a law was promulgated making effective the provisions of the supplementary tariff agreement, whereby the tariff rates or the official valuations on about three hundred items in the Argentine tariff classifications were affected. Under this law the rate or official valuation was reduced, or else the existing rates or valuations were bound. In addition, certain tariff reclassifications were made on certain types of products with the intention of favoring Great Britain. A wide range of products of special interest to the United Kingdom was affected, including certain raw materials, foodstuffs, beverages, automotive products, furniture, jewelry, hardware, machinery, glass, pottery and porcelain, textiles and clothing, dry goods, paints, varnishes, and chemicals. In general, the new law was apparently intended to reduce the Argentine duties on the articles affected by the agreement to approximately the levels of 1930 which, it will be recalled, were those in effect prior to the important tariff increases instituted by the Provisional Government in 1931.

The leading concessions of the Roca-Runciman Treaty on the part of the United Kingdom were: (1) not to restrict the market for Argentine products below a certain level, unless special circumstances warranted such action; (2) to consult Argentina before additional restrictions were imposed on its products; and (3) to extend further restrictions if applied against certain Argentine

products also to similar products from all other countries.[11]

Since the tariff provisions of this treaty were generalized by Argentina, that is, extended gratuitously to other countries, they cannot be said to have constituted a violation of the principle of equality of treatment.[12] It was with respect to the exchange provisions of the treaty that preferential treatment was granted. These exchange provisions will be considered shortly.

On June 30, 1933, a reciprocity treaty was signed with Chile (replacing a temporary agreement dated November 15, 1932), which became effective October 21, 1933. In this treaty, preferential tariff concessions were granted by both countries on a limited number of items. The Argentine concessions were generalized to those countries having unconditional most-favored-nation treaties with Argentina at that time, namely, the United Kingdom, Italy, and France, but not to the United States and other countries with which conditional most-favored-nation treaties were in force.

Reciprocal tariff concessions on a limited number of products exchanged between Brazil and Argentina were granted in an agreement signed and put into force October 11, 1933. Since the concessions were on products of a regional character in which there was no effective competition, they could not be considered discriminatory, although not generalized.[13] An agreement with Italy providing for reciprocal tariff reductions on certain commodities was signed in Rome, September 26, 1933, but was never made effective.

On September 28, 1934, an exchange agreement was signed with Germany which also included provisions granting a seasonal

[11] This agreement was for a term of three years, unless renewed. The United Kingdom gave notice for the termination of the agreement November 7, 1936, but it was continued until a new trade agreement was signed on December 1 and made provisionally effective from November 20, 1936.

[12] In extending the benefit of these concessions to the United States, however, the Argentine Government noted that the Argentine-United States treaty was conditional and stated that the extension was a temporary favor, not a matter of treaty obligation.

[13] The concession to Brazil was confined to pineapples. On May 24, 1935, an unconditional and unlimited most-favored-nation commercial agreement with a considerable number of reciprocal tariff concessions was signed with Brazil, but so far has not been ratified.

reduction by Germany on Argentine grapes, as well as guaranteeing equitable import quotas for Argentine products.

As regards *tariff* policy Argentina has, in general, therefore, maintained the principle of equality of treatment. Its new commercial policy of preferential treatment of certain countries has been effected through another type of weapon in the arsenal of present-day trade controls, that of preferential exchange allocations.

Exchange control was inaugurated, it will be recalled, in October 1931. Since that time the restrictions have been increasingly severe, particularly with reference to those countries with which Argentina has an "adverse" trade balance. Beginning with the Roca-Runciman Treaty in May 1933, Argentina has since negotiated exchange agreements granting special treatment with respect to exchange allocations with the following countries, although a considerable number of the agreements have not yet been declared effective:

	Date of Agreement
Belgium-Luxembourg Union	January 16, 1934
Netherlands	January 31, 1934
Switzerland	May 18, 1934
Germany	September 28, 1934
Spain	December 29, 1934
Brazil	May 24, 1935
Uruguay	December 30, 1935
Finland	December 31, 1935
France	March 4, 1936
Rumania	August 14, 1936
Austria	August 27, 1936
Peru	February 3, 1937
Italy	March 4, 1937

The clause regarding exchange in the Roca-Runciman Treaty of May, 1933, is as follows:

Whenever any system of exchange control is in operation in Argentina, the conditions under which foreign currency shall be made available in any year shall be such as to secure that there shall be available, for the purpose of meeting applications for current remittances from Argentina to the United Kingdom, the full amount of the sterling

exchange arising from the sale of Argentine products in the United Kingdom after deduction of a reasonable sum annually towards the payment of the service of the Argentine public external debts (national, provincial, and municipal) payable in countries other than the United Kingdom.[14]

Subsequent exchange agreements with other countries have in general followed the above provisions. By thus guaranteeing the allocation of exchange to pay for imports at the official or most favorable rate, Argentina formally maintains the policy of favoring products from countries which have an import surplus in their trade with Argentina.

According to a report issued by the Argentine Ministry of Finance, the allocation of sterling exchange for the period May 1933-December 1935, was as follows:[15]

	(thousands of pesos)	
	paper	*gold*
Exchange available:		
Value of "regular" exports to Great Britain	1,310,567	576,649
Exchange allocated:		
Reserved for payment of public debt in other countries	115,622	50,874
Allocated to Great Britain	1,172,439	515,874
Total allocated	1,288,061	566,748
Balance outstanding	22,506	9,901

The distribution of the exchange allocated to Great Britain during the same period was as follows:

(in thousands of pesos at the buying rate of exchange)

	paper	*gold*	*per cent*
Importation of goods	741,976	326,469	57.0
Public debt service	190,769	83,938	14.6

[14] Quoted in United States Tariff Commission, *The Argentine Customs Tariff and Other Trade Restrictions on Imports from the United States Since January 1, 1922* (mimeographed), Washington, D.C., p. 9.

[15] Ernesto Tornquist and Company, Limitada, *Business Conditions in Argentina*, No. 210, April 1936, Buenos Aires, pp. 35-37.

Remittances of public utility companies	335,003	147,401	25.8
Remittances of private individuals	13,349	5,873	1.0
Other transfers (including official expenditures abroad)	20,377	8,966	1.6
Total	1,301,474	572,647	100.0

The exchange sold for payment of imports during the same period (May 1933-December 1935), compared with the official "real" value of imports, was as follows:

	(in thousands of pesos)				Ratio of exchange sold to import values
	Imports		Exchange sold for payment		
	paper	gold	paper	gold	
United Kingdom	794,956	349,781	813,432[a]	357,910	102.32
Other countries	2,387,107	1,050,327	1,647,342	724,830	69.01
Total	3,182,063	1,400,108	2,460,774	1,082,740	77.30

[a] The discrepancy between the 813,432,000 paper pesos of exchange sold in payment of imports from the United Kingdom and the figure of 741,976,000 paper pesos in the preceding table is due to the fact that the exchange sold is based upon the official selling rate of exchange, whereas the 741,976,000 paper pesos of exchange allocated for imports is computed at the official buying rate.

Thus it appears that since the negotiation of the Roca-Runciman Treaty more than sufficient exchange has been made available to cover payment of all imports into Argentina from Great Britain at the official selling rate, whereas payment for approximately 31 per cent of the total imports from other countries must have been cleared through the free market at a rate not less than 20 per cent above the official selling rate.

In contrast, only 35 and 46 per cent of the imports from the United States during 1935 and 1936 were granted permits for payment at the official rate, the remainder presumably having to pay the surcharge of 20 per cent.[16]

We turn in the succeeding section, therefore, after a brief description of previous attempts to negotiate a commercial reciprocity agreement between Argentina and the United States,

[16] According to data compiled by the Bureau of Economic Research of the Central Bank of the Argentine Republic. See Argentine Government, *Prospectus*, *op. cit.* Data for 1933 and 1934 not available.

to a consideration of the possibilities of the negotiation of a commercial agreement with Argentina under the Trade Agreements Act of 1934, and thereby increase the supply of dollar exchange in Argentina which might be made available at the official rate for imports from the United States.

III. COMMERCIAL RECIPROCITY WITH THE UNITED STATES

The existing commercial treaty between the United States and Argentina dates from 1853. On July 27 of that year a "Treaty of Friendship, Commerce, and Navigation" was signed by the representatives of the two governments, and ratifications were exchanged on December 20, 1854. This treaty contains the conditional most-favored-nation clause.[17]

An earlier attempt by the United States to negotiate a commercial agreement with Argentina immediately following the conclusion of the Anglo-Argentine commercial treaty of February 2, 1825, had failed, due to the insistence of the United States upon an executive declaration of reciprocity granting the citizens of each nation equal rights with the citizens of the other in each country, instead of most-favored-nation treatment which the British treaty contained.[18]

Up to the present time, attempts to negotiate a reciprocal trade agreement between the United States and Argentina have been unsuccessful. Following the passage of the McKinley Tariff Act of 1890 in the United States which authorized the President to impose a duty on hides and other products when imported from countries whose treatment of United States products was "unequal and unreasonable," the Department of State entered into correspondence with the Argentine Government in an attempt to secure a treaty.[19] The Argentine Government replied, however, that the duties it imposed on our particular products,

[17] United States Tariff Commission, *Reciprocity and Commercial Treaties*, Washington, D.C., 1919, p. 451. A good summary of the negotiations, as well as earlier diplomatic relations between the United States and Argentina, is contained in Paul Dewitt, *op. cit.* A more detailed account is in H. F. Peterson, *op. cit.*

[18] W. Stewart, "United States-Argentine Commercial Negotiations of 1825," *Hispanic-American Historical Review*, Vol. 13, August 1933, pp. 367-71.

[19] See Ch. VII above, pp. 185-86 for description of Argentine attempt to negotiate a reciprocity agreement in 1867-68.

such as lumber, refined petroleum, agricultural implements, and other manufactures of iron and steel, were not unreasonable in view of the tariff the United States imposed upon wool, which was a major export to the United States at that time. It was intimated during the negotiations, however, that if the United States would remove the duty on wool, the Argentine Government would make generous concessions in favor of United States manufactured goods. Since the Act of 1890 failed to provide for duty *reductions,* there was no legal basis for such an agreement.[20]

The penalty duties authorized in the McKinley Act, however, were not imposed on products from Argentina (although they were imposed on imports from Colombia, Venezuela, and Haiti) for the reason that Argentine duties on United States goods were not considered "reciprocally unequal and unreasonable."[21] The penalty provisions in Section 3 of the Act of 1890 were repealed in the Wilson Tariff Act of 1894 by the Democratic Congress.

Section 4 of the Dingley Tariff Act of 1897 authorized the president to negotiate treaties providing for a reduction of not more than 20 per cent in the duties on any article imported into the United States in exchange for equivalent concessions by any other country. Under this Act, one of several treaties was negotiated with Argentina (the so-called Kasson Treaties). The Argentine Government was unwilling to enter into treaty relations except upon the basis of a reduction of the American duty on wool. In the treaty which was signed, therefore, the United States concession was practically confined to a 20 per cent reduction on wool. In return, Argentina granted a reduction on a number of United States products, together with a modification of the Argentine *aforo* system of arbitrary and variable customs valuations under which the specific duties could be and frequently were increased without legislative action, thus causing uncertainty

[20] See statement by William C. Curtis presented by the House Committee on Ways and Means, June 6, 1896, 54th Congress, First Session, House of Representatives, No. 2263, Supplement B, quoted in *Reciprocity and Commercial Treaties,* p. 156.

[21] Section 3, Act of 1890, quoted in *op. cit.,* p. 148.

TABLE

UNITED STATES IMPORTS FROM ARGENTINA AND FROM ALL COUNTRIES OF
IN 1928, 1934,
(values in thou

Rank of Argentina as a source in				Commodity	1928[a]			
1928	1934	1935	1936		Argentina	Per cent[b]	All countries	Per cent[c]
				Group "A"—Free under Act of 1930				
2	2	2	2	Sheep and lamb skins	3,402	3.4	20,731	16.4
7	6	5	4	Goat and kid skins	1,693	1.7	41,740	4.1
8	9	7	8	Furs, undressed	4,423	4.5	108,783	4.1
1	1	1	1	Bones, hoofs, horns, unmanufactured	916	0.9	1,727	53.0
1	1	2	2	Horsehair, tails and manes	868	0.9	2,112	41.1
2	4	5	4	Sausage casings	1,901	1.9	12,586	15.1
[e]	2	1	1	Tankage	[e]	—	[e]	—
1	1	1	1	Quebracho wood	1,228	1.2	1,228	100.0
[d]	2	2	1	Carpet wool	[d]	—	[d]	—
				Total Group "A"	14,431	14.5	188,907	7.7
				Total free imports	[g]	—	[g]	—
				Group "B"—Dutiable under Act of 1930				
1	1	1	1	Cattle hides (free under Act of 1922)	32,381	32.6	63,694	50.8
1	2	1	1	Corn	275	0.3	609	45.2
6	2	1	1	Carpet wool[d]	1,977	2.0	33,014	8.0
3	5	6	4	Combing wool	4,217	4.2	31,729	13.3
1	1	1	1	Flax seed	26,046	26.2	31,245	83.4
1	1	1	1	Canary seeds	338	0.3	501	87.5
1	1	1	2	Casein or lactarine	2,951	3.0	3,678	80.2
1	1	1	1	Quebracho extract	4,239	4.3	4,320	98.1
1	1	1	1	Poultry, dead	746	0.8	1,564	47.7
1	2	2	2	Meats, canned	3,489	3.5	6,644	52.5
1	2	1	1	Grapes	223	0.2	318	70.1
				Total Group "B"	76,782	77.2	177,316	43.3
				Total dutiable imports	[g]	—	[g]	—
				Total Groups "A" and "B"	91,313	91.8	366,223	24.9
				Total free and dutiable imports	99,438	100.0	4,091,444	2.4

[a] General imports in 1928; Imports for Consumption, 1934–36.
[c] Per cent of corresponding imports from all countries obtained from Argentina.
[d] Figures for 1928 cover carpet wools which were free of duty under tariff act, but reported as duti-
Imports in 1928. All carpet wool not entered for immediate consumption at time of arrival goes into bonded warehouse, it is marked free under bond for manufacture of carpets, etc., or dutiable, depending
[e] Not classified separately in 1928.
[g] Data not available.

XXIX

Articles Important in United States Import Trade with Argentina

1935, and 1936

sands of dollars)

1934[a]				1935[a]				1936[a]			
Argen- tina	*Per cent*[b]	*All countries*	*Per cent*[c]	*Argen- tina*	*Per cent*[b]	*All countries*	*Per cent*[c]	*Argen- tina*	*Per cent*[b]	*All countries*	*Per cent*[c]
1,197	4.1	6,532	18.3	945	1.5	6,699	14.1	2,345	3.6	10,348	22.7
799	2.7	17,159	4.7	1,093	1.7	19,018	5.7	1,356	2.1	21,544	6.3
1,237	4.2	38,165	3.2	1,955	3.1	48,247	4.1	2,284	3.5	74,721	3.1
405	1.4	681	59.5	334	0.5	609	54.8	429	0.7	786	54.6
83	0.3	562	14.8	167	0.3	854	19.6	365	0.6	1,623	22.5
924	3.1	8,887	10.4	899	1.4	10,131	8.9	657	1.0	6,664	9.9
109	0.4	301	36.2	372	0.6	857	43.4	869	1.3	1,715	50.7
747	2.5	747	100.0	409	0.6	409	100.0	296	0.5	296	100.0
1,895	6.4	9,791	19.4	4,411	6.9	20,794	21.2	5,473	8.4	23,282	23.5
7,396	25.1	82,825	8.9	10,585	16.6	107,618	9.8	14,074	21.5	140,979	10.0
10,521	35.7	991,161	1.1	12,427	19.5	1,205,987	1.0	15,966	24.4	1,382,376	1.2
2,845	9.7	5,224	54.5	6,137	9.6	11,647	52.7	7,912	12.1	13,924	56.8
81	[f]	1,530	0.1	14,795	23.2	20,292	72.9	11,758	18.0	16,055	73.2
447	1.5	1,383	32.3	944	1.5	2,516	37.5	2,674	4.1	6,228	42.9
261	0.9	4,273	6.1	244	0.4	5,077	4.8	1,120	1.7	20,443	5.5
8,187	27.8	15,028	54.5	14,021	22.0	15,623	89.7	14,287	21.9	17,653	80.9
230	0.8	406	56.7	333	0.5	530	62.8	301	0.5	655	46.0
82	0.3	143	57.3	140	0.2	262	53.4	547	0.8	1,368	40.0
2,615	8.9	2,870	91.1	2,694	4.2	3,172	84.9	2,907	4.5	3,356	86.6
34	0.1	51	66.7	22	[f]	25	88.0	61	0.1	124	49.2
1,155	3.9	3,048	37.9	2,417	3.8	5,625	43.0	3,982	6.1	8,404	47.4
294	1.0	647	45.4	356	0.6	397	89.7	433	0.7	495	87.5
16,231	55.1	34,603	48.8	42,103	65.9	65,166	64.6	45,982	70.4	88,705	51.9
18,914	64.3	644,842	2.9	51,420	80.5	832,918	6.2	49,345	75.6	1,039,088	4.7
23,627	80.3	117,428	20.1	52,688	82.5	172,784	30.5	60,056	92.0	229,684	26.2
29,435	100.0	1,636,003	1.8	63,847	100.0	2,038,905	3.1	65,311	100.0	2,421,464	2.7

[b] Per cent of total imports from Argentina.

able. Imports for consumption of carpet wool in 1934, 1935, and 1936 not comparable with General bonded warehouse, and is automatically noted as dutiable. At time of release for consumption from on purpose for which released.

[f] Less than 0.1 per cent.

Source: United States Tariff Commission.

and frequent loss to importing interests.[22] The treaty was not ratified by the United States Senate, however, and thus never became effective.

No other attempts were made by the United States to effect a reciprocity agreement with Argentina until 1933, when preliminary conversations were held between the representatives of the two governments regarding the possibility of negotiating a reciprocal trade agreement. Nothing definite, however, was achieved. Up to the present time (May 1937), no official announcement has been made of the opening of negotiations with Argentina under the provisions of the Trade Argeements Act of June 1934.

Such an agreement would be highly desirable since, as has been already pointed out, the expansion of United States exports to Argentina is conditioned to a considerable degree, under Argentina's present foreign commercial policy of bilateralism, upon the creation of additional dollar exchange in Argentina. The problem is a difficult one, due to the political strength of the farm bloc in the United States. That some basis exists for the granting of concessions by the United States on Argentine imports will be indicated in the following paragraphs.

The leading commodities which the United States imports from Argentina are shown in Table XXIX. An analysis of the data contained in this table reveals that the imports best adapted to the granting of concessions by the United States under the Trade Agreements Act of 1934 may be grouped as follows:

Major products:
Dutiable:
- flaxseed
- cattle hides
- quebracho extract

Minor products:
Dutiable:
- casein
- grapes
- canary seed

Free:
- bones, hoofs, horns, unmanufactured
- quebracho wood

[22] *Ibid.*, p. 219.

With respect to each of these commodities, Argentina, during recent years, has generally been the principal source of supply, providing in 1936 from 40 per cent of total imports for casein to 100 per cent for quebracho wood.[23] Thus they conform to the

TABLE XXX

UNITED STATES TARIFF TREATMENT OF THE PRINCIPAL DUTIABLE COMMODITIES IMPORTED FROM ARGENTINA

Commodity	*Rate of Duty*			*Ad valorem equivalent*			
	Act of 1913	*Act of 1922*	*Act of 1930*	*1929*	*1931*	*1935*	*1936*
				Per cent			
All dutiable commodities........				26.0	47.6	57.1	50.4
Cattle hides	Free	Free	10%	—	10.0	10.0	10.0
Combing wool....	Free	30¢ or 31¢ lb.	Various; chiefly 34¢ lb.	60.8	142.7	150.4	97.5
Carpet wool[a]......	Free	Free	Free				
Flaxseed[b].........	20¢ bu.	40¢ bu.	65¢ bu.	24.2	67.8	74.9	59.9
Canary seed......	1¢ lb.	1¢ lb.	1¢ lb.	26.8	41.7	42.3	26.2
Casein...........	Free	2½¢ lb.	5½¢ lb.	21.1	150.2	72.9	63.6
Quebracho extract.	Free	15%	15%	15.0	15.0	15.0	15.0
Poultry, dead.....	Free	6¢ lb.	10¢ lb.	18.9	51.4	81.8	68.9
Meats, canned....	Free	20%	6¢ lb., but not less than 20%	20.0	47.4	79.1	60.2
Grapes...........	Free	25¢ cu. ft.	25¢ cu. ft.	12.9	12.2	17.1	18.7
Corn.............	Free	15¢ bu.	25¢ bu.	12.7	61.1	56.5	54.5

[a] Free of duty, but reported as dutiable.

[b] Rates are for a bushel of 56 pounds; duty was increased by Presidential proclamation, effective June 13, 1929, to 56¢ per bushel.

Source: United States Tariff Commission. Compiled from *Comparison of Tariff Acts of 1913, 1922, and 1930.*

principles so far enunciated in the administration of the Trade Agreements Act, namely, the granting of concessions on articles of which the particular country is the chief supplier, in order

[23] In 1936 Argentina ranked second as a supplier of casein. In previous years, however, she ranked first, providing in 1928, 1934, and 1935, 80.2, 57.3, and 53.4 per cent, respectively, of total imports. The marked increase in imports of corn and tankage during 1935 and 1936 is presumably temporary, due to the feed shortage resulting from the drouth.

that the concession may be generalized under the unconditional interpretation of the most-favored-nation clause.[24]

All except two of the minor products, unmanufactured bones, hoofs, and horns, and quebracho wood, are dutiable under the Tariff Act of 1930. These two items, however, might be bound to the free list.

The tariff treatment since 1913 of the principal commodities imported from Argentina is summarized in Table XXX.

The leading import into the United States from Argentina in recent years has been flaxseed, which for the selected years accounted for the following percentages of the total value of imports from Argentina, and of total imports of flaxseed from all countries:

UNITED STATES IMPORTS OF FLAXSEED

Calendar year	*Per cent of total value of imports from Argentina*	*Per cent of total value of flaxseed imports from all countries*
1928	26.2	83.4
1933	31.9	79.9
1934	27.8	54.5
1935	22.0	89.7
1936	21.9	80.9

Analysis of the figures covering the production and import of flaxseed appears to support the conclusion that some relief to Argentina from the present duty of 65 cents per bushel is warranted.[25] During the decade of the twenties net imports of flaxseed into the United States were equivalent, roughly, to total domestic production.[26] For the four-year period July 1,

[24] The alleged inconsistency claimed by certain critics of this interpretation and administration of the unconditional most-favored-nation clause cannot be discussed in detail here, namely, that by restricting the concessions to "chief supplier" commodities, the generalization of such concessions is meaningless, or nearly so, and that thus, in the actual operation of the Act, the conditional interpretation is followed, in fact if not in theory.

[25] In 1934, 1935, and 1936 this specification of 65 cents per bushel was equivalent to an ad valorem duty of 120, 75, and 60 per cent, respectively.

[26] United States Department of Agriculture, *Yearbook*, 1935, p. 408. Exports were negligible, never totaling as much as 500,000 bushels in any one year.

1927-June 30, 1931,[27] imports averaged 84.7 per cent of total domestic production. Notwithstanding an increase in the duty from 40 cents to 65 cents a bushel in 1929 and 1930, however, the ratio of domestic production has not increased. On the contrary it has declined. As shown in Table XXXI, imports for the five-year period July 1, 1930-June 30, 1936, equaled 138.0 per cent of domestic production.

TABLE XXXI

UNITED STATES FLAXSEED PRODUCTION AND IMPORTS, 1927-35

Year	*Acreage Seeded*	*Acreage Harvested*	*Production*	*Imports*[a]			
				Total		*Argentina*	
	1,000 acres	*1,000 acres*	*1,000 bushels*	*1,000 bushels*	*Per cent of domestic production*	*1,000 bushels*	*Per cent of total imports*
Average, 1927-30	3,307	3,039	20,380	17,268	84.7	15,580	90.2
1931	3,716	2,416	11,798	13,850	117.4	13,342	96.3
1932	2,570	1,975	11,671	6,213	53.2	5,495	88.4
1933	1,700	1,328	6,947	17,901	257.7	12,736[b]	71.1
1934	1,499	969	5,213	15,332	294.1	12,146[b]	79.2
1935	2,252	2,014	14,128	15,388	108.9	13,656[b]	88.7
Average, 1931-35	2,347	1,740	9,951	13,737	138.0	11,475	83.5

[a] Year ended June 30; i.e., 1927 figure is for year ended June 30, 1928, to correspond with consumption period for 1927 domestic crop.

[b] In 1933, 1934, and 1935, 4,311, 2,233, and 1,219 thousand bushels, respectively, were imported from British India.

Source: United States Department of Agriculture, *Agricultural Statistics*, 1936, pp. 60, 320.

The production of flaxseed in the United States is a highly localized and relatively small industry, the average total acreage harvested annually for the period 1927-30 being only 3,039,000 acres, or less than one per cent of total acreage of farm crops.[28] During the five-year period since the import duty was increased from 40 cents to 65 cents per bushel (1931-35) total acreage harvested declined to an annual average of 1,740,000 acres, or

[27] Crop year basis.

[28] United States Department of Agriculture, *Yearbook*, 1935, p. 409.

43 per cent below the annual average for the period 1927-30. It is true that three of these five years, 1931, 1933, and 1934, were severe drouth years, and thus years in which the ratio of acreage harvested to acreage seeded was abnormally low. Nevertheless, the total acreage seeded declined from an annual average of 3,307,000 acres for the period 1927-30 to an annual average of 2,347,000 acres for the period 1931-35, or by 29 per cent.

Flaxseed is produced as an alternate crop on land suitable for other grains. Furthermore, it is classified as a soil-depleting crop under the existing Soil Conservation Act; thus, a portion of the areas now devoted to flaxseed production, with the attendant low ratios of acreage harvested to acreage planted, might be advantageously diverted, under the soil conservation program, to soil-building crops. It would seem, therefore, that the restoration of at least the rate of duty effective prior to 1929, namely, 40 cents per bushel, as against the present rate of 65 cents per bushel, would be a desirable concession to make to Argentina.

Second to flaxseed in value among United States purchases from Argentina (under normal conditions) are cattle hides.[29] In recent years Argentina has supplied from one-half to two-thirds of total imports of cattle hides by the United States. Prior to 1930 cattle hides were entered free of duty, but in the Smoot-Hawley Bill were placed on the dutiable list at ten per cent ad valorem. This duty is primarily a revenue duty, since it cannot be said to provide a very great measure of protection to domestic producers of cattle hides which are primarily a by-product of the beef and dairy industries. A reduction of 50 per cent in the duty, that is, from ten to five per cent ad valorem, would presumably not seriously affect the total customs rev-

[29] In 1935 and 1936 imports of corn from Argentina ranked first and second, respectively, in value, as follows:

	1935	*1936*
	(thousands of dollars)	
Flaxseed	14,021	14,287
Corn	14,795	11,758
Cattle hides	6,134	7,912

enues received, since the duty derived from imports of cattle hides has averaged less than five million dollars annually. In fact, the total duty obtained might be increased, as a result of increased imports.

The third major product upon which a concession might be made is quebracho extract, which in recent years has contributed from five to ten per cent of total imports from Argentina. Furthermore, of total imports of quebracho extract, Argentina supplied 91.1, 84.9, and 86.6 per cent in 1934, 1935, and 1936, respectively.

There appears to be little economic reason for the 15 per cent ad valorem duty which was imposed in 1922 and retained in the Act of 1930,[30] the purpose of which apparently was to promote the import of quebracho wood for extraction in this country. A much less economic situation is difficult to imagine, since the ratio of the weight of the extract obtained from quebracho wood is about 24 per cent. The removal of the duty on quebracho extract, therefore, seems highly desirable.

The commodity which normally ranks fourth in value of imports from Argentina is canned meat,[31] of which Argentina supplies nearly one-half of the total United States imports. Practically all of the remainder, however, is obtained from Uruguay, which ranks first as a source of canned meat imports. During the four-year period 1933-36 Uruguay and Argentina supplied 54.0 and 42.8 per cent, respectively, of the total volume of imports of canned meat which averaged 63.6 million pounds annually. In accordance with the "chief supplier" doctrine, therefore, a concession could not be granted to Argentina on canned meat.

Under the Tariff Act of 1922 imports of canned meat were subject to an ad valorem duty of 20 per cent. In 1930, however, the duty was changed to six cents a pound, but not less than 20 per cent ad valorem. So far this supplementary provision has been superfluous, since the result of the six-cent duty, as well as

[30] See Table XXX.

[31] Practically all corned beef, which cannot be produced on a competitive basis in the United States.

lower prices, was to raise the ad valorem rate on canned beef to the following percentages:

1931	51	1934	92
1932	69	1935	82
1933	93	1936	60

Between 1929 and 1932 the value and volume of total imports of canned meat into the United States declined 82.9 and 55.1 per cent, respectively. The general decline in all imports between 1929 and 1932, which amounted to 70.0 per cent, by value, accounts of course, for a considerable portion of this decrease. The sharp reduction in meat supplies in the United States since 1934, however, has resulted in a marked increase in canned meat imports, which in 1936 equaled 87.9 million pounds, valued at 8.4 million dollars, or approximately the quantity imported in 1929 of 89.9 million pounds. If a trade agreement should be subsequently negotiated with Uruguay which includes a concession on canned meats, Argentina would benefit therefrom, under the existing policy of generalizing concessions, only slightly less than Uruguay, and imports of canned beef from both countries might be still further augmented.

Minor Products

1. *Grapes*

Although still a relatively small per cent of the total value of United States imports of Argentine products (from 1 to 3 per cent), fresh grapes constitute an item the export of which has been of especial interest to Argentina in recent years. Imports of grapes into the United States from Argentina have recently shown a marked increase, as the following figures indicate:

UNITED STATES IMPORTS OF FRESH GRAPES FROM ARGENTINA

(in thousands of cubic feet)

1925/29 Avg.	71
1930	194
1932	219
1934	281
1935	245
1936	326

Argentina is the chief source of grape imports, providing generally from 80 to 90 per cent of the total in recent years.

Argentina desires relief, however, from the duty of 25 cents per cubic foot, which on an ad valorem basis equalled 19.1, 17.1, and 18.8 per cent in 1933, 1935, and 1936, respectively. Since Argentine grapes are marketed largely in the late winter and spring months (in the northern hemisphere), a seasonal reduction in duty might be effected covering those months when the United States domestic crop was not in a competitive position.

2. *Casein, or lacterene*

Another Argentine product, the import of which has been sharply curtailed in recent years, is casein, or lacterene. Of total United States imports of casein, Argentina supplied until recently about 80 per cent. As shown in Table XXIX Argentina's share in 1934, 1935, and 1936 was reduced to 57.3, 53.4, and 40 per cent, respectively. As indicated in Table XXX, a duty of 2½¢ per pound was levied on casein in 1922, and increased in 1930 to 5½¢ per pound. This increased duty, coupled with lower prices, resulted in an ad valorem rate on casein imports in 1932, 1935, and 1936, of 141.0, 72.9, and 63.6 per cent, respectively. The decline in the volume of United States imports of casein since 1928 is shown in the following figures:

UNITED STATES IMPORTS OF CASEIN

(thousands of pounds)

	Argentina	*Total*
1928	23,139	28,651
1932	803	1,201
1933	6,927	8,142
1934	1,097	1,491
1935	1,853	3,229
1936	6,320	16,203

The restoration of the duty of 2½¢ per pound imposed from 1922 to 1930 would seem to be a not unreasonable concession.

3. *Canary seed*

Another minor import of which Argentina is the chief source of supply is canary seed. Subject to a duty of one cent per pound,

the ad valorem equivalent for the years 1933, 1935, and 1936 was 73.6, 42.3, and 26.4 per cent, respectively. Notwithstanding the drastic general decline in imports, total United States purchases of canary seed from abroad increased from 16,763 thousand pounds in 1928 to 19,622 thousand pounds in 1932, of which Argentina supplied 11,582 and 10,775 thousand pounds, respectively. In 1936 total imports equaled 16,808 thousand pounds, of which Argentina supplied 7,938 thousand pounds, with Turkey and Morocco furnishing 6,462 and 2,166 thousand pounds, respectively. A reduction of 50 per cent, or even the complete elimination of the present duty, might add something (if only slightly) to the supply of dollar exchange in Argentina available for remittances to cover purchases of United States exports.

In addition to the question of duty concessions to Argentina, there remains the question of the sanitary embargo on fresh meat imports into the United States from Argentina. It may be that Argentina will adopt the position that the removal of this quarantine must be a part of any agreement for mutual concessions by the two countries. Whether the ratification of the Sanitary Convention signed in May 1935 by the United States Senate will be accomplished in the near future is problematical. As stated previously,[32] this Convention has the strong support of both the Departments of Agriculture and State, yet the beef producers, through the politically powerful farm bloc, have so far been successful in preventing its consideration by the Senate.

[32] See Chapter VII, p. 187.

X

CONCLUSIONS

THE FIFTY years from 1880 to 1930 was a period of rapid expansion in Argentina. A tremendous volume of wealth was created, based primarily upon the fertility of the broad, treeless pampas. This development of a relatively simple economy based primarily upon agricultural and pastoral pursuits has resulted in a large volume of foreign trade; exports consisting primarily of foodstuffs and raw materials, and imports of a wide variety of manufactured products. Coupled with a large volume of foreign borrowing, this type of development has made the Argentine economy particularly susceptible to international economic influences. This susceptibility has been reflected in the wide fluctuations in the country's international accounts. These fluctuations have been accentuated by the inelasticity in both demand and supply of Argentina's major exports, plus the fact that the cessation of demand for the country's exports has been generally paralleled by a sharp decline in foreign capital supplies. Trade and capital items have been the dominant factors in the country's international balance of payments.

Under a gold standard, these wide fluctations would have operated as severe shocks to the Argentine domestic economy, particularly since its monetary and banking system was highly rigid and inelastic. In times of world economic breakdowns restoration of equilibrium in the country's international accounts would have required, presumably, drastic deflations and price declines. During such crises in the past, however, Argentina has not chosen the gold standard mechanism of restoring equilibrium in its international balance of payments. Since 1910 the country has gone through three major crises; the first, upon the outbreak of the World War in 1914; the second, the post-war deflation of 1920-21; the third, the breakdown of 1929-33. During none of

these periods of readjustment did Argentina maintain the gold standard. In fact, during the twenty-year period 1914-34, Argentina operated under a gold standard for only two years, or from August 1927 to December 1929. Instead, gold payments were suspended,[1] the peso was allowed to depreciate, and thus the mechanism of an inconvertible currency was utilized to restore equilibrium in the country's international accounts.[2] The result has been external instability in the Argentine peso, but relative internal stability; i.e., a relatively stable price level.

With its international accounts subject to such wide fluctuations, future external stability of its currency appears to require the creation and maintenance of a short-term creditor position abroad, thus providing a reserve upon which to draw when a deficit occurs in the balance of payments. Whether the recent complete reorganization of the country's banking system, implemented by an exchange equalization fund, will enable Argentina to maintain *relative* stability in both the external and internal value of its currency, remains to be seen. With a continued recurrence in the future of world economic crises and breakdowns, it is difficult to see how Argentina, or any country whose economy is so interrelated with international economic forces, can hope to maintain the gold standard. This situation is, perhaps, the chief justification of Argentina's new economic policy of promoting a greater degree of self-sufficiency and diversification in its domestic economy.

Between 1910 and 1934 estimated foreign investments in Argentina increased approximately one hundred per cent, or from 2,255 million to 4,300 million gold pesos. The estimated increase during the decade of the twenties was about one billion pesos, or some 100 millions annually. This was, however, only about one-half the rate of growth in the years immediately preceding the World War, since between 1910 and 1913 the esti-

[1] Or else not restored; that is, when the balance of payments turned against Argentina in 1920, it will be recalled, the release of gold for export was not permitted, although large gold stocks existed within the country.

[2] Since 1931 higher tariff duties, plus exchange control with the rationing of foreign exchange, has supplemented currency depreciation in effecting equilibrium.

mated growth was also about one billion gold pesos, or over 200 million pesos annually.[3] In sharp contrast to the pre-war borrowings, however, a major portion (about 75 per cent) of the new funds obtained abroad during the twenties originated in the United States. Approximately 30 per cent of the increase during the twenties was public borrowing, the balance representing investment in private undertakings in Argentina. Nevertheless, the estimated total public debt held abroad (including national, provincial, and municipal) in 1930 was only 60 million gold pesos larger than in 1914 (675 million pesos in 1914 and 734 millions in 1930). Between 1930 and 1934, however, estimated total public borrowings from abroad increased from 734 to 900 million gold pesos, due primarily to the funding of commercial balances blocked in Argentina under the exchange restrictions in effect.

As pointed out in Chapter V, this external debt burden has not been excessive in the light of the expansion of Argentina's internal income and revenue producing capacity. But, in view of the wide fluctuations in the income items in Argentina's balance of payments, to the extent that these foreign borrowings involve fixed foreign debt service remittances, a serious transfer problem results. By placing itself in a favored position with respect to obtaining foreign currencies under the exchange control system in effect since 1931, however, the National Government has maintained its external debt service, notwithstanding the additional burden resulting from the abrupt price declines and peso depreciation. Since November 1933 the Government has, however, recouped its exchange losses from the profits accruing from sales of foreign currencies to private purchasers.

A considerable portion of the burden of restoring and maintaining equilibrium in the Argentine international accounts since 1929 has fallen, therefore, upon the owners of the large volume of foreign *private* investments in Argentina, due to the difficulty of transferring abroad the earnings of these investments. The

[3] During the prosperous war and post-war years, it will be recalled, Argentina reduced its total foreign borrowings about 200 million gold pesos, in addition to lending foreigners (net) some 180 million gold pesos.

conclusion was reached that an aid to the solution of this difficulty for the future was in having the country's foreign borrowings in the form of equities, rather than fixed-income securities. Thus, with such a national "capital structure," large earnings during years of prosperity might be easily transferred in order to offset the inability to transfer earnings (even when earned) during periods of relatively low levels of economic activity. With respect to public borrowings, the solution appears to rest in building up a short-term creditor position abroad, as already indicated, which may serve as a reserve upon which to draw when normal international income items fail.[4]

During the twenty-year period covered by this study, marked changes occurred in the volume, composition, and direction of Argentina's foreign trade. Due to the character of Argentina's major exports, both their volume and value fluctuate widely from year to year, the effect of which on the country's international accounts has already been described. The large export surpluses built up during the War and post-war years were succeeded during the twenties by alternating periods of export and import surpluses. The decline in exports which began in 1929 and continued through 1933 brought the value of Argentina's exports in pesos in the latter year to less than 50 per cent of the 1929 level. In terms of gold currencies, the decline in value was nearly 75 per cent. Imports dropped correspondingly, from about 800 million gold pesos in 1929 and 1930 to slightly under 400 millions in 1932 and 1933.

The United Kingdom and the United States have been the chief suppliers of Argentina's imports, accounting for nearly half the total. The United Kingdom is also the leading market for Argentine exports, taking approximately one-third of the total. Thus the United Kingdom, during the period of this study, accounted for about one-fourth of Argentina's total foreign trade, and the United States (whose purchases from

[4] Since the above was written, it is reported that the Argentine National Government proposes to retire its foreign debt from the proceeds of new domestic issues. See footnote 36, Chapter V, p. 122.

Argentina have been generally less than 10 per cent of Argentina's total exports, except during the war years) from 10 to 15 per cent. Prior to the War the United Kingdom ranked first by a wide margin in the Argentine import trade, supplying about 30 per cent, compared with 17 per cent for Germany, and 15 per cent for the United States. During the War the share of the United States increased to 35 per cent, while the United Kingdom's share dropped to 24 per cent, and Germany's to less than one per cent. After the War the United Kingdom regained first position, which she held until 1925 by a small margin over the United States. From 1925 through 1930, however, the United States held first position, in 1929 supplying 26.3 per cent of Argentina's total imports, compared with 17.6 per cent for the United Kingdom.

In 1931 the United Kingdom regained first position, due in part to a marked decline in the percentage supplied by the United States, the comparative figures being 21.0 per cent for the former and 15.8 per cent for the latter. During the three years 1932-34, the United Kingdom supplied 22.5 per cent of Argentina's total imports, compared with 13.4 per cent for the United States. In 1935 the respective figures were 24.7 and 13.6 per cent. Preliminary figures for 1936 (based on tariff values) show a decline again in the share of the United Kingdom, which equaled 20.4 per cent, compared with 14.6 per cent for the United States. This marked decline in the relative position of the United States has been due primarily, as described in the above pages, to the preferential treatment accorded the United Kingdom by Argentina under its new foreign commercial policy of bilateralism, and not to any marked change in the preference of Argentinians for "Made in the U. S." merchandise. On the contrary, under conditions of equal opportunity in the Argentine market, there is every reason to believe that Argentina would continue to purchase from the United States those types of products which were supplied prior to 1931, in the production of which the United States has an international competitive advantage; namely, articles adapted to mass production (as well as mass con-

sumption within the United States), such as automobiles and related products, office and household equipment, industrial, mining, and agricultural machinery.[5]

Argentina's adoption of a foreign policy based upon preferential treatment, after a hundred years of devotion to the principle of equality of treatment, was involuntary; that is, it was due to world conditions over which Argentina had no control. Faced with a rapid curtailment of outlets for the large volume of agricultural and pastoral exports upon which the economic life of Argentina depends, it has been forced to adopt a bargaining policy. This policy first found significant expression in the Roca-Runciman Agreement as an attempt to offset the detrimental effects of the Ottawa Agreements of 1932 which had a profound influence in Argentina.

As a corollary to its new foreign commercial policy of bilateralism, Argentina has, since 1931, also embarked upon a program of increasing national economic self-sufficiency, as an aid in alleviating the country's dependence upon international conditions. This encouragement of greater diversification in the country's domestic economy is probably a permanent policy, from which there will be no turning back. The same conclusion cannot be drawn, however, respecting Argentina's foreign commercial policy. World conditions permitting, Argentina still prefers the open system based upon equality of treatment and multangular settlement of its international balances.

The United States has not been backward in restricting Argentina's market for its products in the former country. Since 1920

[5] The trend of Argentina's import trade during recent months tends to substantiate the above statement, which was originally written in May 1936. As indicated in Chapter VI, Argentine purchases of United States products during the early months of 1937 equaled 17 per cent of total imports, compared with 19 per cent from the United Kingdom. This increase occurred notwithstanding the continuance of the 20 per cent premium charged in the free exchange market, although it is reported that official permits are now being granted for much larger quantities of merchandise from the United States. Furthermore, it is stated that the decline in the United Kingdom's share is in part attributable to her inability to fill foreign orders because of the current British rearmament program.

sharp tariff increases, plus sanitary embargoes, have effectively curtailed the import of large quantities of Argentine products. The result has been a large import surplus for Argentina in its trade with the United States which, during the decade of the twenties, averaged slightly over 100 million gold pesos annually, although reduced in the four-year period 1931-34 to an annual average of less than 30 million pesos.[6] Although large capital imports by Argentina from the United States provided a basis of settlement for about half[7] of this import surplus of approximately one billion gold pesos, the balance had to be covered by multangular payments through other countries.

Under Argentina's present policy of bilateralism an expansion of United States exports is contingent to a considerable degree, therefore, upon an increase in imports by the United States from Argentina. Renewed lending to Argentina by the United States would not improve the relative position of American importers in securing dollar exchange, since, under the existing system of exchange control, foreign exchange derived from capital imports is sold in the free market, where the cost of foreign currencies cannot be less than 20 per cent above the official selling rate. With a continuance of Argentina's policy of fostering industrial development, however, new investments of United States capital in Argentina will no doubt be continued, primarily in the form of direct investments in private undertakings. Such investments, by increasing the supply of foreign exchange available, would tend to reduce exchange rates in the free market. If the free market rates should go below the official rates, presumably some modification of the existing exchange control system would be forthcoming.

With respect to a permanent increase in purchases by the United States of Argentine products the outlook is not very

[6] As pointed out in Chapter VIII, during 1935 and 1936 Argentine exports of grain to the United States increased rapidly, due to presumably temporary conditions in the latter country, resulting in Argentina's having a small export surplus in its trade with the United States.

[7] That is, *net* capital balance after deducting estimated debt service remittances to the United States.

favorable. That some opportunities exist, however, has been indicated in the above pages. The negotiation of an agreement by the United States with Argentina under the Trade Agreements Act of 1934 would presumably promote such purchases, thus creating increased supplies of dollar exchange in Argentina available for the acquisition of exports from the United States.

APPENDIX I

THE ARGENTINE INTERNATIONAL ACCOUNTS

BECAUSE of the importance of international factors in the economic life of Argentina, the country's international accounts have been quite naturally a subject of great interest to Argentine economists and financiers. From 1911 to 1931 an annual statement of the Argentine balance of payments was compiled by Sr. Carlos A. Tornquist, an eminant Argentine banker.[1] These statements covered what Sr. Tornquist termed the "economic" year, that is, October 1 to September 30, which he justified on the grounds that the Argentine agricultural productive cycle begins in October (spring in Argentina), and the major portion of that season's crop is marketed by the end of the following winter (June-September).[2]

Beginning with the "economic" year 1914-15, these statements were published by Sr. Tornquist, and have been reprinted in several other sources, as indicated below. The statement for the "economic" year 1914-15 also contained a summary for 1913-14.[3] An earlier monograph, *La República Argentina, Su Situación Económica y Financiera*, Buenos Aires, 1914,[4] contains certain

[1] Until recently head of the great private banking firm of Ernesto Tornquist and Company, Buenos Aires. This organization, it is interesting to observe, was founded by his grandfather, who was an emigrant to Argentina from Baltimore early in the nineteenth century.

[2] Estimates of the Argentine balance of payments for the calendar years 1904 and 1908 were also compiled by the Argentine statistician, A. B. Martinez, and for the years 1916 and 1917 by Alejandro Bunge, at that time Director-General of National Statistics.

[3] Carlos A. Tornquist, *El Balance de Pagos de la República Argentina En el Primer Año Económico Pasado Bajo Los Efectos de la Guerra Europea*, Buenos Aires, 1916.

[4] English translation, *The Argentine Republic, Its Economic and Financial Situation*, Washington, D.C., January 1915.

balance-of-payments estimates for 1913-14; these do not check entirely, however, with the summary figures for 1913-14 contained in the 1914-15 statement. The breakdown of certain of the data contained in the 1913-14 summary figures used in Chapter II is, therefore, an estimate based in part upon the figures for similar items in succeeding years.

Although unable to obtain complete data for the years 1911-12 and 1912-13, the writer was able to obtain a summary for these years which is reproduced below:[5]

ARGENTINE BALANCE OF PAYMENTS, 1911-12

(in millions of gold pesos)

Credit:		*Debit:*	
Exports	428.5	Imports	368.0
Balance	235.4	Estimated difference in imports	41.0
		Financial Service	167.9
		Immigrant Remittances	43.0
		Tourist Expenditures	44.0
	663.9		663.9

ARGENTINE BALANCE OF PAYMENTS, 1912-13

Credit:		*Debit:*	
Exports	512.2	Imports	418.5
Balance	195.7	Estimated difference in imports	41.9
		Financial Service	160.5
		Immigrant Remittances	43.0
		Tourist Expenditures	44.0
	707.9		707.9

The statements since 1914-15 have been published in Spanish through 1922, and in both Spanish and English from 1922 through 1931. Summary statements since 1918 are also contained in *Business Conditions in Argentina* (quarterly) published

[5] Obtained from the library of Ernesto Tornquist and Company, Buenos Aires, through the coöperation of Mr. C. E. Babcock, Librarian, Columbus Memorial Library, Pan-American Union, Washington, D.C.

by Ernesto Tornquist and Company, Buenos Aires. Beginning with the year 1917-18 the statements also appear in *Revísta de Economía Argentina*, Buenos Aires. Translations of the complete statements may be also found in the *Review of the River Plate*, Buenos Aires, and the *South American Journal*, London. Tornquist's studies are also the basis of the Argentine balance of payments contained in the *Memoranda on Balance of Payments* published by the League of Nations, which for Argentina, date from 1918.

In his original statements for the "economic" years 1913-14, 1914-15, and 1915-16 Sr. Tornquist made adjustments for estimated errors in the official Argentine foreign trade statistics, which were due to undervaluation resulting from the use of the official valuation system based upon 1906 prices.[6] Official revision of these statistics in 1916, however, were sufficiently at variance with his original adjustments as to cause Sr. Tornquist to revise his figures for these years. These revised figures were included in his statement for 1916-17, along with the original figures.[7]

The revision of the Argentine official trade statistics just referred to was made following the appointment of Sr. Alejandro Bunge as Director of the National Statistical Bureau. Furthermore, during the first two years of Sr. Bunge's administration, an official calculation was compiled of Argentina's balance of payments, or "Economic Balance" (*Balance Económico*), as it was called in the official bulletins.[8] Although a comparison of Bunge's compilation with that of Tornquist shows wide variations in individual items (even allowing for the lag of three months for different periods covered), the total net differences are relatively small, especially when it is recalled that most of these estimates must of necessity be of a conjectural character.

For certain years the Tornquist statements contain a rela-

[6] See p. 203 above for description of this system.

[7] English translation in *Review of the River Plate*, Mar. 29, 1918, p. 760.

[8] *El Intercambio Económico de la República Argentina en 1916 (Informe)*, República Argentina, Dirección General de Estadística de la Nación, Buenos Aires, 1917, p. 30; *El Intercambio Económico de la República en los Años 1910 a 1917*, Buenos Aires, 1918.

tively large residual, or unaccounted-for, figure. With the exception of the following adjustments which were made by the writer, these residual balances have been included with short-term capital items in Table II, "Estimated International Capital Transactions of Argentina, 1913-1934," Appendix II, pp. 240-41.

For the "economic" year 1917-18 the residual figure was 160.19 million pesos. Apparently this large discrepancy was due to the fact that during that year the Argentine Government made a loan to the British and French Governments totaling 177.30 million gold pesos (net) which Tornquist included as a "debit" item only. The funds must never have been transferred, however, and therefore should also have been included as a short-term loan ("credit") to Argentina.

The figures for the "economic" years 1920-21 and 1921-22 were combined in one statement, which contained a residual figure totaling 269.9 million pesos. According to Tornquist, this balance was due in large part to losses on imports; that is, imports were recorded in the official statistics, but the funds were never remitted abroad to pay for them. The official figures for imports for these two years have been reduced, therefore, by 225 million pesos, or approximately 15 per cent, which reduces the residual figure to some 45 million gold pesos. Tornquist makes a similar adjustment for the two-year period 1923-25, although his deduction is only two per cent. Losses incurred by foreigners on Argentine imports in 1920-22 were much greater, however, than in 1923-25.

For the following "economic" year, 1922-23, the reduction of the official import statistics was placed by the writer at ten per cent. For this year the residual figure in Tornquist's statement was 240 million gold pesos, which the above adjustment of ten per cent reduced to 155 million pesos. A considerable portion of this remainder of 155 million pesos may have been due to an increase in commercial credits granted to Argentine importers. During the year a large volume of merchandise was brought into the country in anticipation of higher import duties under a bill which was before the Argentine Congress from December 1922 to December 1923. This sum was included, therefore, as an in-

crease in Argentine short-term borrowing, that is, commercial credits.

In the 1925-26 statement the residual item was again very large, totaling 210.30 million pesos. In accounting for this large sum, Tornquist enumerated the following factors:

1. Statistical over-valuation of imports.
2. Imported merchandise not withdrawn from Customs House.
3. Merchandise received on credit and not paid for.
4. Investments of foreigners not numerically ascertainable.
5. Amounts not remitted abroad.
6. Commercial credits.
7. Losses on merchandise imported.

After a careful analysis and comparison with other years, 100 million pesos of this residual was more or less arbitrarily allocated to current items; that is, it was assumed that actual remittances for imports were less than the official figures for imports by that amount. This was a reduction in the official figures of approximately 12 per cent. The remainder of 110.3 million pesos was included in changes in short-term credits. The *South American Journal*, in discussing Tornquist's statement, emphasized the fact that during this period there was a large influx of short-term banking credit into Argentina, as well as much merchandise received on credit.[9]

For the following "economic" year, 1926-27, the unaccounted-for item was again reduced to a relatively negligible figure, totaling only 13 million gold pesos. Since it was an excess of "credits," however, in contrast to the previous year, Tornquist believed that it represented repayments of commercial credits raised abroad in the preceding year.

The unspecified balance in the 1927-28 statement (as finally corrected in the 1928-29 statement) was 51.75 million pesos (excess of "debits"), and in the 1928-29 statement 35.34 million pesos (excess of "credits"). For 1929-30 the unspecified balance was 85.70 million pesos, a portion of which was attributed by Tornquist to the retention of certain remittances in Argentina

[9] *South American Journal*, Jan. 21, 1928, p. 91.

awaiting more favorable exchange rates; that is, short-term borrowing by Argentina.

As stated previously, the last statement to be compiled by Sr. Tornquist covered the "economic" year, 1930-31, at the end of which, it will be recalled, exchange control was instituted. Estimates of the Argentine balance of payments for the calendar years 1932-35 inclusive have been compiled, however, by the new Argentine Central Bank.[10] These statements, plus the original Tornquist data, constitute the basis of Table I, "International Income Account of Argentina, 1914-1935," which follows, as well as Table II, "Estimated International Capital Transactions of Argentina, 1913-1934," Appendix II, pp. 240-41. These two tables present in standardized form estimates of the Argentine international accounts for the period covered by this study, and thus reflect the changes in the country's international economic position during the past two decades. They provide the basis for the summary statements of Argentina's international accounts which are used in Chapters II, III, and IV.

[10] These statements were placed at the writer's disposal through the courtesy of Sr. C. Alonso Irigoyen, Financial Attaché, Argentine Embassy, Washington, D.C.

THE INTERNATIONAL ECONOMIC POSITION OF ARGENTINA

THE INTERNATIONAL ECONOMIC POSITION OF ARGENTINA

By

Vernon Lovell Phelps

Philadelphia

UNIVERSITY OF PENNSYLVANIA PRESS

London

Humphrey Milford: Oxford University Press

1938

1926–27	1927–28	1928–29	1929–30	1930–31	Oct.–Dec. 1931	1932	1933	1934	1935
960.95	1,048.90	1,001.05	661.30	606.10	165	574	500	730	766
						18[9]	15[9]	22[9]	23[9]
[.95]	[.75]	[.40]	[.50]	[.50]		8[10]	7[10]	7[10]	8[10]
.95	.75	.40	.50	.50		2[11]	2[11]	3[11]	3[11]
						22[12]	13[12]	18[12]	24[12]
6.00[6]	8.00	12.00	12.00	10.00	2				
			64.00	171.20	24	8	19	7	7
		124.50							
967.90	1,057.65	1,137.95	737.80	787.80	191	632	556	787	831
816.60	843.50	881.70	778.90[7]	546.60	101	368	395	484	524
[178.50]	[188.50]	[197.50]	[180.50]	[163.50]	40	[211]	[191]	[221]	[215]
58.00	64.00	68.00	68.00	70.00		88	77	93	85
7.50	7.50	7.50	7.50	7.50					
						123	114	128	130
78.00	79.00	80.00	70.00	56.00					
35.00	38.00	42.00	35.00	30.00					
37.00	34.00	33.00	30.00	20.00 }	12	79[13]	40[13]	44[13]	48[13]
28.00[6]	28.00	30.00	25.00	20.00 }					
							5[14]	9[14]	10[14]
35.80	150.50			.20		26[12]	15[12]	22[12]	22[12]
1,095.90	1,244.50	1,142.20	1,014.40	750.30	153	684	646	780	819
+128.00	+186.85	+4.25	+276.60	−37.50	−38	+52	+90	−7	−12
162.40	165.35[8]	62.60	283.20[8]	59.00	}	61[8]	112[8]	67	67
	35.20		16.80	50.10					
162.40	200.55	62.60	300.00	109.10					
23.20[8]	13.70	40.65[8]	3.40	106.60[8]	}	9	22	74[8]	79[8]
11.20		17.70	20.00	40.00					
34.40	13.70	58.35	23.40	146.60					
+128.00	+186.85	+4.25	+276.60	−37.50		+52	−90	+7	−12

110.30
12.80
51.75
35.35
85.70
39.50
54.00
99.00
74.00
70.00

[9] Exporters' Profits.
[10] Port Dues.
[11] Diplomatic Expenses.
[12] Miscellaneous.
[13] Includes other private remittances.
[14] Diplomatic and other national expenses.
[15] Tornquist gives figures for 1920/21–1921/22 and for 1923/24–1924/25 together. No breakdown has been attempted of the capital items.

Table I

ternational Income Account of Argentina, 1914–1935
(in millions of gold pesos)

918–19	1919–20	1920–21	1921–22	1922–23	1923–24	1924–25	1925–26
900.15	1,172.04	714.31	675.15	767.00	947.74	903.56	792.50
1.60		2.00	2.30				
[8.40]	[7.51]	[5.60]	[5.01]	[3.70]	[.95]	[.95]	[.95]
7.30	6.21	3.00	2.61	1.70	.95	.95[4]	.95
1.10	1.30	2.60	2.40	2.00			
4.20	6.00	5.00	4.50	6.00	7.00	7.00	8.00
		17.25	1.45	1.90	40.00		
914.35	1,185.55	744.16	688.41	778.60	995.69	911.51	801.45
599.35	844.20	712.02[5]	567.74[5]	761.00[5]	822.59[5]	850.84[5]	744.70[5]
[157.30]	[151.95]	[151.10]	[120.59]	[161.20]	[170.28]	[166.22]	[154.30]
44.39	42.50	45.00	42.10	52.00	55.00	53.00	47.00
5.00	3.90	6.86	7.09	6.90	5.00	4.80	5.00
20.10	9.90						
44.60	42.75	60.30	40.00	69.50	77.00	75.90	77.30
43.21	52.90	35.00	31.40	32.80	33.28[3]	32.52	25.00
		3.94					
49.20	45.40	36.00	32.00	38.00	40.00	30.00	30.00
20.00	27.00	25.00	18.00	12.00	16.00	14.00	15.00
1.50							
11.90	78.52					9.00	1.65
839.25	1,147.07	924.12	738.33	972.20	1,048.87	1,070.06	945.65
-75.10	−38.48	+179.96	+ 49.92	+193.60	+ 53.18	+158.55	+144.20
21.90	109.79[8]	[15]	211.16[8]	213.10[8]	[15]	231.43[8]	166.20[8]
57.40	7.10		91.20				
79.30	116.89		302.36	213.10		231.43	166.20
141.80	111.50		70.18	18.70		19.70	5.70
12.60	43.87		2.30	.80			16.30
154.40	155.37		72.48	19.50		19.70	22.00
-75.10	−38.48		+229.88	+193.60		+211.73	+144.20

ses on imported merchandise. See

Tornquist gives only net figure of

million pesos for estimated losses

unted-for figure, as follows:

nquist (1913-31), and the Central

	(millions of gold pesos)	
1917/18	160.19	1925/26
1919/20	79.79	1926/27
1920/21, 1921/22	44.91	1927/28
		1928/29
1922/23	159.00	1929/30
1923/24, 1924/25	3.33	1930/31
		1932
		1933
		1934
		1935

	1913–14	*1914–15*	*1915–16*	*19*
A. *Income:*				
1. Exports:				
A. Commodities	404.25	556.90	505.50	5
B. Sale of Ships			3.00	
2. Interest and Dividends: Total				
A. Interest on Credit to France and U.K.				
B. Interest on Foreign Securities				
C. Interest on Foreign War Bonds				
3. Expenditures of Foreigners in Argentina				
4. Gold Exports: Net[1]				
A. Actual	32.60			
B. Decrease in Ear-marked (in legations)			10.70	
Total Income	436.85	556.90	519.20	61
B. *Outgo:*				
1. Imports	392.10	268.00	365.70	35
2. Foreign Debt Service: Total[2]	[139.30]	[138.10]	[146.20]	[14
A. Public Debt	50.00	46.70	48.50	4
B. Cedulas	10.00	10.20	9.90	
C. Private				
1. Mortgage Loans	17.00	20.00	18.00	1
2. Railways—Interest & Dividends	38.30	37.20	45.80	4
3. Other Foreign Capital	24.00	24.00	24.00	3
D. Interest Payment to U.K.				
3. Immigrant Remittances	30.00	20.00	10.00	1
4. Expenditures Abroad by Argentines	8.00	15.00	5.00	
5. Gifts: (charitable contributions)			2.00	
6. Gold Imports: Net				
A. Actual		3.40	21.31	3
B. Increase in Ear-marked		71.00		
Total Outgo	569.40	515.50	550.21	55
C. *Net Increase* (+) *or Decrease* (−) *in Debtor Position*	+132.55	−41.40	+31.01	−6
D. *Capital Transactions: Summary*				
1. Receipts:				
A. Borrowing from Foreigners	132.55	35.20	59.60	1
B. Repayments by Foreigners		8.00		
Total Receipts	132.55	43.20	59.60	1
2. Payments:				
A. To Foreigners		84.60	19.59	7
B. Loans to Foreigners			9.00	
Total Payments		84.60	28.59	7
E. *Net Increase* (+) *or Decrease* (−) *in Debtor Position*	+132.55	−41.40	+31.01	−6

[1] The figures for gold movements are not the official statistics of exports and imports of gold, but are based upon estimated net changes in the country's total gold stocks, as shown by the holdings of the Conversion Office and the banks. See Appendix III.

[2] Includes amortization in some cases.

[3] According to League of Nations "Memorandum on International Trade and Balance of Payments, 1912–1926," Vol. I, p. 56.

[4] France on

[5] Net after
pp. 8–10 above

[6] Estimated
20 million peso

[7] Net after
on imported m

[8] Includes r

Source: Computed from the Balance of Payments statements of Argentina compile
Bank of Argentina (1932-35).

APPENDIX II

GROWTH OF FOREIGN INVESTMENTS IN ARGENTINA, 1910-34

CHANGES in the value of a country's foreign investments may be computed either "directly" or "indirectly"; that is, by taking a census or inventory periodically, or by an analysis of the capital items in the international accounts.[1]

In attempting to trace the growth of foreign investments in Argentina, the writer has utilized both methods. The results of the "indirect" method are reflected in Table I, "International Income Account of Argentina, 1913-1935," Appendix I, supplemented by the accompanying table (Table II, "Estimated International Capital Transactions of Argentina, 1913-1934"), which contains summaries by periods of the international capital transactions of Argentina. Since the estimates of the international accounts are subject to a wide margin of error, these data of course cannot be considered as conclusive. At best they are approximations.[2] Furthermore, they do not take into account capital gains or losses on investments of foreign capital in Argentina, a factor which becomes, of course, of increasing importance as the data are projected through a considerable period of time.

Due to the great importance of foreign capital in the economic life of Argentina, the subject has always been of great interest, and "direct" estimates (of varying degrees of accuracy and thoroughness) have been made from time to time of the volume of such investments. By checking these "direct" inventories which the writer has encountered with the data obtained from the an-

[1] See Cleona Lewis, *The International Accounts*, The Brookings Institution, 1927, for an extended analysis of this methodology and the problems involved therein.

[2] One specific inaccuracy is the fact that debt service remittances in Table I include, to a large degree, amortization payments as well as interest and dividends, which it was impossible to segregate with existing data.

TABLE II

ESTIMATED INTERNATIONAL CAPITAL TRANSACTIONS OF ARGENTINA, 1913–1934
(in millions of gold pesos)

	1913–1917	1917–1920	1920–1923	1923–1927	1927–1931	1913–1920	1921–1931	1931–1934
I.								
A. *Borrowing from foreigners:*								
1. *long-term*								
a. new borrowing	157.40	71.90	127.55	434.10	320.20	229.30	881.85	—
b. repayments	48.28	268.50	88.88	35.80	79.50	316.78	204.18	—
Net Change:								
Increase	109.12		38.67	398.30	240.70		677.77	86.00
Decrease		196.60				87.48		
2. *short-term*								
a. new borrowing	81.65	239.98	296.61	125.93	137.45	321.63	672.49	154.00
b. repayments	126.19	37.50	—	12.80	84.85	163.69	97.65	143.00
Net Change:								
Increase		202.48	296.61	113.13	52.60	157.94	574.84	11.00
Decrease	44.54							
Total Borrowings:								
Net Change:								
Increase	64.58	5.88	335.28	511.43	293.30	70.46	1,140.01	97.00
B. *Loans to foreigners:*								
1. *long-term*								
a. new loans	11.50	238.87	3.10	—	6.30	250.37	9.40	—
b. repayments by foreigners	—	59.40	90.20	—	6.30	59.40	96.50	—
Net Change:								
Increase	11.50	179.47		—	—	190.97		
Decrease			87.10				87.10	—
2. *short-term*								
a. new loans	6.00	7.60	—	27.50	71.40	13.60	98.90	—
b. repayments by foreigners	13.50	8.25	1.00	—	95.80	21.75	96.80	—
Net Change:								
Increase				27.50			2.10	—
Decrease	7.50	.65	1.00		24.40	8.15		
Total Loans:								
Net Change:								
Increase	4.00	178.82		27.50		182.82		
Decrease			88.10		24.40		85.00	—
Total Net Foreign Indebtedness:								
Increase	60.58		423.38	483.93	317.70		1,225.01	97.00
Decrease		172.94				112.36		

TABLE II (*continued*)

	1913–1917	*1917–1920*	*1920–1923*	*1923–1927*	*1927–1931*	*1913–1920*	*1921–1931*	*1931–1934*
II.								
A. *Long-term:*								
1. *Borrowing from foreigners:*								
Net Change:								
Increase	109.12		38.67	398.30	240.70		677.67	86.00
Decrease		196.60				87.48		
2. *Loans to foreigners:*								
Net Change:								
Increase	11.50	179.47		—	—	190.97		—
Decrease			87.10				87.10	
Total Net long-term Foreign Indebtedness:								
Increase	97.62		125.77	398.30	240.70		764.77	86.00
Decrease		376.07				278.45		
B. *Short-term*								
1. *Borrowing from Foreigners:*								
Net Change:								
Increase		202.48	296.61	113.13	52.60	157.94	574.84	11.00
Decrease	44.54							
2. *Loans to foreigners:*								
Net Change:								
Increase				27.50			2.10	—
Decrease	7.50	.65	1.00		24.40	8.15		
Total net short-term Foreign Indebtedness:								
Increase		203.13	298.61	85.63	77.00	166.09	572.74	11.0
Decrease	37.04							

Source: Computed from the Balance of Payments statements of Argentina compiled by Sr. Tornquist (1913–31), and the Central Bank of Argentina (1932–34).

nual balance of payments statements, the writer has compiled estimates of the growth of foreign investments in Argentina during the period under review.

Furthermore, these "direct" estimates furnish some basis for comparative analysis, since they include not only estimates by Argentine writers of total foreign investments in Argentina, but also independent estimates of the holdings of Argentine investments by individual foreign countries, particularly Great Britain and, in recent years, the United States. Since these two countries have become Argentina's two leading creditors, accounting in recent years for approximately two-thirds of total foreign investments in Argentina, such interest is to be expected, and these estimates provide a check on Argentine estimates.

A comprehensive compilation was made in 1910 by Sr. Guillermo A. Schwenke.[3] According to Schwenke, the foreign capital invested in Argentina in 1910 totaled 2,256 million gold pesos.[4] The accompanying table (Table III) contains a summary of the individual items in Schwenke's compilation:

TABLE III

FOREIGN CAPITAL INVESTED IN ARGENTINA, 1910

	gold pesos
Loans and Various Argentine Bonds	691,831,000
Railways	804,413,000
Banks	37,511,000
Ports	22,163,909
Tramways	91,576,270
Refrigerating Plants	8,391,500
Gas, Electric, Water, and Drainage Works	58,035,015
Land and Mortgage Companies	150,959,285
Various Companies	41,650,100
Mortgage and Real Estate	150,000,000
Commerce and Credit	200,000,000
Total	2,256,531,079

Source: *Review of the River Plate*, January 20, 1928, p. 24.

The total foreign capital invested in Argentina at the end of 1911 was estimated by A. B. Martinez, another well-known Argentine statistician and economist, at 2,752,142,333 gold pesos.[5] Martinez's estimate gives great detail by individual com-

[3] According to Sr. Alejandro Bunge, the well-known Argentine economist, who has also given much attention to this subject, Schwenke's study was the "first scientific inventory" of the amount of foreign capital in Argentina. Alejandro Bunge, "Foreign Capital in the Argentine Republic," *Review of the River Plate*, January 20, 1928, p. 23.

[4] John H. Williams, in *Argentine International Trade Under Inconvertible Paper Money, 1880-1900*, Harvard University Press, 1920, estimated the total "foreign liabilities of Argentina, January 1, 1892" at 922,545,000 gold pesos. See also his references to other estimates of foreign investments in Argentina by countries, *ibid.*, p. 150, referred to below, footnotes 17, 18, and 19, p. 249.

[5] A. B. Martinez, *Annuaire Economique et Financier de la République Argentine*, 1913, pp. 155-58.

panies, etc. A summary statement of his estimate is given in Table IV.

This meant an increase in foreign estimates in the period intervening between the two estimates of approximately 500 million gold pesos. If Schwenke's estimate is as of the end of 1909 (thus making a two-year interval, from December 31, 1909 to December 31, 1911) this increase is in line with other estimates.

TABLE IV

FOREIGN CAPITAL INVESTED IN ARGENTINA, DECEMBER 31, 1911

		gold pesos	
Public (total)			835,949,909
a. National			
1. External	303,974,989		
2. Internal gold	161,378,600		
3. Internal paper	36,000,000	501,352,789	
b. Cedulas[a]		110,692,420	
c. Provincial		174,597,598	
d. Municipal		49,306,502	
Railroads			1,001,346,000
Banks			39,018,000
Navigation, Ports, etc.			22,240,000
Tramways			95,345,000
Refrigerating Plants			10,934,000
Public Utilities			58,035,000
Mortgage Companies			251,572,000
Miscellaneous			37,701,000
Mortgages			200,000,000
Commerce and Credits			200,000,000
Total			2,752,142,909

[a] National Mortgage Bank Bonds

If it covers only one year it is doubtful if as much as 500 million pesos of new capital was invested in Argentina in 1911. According to Sr. C. A. Tornquist, the importation of new capital during the last three years before the outbreak of the World War averaged 200 million dollars (U.S.) annually.[6]

According to data compiled by Sir George Paish,[7] the total net new capital publicly invested by Great Britain in Argentina dur-

[6] C. A. Tornquist, *The Argentine Republic of Today*, 1916.

[7] *The Statist* (Supplement), February 14, 1914, pp. v and vi.

ing 1910 and 1911 was 83,638,901 gold pesos and 77,877,536 gold pesos respectively.[8] Great Britain was by far the heaviest foreign investor in Argentina. An estimate by Sr. Bunge places the total foreign capital invested in Argentina "up to 1914" at 3,520,000,000 gold pesos.[9]

If Schwenke's estimate in 1910 of 2,256 million gold pesos is accepted as approximately correct, this would mean an increase during the four-year period 1910-1914 of some 1,264 million gold pesos, or an annual average of about 320 millions. This is 120 million pesos per year greater than Tornquist's estimate. Presumably, Bunge's estimate of 3,520 million pesos for 1914 was too high. Assuming an annual increase in the four years preceding 1914 of 250 million pesos, added to Schwenke's estimate of 2,256 million pesos in 1910 (end of 1909 presumably), gives a figure of approximately 3,250 million pesos. This sum the writer assumes as a more nearly correct estimate of the total foreign investments in Argentina at the beginning of 1914. Furthermore, this figure of 3,250 million pesos more nearly corresponds to post-war estimates after allowing for changes during the intervening period.

In 1918 Sr. A. B. Martinez stated that the foreign investments in Argentina amounted to four billion gold pesos and possibly four and one-half billions. A few days later he published the details of this estimate, which are given in Table V, the total of which, it will be observed, was only 3,882 million pesos. This estimate was not an original compilation, but a revision of Schwenke's estimate of 1910.[10]

Martinez's estimate of from four to four and one-half billions must have been a considerable overstatement, and presumably his later figure of 3,882 million pesos was some 500 millions too large. According to Bunge, Martinez's figure of 3,882 million pesos involved a duplication of certain railway and industrial

[8] Converted at par of exchange.

[9] República Argentina, Dirección General de Estadística de la Nación, A. E. Bunge, Director General, *Analisis del Comercio Exterior Argentino en los Años 1910 a 1922*, Buenos Aires, 1923, p. 10.

[10] A. E. Bunge, "Foreign Capital in the Argentine Republic," *Review of the River Plate*, Jan. 20, 1928, p. 23.

investments plus commercial credits and investments ranging from 700 to 900 million pesos.[11] In the writer's opinion, this is too great a deduction from Martinez's total of 3,882 million pesos for the following reasons: (1) According to Martinez's figures, the total miscellaneous foreign capital in Argentina in 1917 (excluding public loans, railway mortgages, and commercial capital) was approximately 910 million pesos. Tornquist's estimate of this item, however, in his various balance-of-payments statements from 1914 to 1918, ranged from 400 to 463 million pesos. Also, Bunge, in his estimate of the balance of payments for the calendar year 1916,[12] gives a figure of 460 million pesos for miscellaneous foreign capital. Assuming that Martinez's estimate of miscellaneous foreign capital of 910 million pesos (compared with those of Bunge and Tornquist in the neighborhood of 450 million pesos) was too great by some 460 million pesos,

TABLE V

FOREIGN CAPITAL INVESTED IN ARGENTINA, 1917

	gold pesos
Loans and Various Argentine Bonds	657,303,460
Railways	1,344,326,465
Banks	51,891,022
Ports	22,163,909
Tramways	109,496,149
Refrigerating Plants	40,916,439
Public Utilities	78,373,018
Land Mortgage Companies	79,681,618
Mortgages	500,015,962
Insurance	3,886,464
Industrial Establishments	507,760,000
Telegraph and Radiographic Companies	21,340,000
Commerce and Credits	465,169,244
Totals	3,882,323,750

Source: *Review of the River Plate*, January 20, 1928, p. 28.

[11] This criticism by Bunge first appeared in an article in the *Revista de Economía Argentina*, Vol. I, p. 182, 1918, and was repeated in his article "Foreign Capital in the Argentine Republic," *Review of the River Plate.*

[12] See Appendix I, p. 235.

and deducting this amount from his total figure of 3,882 millions, we arrive at an estimated total of foreign capital in Argentina in 1917 of 3,420 million pesos. (2) A second reason for feeling that Martinez's estimate was too high, and Bunge's too low, is the fact that, according to Tornquist's balance-of-payments statements, the estimated net increase in long-term borrowing from October 1913, to October 1917, was 109,120,000 gold pesos, offsetting which there was an estimated decrease in short-term borrowing of 44,540,000 pesos. Combining the figures for both long-and short-term operations, the result is a net increase in foreign borrowing approximating only 65 million gold pesos for the four-year period.[13] If this 65 millions is added to the 1913 estimate of 3,250 millions, the result is an estimated total of foreign capital in Argentina in 1917 of 3,315 million pesos. The writer uses, therefore, the figure of 3,350 million pesos, or some 530 millions less than Martinez's estimate, as representing the total amount of foreign capital in Argentina in 1917. These corrected estimates are those used in Table VI.

TABLE VI

ESTIMATED FOREIGN INVESTMENTS IN ARGENTINA BY COUNTRIES
(in millions of gold pesos)

	1910	*1913*	*1917*	*1920*	*1923*	*1927*	*1931*	*1934*
Great Britain	1,475	1,928	1,950	1,825	1,975	2,075	2,100	2,285
United States	20	40	85	75	200	505	807	590
Germany	200	250	275	265	285	285	300	315
France	410	475	465	410	415	415	425	450
Others	150	557	575	575	325	320	468	660
Total	2,255	3,250	3,350	3,150	3,200	3,600	4,100	4,300

The figures in Table VI for total foreign capital invested in Argentina are further supported by independent estimates of the investments of individual foreign countries. The estimates

[13] See Table II, "Estimated International Capital Transactions of Argentina, 1913-1934." This is not *net* change in foreign indebtedness, since it does not include Argentine loans to foreigners and their repayment. Furthermore, it must be emphasized that all these estimates of capital movements, especially short-term, can be accepted only as very rough approximations.

according to countries are based upon the following data:

A widely used estimate of British investments in Argentina is that which has been compiled annually by the *South American Journal* (London) since 1923. Estimates were also compiled for the years 1910, 1913, and 1918. These estimates present a good picture of the trend in the growth of British investments in Argentina for this period. They are not strictly accurate, however, since they are based upon the nominal value of Argentine securities quoted on the London Stock Exchange as of the end of each year. Although some of these securities are owned outside of Great Britain, especially on the continent of Europe, the *South American Journal* feels that these foreign-owned securities are offset by the large amount of British funds invested in Argentina which are not in quoted securities; therefore, "approximate totals can be obtained by accepting the figures quoted on the London Stock Exchange."[14] These compilations of the *South American Journal* are classified by type of investments, and also include estimates of income earned from the investment. These data are reproduced in Table VII, together with conversions in gold pesos at the par of exchange.

Other estimates of British capital invested in Argentina have also been compiled which may be used as a check on the *South American Journal* figures. In 1909 total British investments in Argentina were estimated at 1,285 million gold pesos (254 million pounds sterling).[15] In 1911 Sir George Paish estimated that at the end of 1909 and 1910, respectively, British investments in Argentina were 1,272 million gold pesos and 1,366 million gold pesos (£252.4 million and £269.0 million). Paish's figures are based upon the issue price (not nominal value) of net new issues in London, i.e., excluding refunding issues.[16] Paish's figures also omit direct investments, the world total of which he estimates at roughly £300 million. In view of this omission, plus

[14] *South American Journal*, September 4, 1915, p. 190.

[15] A. B. Martinez and M. Lewandowski, *The Argentine in the Twentieth Century*, London, 1911, p. 361. All the figures used in this discussion when given in a foreign currency have been converted to gold pesos at the par of exchange.

[16] *Journal of Royal Statistical Society* (London), January 1911, p. 167.

Table VII

British Investments in Argentina
(in millions)

Total Investments

	Amount		*Total Interest*			*Amount paying no Interest*	
	sterling	*gold pesos*	*sterling*	*gold pesos*	*per cent*	*sterling*	*gold pesos*
1910	290.63	1,464.78	13.96	70.36	4.8	—	—
1913	357.74	1,803.01	17.66	89.01	4.9	8.84	44.55
1918	379.49	1,912.63	14.58	73.48	3.8	42.66	215.01
1923	396.11	1,996.39	18.83	94.90	4.7	37.34	188.19
1927	411.94	2,076.18	22.14	111.59	5.3	12.28	61.89
1931	429.70	2,165.69	15.67	78.98	3.6	64.31	324.12
1934	453.11	2,283.67	10.72	54.03	2.3	217.96	1,098.52

Government Bonds

	Amount		*Total Interest*			*Amount paying no Interest*	
	sterling	*gold pesos*	*sterling*	*gold pesos*	*per cent*	*sterling*	*gold pesos*
1913	81.58	411.16	3.56	17.94	4.3	—	—
1918	82.79	417.31	3.70	18.65	4.4	.15	.76
1923	79.13	398.82	3.52	17.74	4.4	.15	.76
1927	69.86	352.09	3.09	15.57	4.4	.15	.76
1931	56.00	282.24	2.44	12.30	4.3	.30	1.51
1934	79.27	399.52	3.13	15.78	3.9	2.32	11.70

Railways

	Amount		*Total Interest*			*Amount paying no Interest*	
	sterling	*gold pesos*	*sterling*	*gold pesos*	*per cent*	*sterling*	*gold pesos*
1913	215.00	1,083.60	10.36	52.21	4.8	6.36	32.05
1918	226.55	1,141.81	6.94	34.98	3.0	23.77	119.80
1923	232.93	1,173.97	11.59	58.41	4.9	15.09	76.05
1927	243.88	1,220.40	13.34	67.23	5.5	3.27	16.48
1931	271.40	1,367.86	8.17	41.18	3.0	44.08	222.16
1934	276.97	1,395.93	4.50	22.68	1.6	177.09	892.53

Miscellaneous

	Amount		*Total Interest*			*Amount paying no Interest*	
	sterling	*gold pesos*	*sterling*	*gold pesos*	*per cent*	*sterling*	*gold pesos*
1913	61.16	308.25	3.74	18.85	6.1	2.48	12.50
1918	70.04	353.04	3.94	19.86	5.6	18.75	94.50
1923	84.46	425.68	3.72	18.75	4.4	22.11	111.43
1927	98.20	494.93	5.71	28.78	5.8	8.87	43.70
1931	102.30	515.59	5.06	25.50	4.8	19.93	100.45
1934	96.86	488.17	3.09	15.57	3.2	38.55	194.29

Source: *South American Journal,* Mar. 30, 1935, p. 326 and Sept. 4, 1915, p. 190.

the fact that the *South American Journal* figure for 1910 approximated 1,473 million pesos, the writer has placed the estimated total of British investments in Argentina as of the end of 1910 at 1,475 million pesos.[17]

The next largest foreign investor in Argentina before the War was France, whose total investment in 1910 was estimated at approximately 410 million gold pesos.[18] Germany held third place with investments in Argentina in 1910 estimated roughly at 200 million gold pesos.[19]

[17] Sr. Ernesto Nelson's estimate of 1,554 million pesos (1,500 million dollars, U. S.) for total British investments in Argentina in 1903, is undoubtedly too high. See *Annals of the American Academy of Political and Social Science*, July, 1903, p. 175. Williams cites an estimate of Tornquist and Company which put the total British investments in Argentina in 1900 at 945,202,000 gold pesos, distributed as follows:

Public Loans	366,215,000
Railways	477,345,000
Miscellaneous	101,642,000

John H. Williams, *Argentine International Trade Under Inconvertible Paper Currency, 1880-1900*, footnote, p. 150. Sir George Paish estimated that during 1907-1913 inclusive, Great Britain invested approximately 600 million pesos in Argentina, most of it in railway construction. Paish, "The Export of Capital and the Cost of Living," *The Statist* (Supplement), February 14, 1914, p. v.

[18] Martinez and Lewandowski, *op. cit.*, p. 361. Their figure was based upon Paris Bourse quotations. French and Belgian investments combined were estimated by Martinez in 1904 at 185 million gold pesos. See John H. Williams, *op. cit.*

[19] Martinez and Lewandowski, *op. cit.*, p. 363. In 1904 German investments were estimated at 150 million gold pesos. John H. Williams, *op. cit.*

United States investments in Argentina were estimated in 1909 to approximate ten million dollars.[20] Another estimate published in May 1912 stated that the volume of American capital in Argentina totaled 40 million dollars "at the present time."[21] Total United States investments in Argentina upon the outbreak of the War are generally estimated at approximately 40 million dollars.[22] Only one issue of Argentine securities had been publicly sold in the United States prior to 1914. In 1909 one-fifth of a national loan for ten million pounds was floated in New York through J. P. Morgan and Company. In 1914 this issue was the only South American national government bond listed on the New York Stock Exchange.[23] Including this issue total United States investments in Argentina in 1910 may be estimated roughly at 20 million dollars. In 1907 the first Swift packing plant was built in Argentina, followed by one by Armour and Company in 1909.

Deducting the sum of these estimates for Great Britain, Germany, France, and the United States from Schwenke's figure of total foreign investments in 1910, a remainder of 150 million pesos is left as the estimated investment of other foreign capital, primarily Dutch, Belgian, and Italian.

The total British investments in Argentina in 1913 are estimated at 1,928 million gold pesos. This is the approximate figure used by Winkler,[24] whose estimate is, apparently, an adaptation

[20] Charles F. Speare, "Foreign Investments of the Nations," *North American Review*, Vol. 190, July 1909, p. 88. An estimate in 1900 placed the total United States capital invested in "Buenos Aires and the dependent country" at three million dollars. Nathaniel T. Bacon, "America's International Indebtedness," *Yale Review*, November 1900, p. 276.

[21] J. B. Osborne, "American Commerce and Capital Abroad," *North American Review*, May 1912, p. 687.

[22] Max Winkler, *Investments of United States Capital in Latin America*, World Peace Foundation, 1928, p. 68.

[23] H. E. Peters, *op. cit.*, p. 76. Chapters III and IV of Peters' study contain an excellent comprehensive description of the history of the Argentine public debt during this period, particularly with reference to the New York money market.

[24] Max Winkler, "United States Capital in Latin America," *The Index*, New York Trust Company, June 1930; also, Winkler, *Investments of United States Capital in Latin America.*

of the *South American Journal* estimate for 1913 of 1,803 million gold pesos. Sir George Paish estimated the total value of publicly offered Argentine securities in Great Britain as of December 31, 1913, at 1,611 million gold pesos. An additional sum of 300 million pesos to cover direct investments not included in Paish's estimate does not seem unreasonable. On the other hand, Paish's estimate of new Argentine publicly offered issues in London from 1910 to 1913 inclusive was only 250 million gold pesos.[25] Assuming the total increase to be 453 million pesos (see Table VI, p. 246) this would leave a remainder of 200 million pesos to be accounted for by direct investments from 1910 to 1914. Presumably, therefore, the figure of 1,928 million pesos may be too high by some 100 millions.

The figure of 250 million pesos used in Table VI above as representing total German capital invested in Argentina in 1913 is a rough approximation, based upon an estimate of 260 million pesos (250 million dollars), as the amount of German capital in Argentina in 1916.[26] Presumably very little, if any, German capital was invested in Argentina after the outbreak of the War, and an increase of 50 million pesos over the estimate of 200 million pesos for 1910 does not seem unreasonable.

French investments in 1913 are placed at 475 million gold pesos. Two estimates for 1916 give the figures of 414 million gold pesos (400 million dollars)[27] and 518 million gold pesos (500 million dollars),[28] respectively, for total French capital in Argentina.

Adding the United States investment estimated above at roughly 40 million gold pesos leaves a remainder as of 1913 of 557 million gold pesos for investments of other countries in

[25] *The Statist* (Supplement), February 14, 1914, pp. v and vi.

[26] T. M. Poblete, "Influence du Capital Étranger dans le Development Economique de L'Amérique Latine," *Revue de l'Amérique Latine*, Vol. 23, pp. 245-60, which also contains numerous other estimates for different years of foreign capital in Argentina. Halsey also gives the figure of 250 million dollars for German investments as of 1916. "Investments in Latin America, I: Argentina," *Trade Information Bulletin* No. 362, United States Bureau of Foreign and Domestic Commerce, Washington, D.C., 1925, p. 4.

[27] Halsey, *op. cit.*

[28] Poblete, *op. cit.*

Argentina, if the figure of 3,250 million pesos of total foreign capital is accepted.

According to Halsey,[29] British investments in Argentina in 1916 totaled 1,966 million gold pesos (1,898 million dollars). The *South American Journal* figure for 1918 places the total at 1,920 million pesos (379.49 million pounds). These estimates are the basis of the writer's figure in Table VI of 1,950 million pesos as the total British investment in 1917.[30]

The increase of 25 million pesos in German investments in 1917 over 1913 includes funds impounded in Argentina which were remitted after the War.[31]

The French estimate for 1917 of 465 million gold pesos is based primarily upon two estimates for 1916 referred to previously. It is assumed that increases in French investments between 1913 and the outbreak of the War were more than offset by decreases thereafter.

Total investments of the United States in Argentina in 1917 are estimated roughly at 85 million dollars, based upon the following data. During the War, the Argentine National Government negotiated short-term loans in New York which reached a maximum of 80 million dollars at the end of December 1916, but which were reduced to 25 million dollars by the end of 1917 and were entirely liquidated by the end of 1920.[32] In February 1917 the Province of Buenos Aires floated a loan of 2,800,000 dollars in New York. According to compilations of the United States Bureau of Foreign and Domestic Commerce there were also two private corporate issues publicly floated in the United States during 1916 and 1917, the proceeds of which were destined for Argentina, as follows:[33]

[29] "Investments in Latin America," *Special Agents Series* No. 169, United States Bureau of Foreign and Domestic Commerce, Washington, D.C., 1918.

[30] During the first six months of 1914 a total of 12,809,200 pounds, or roughly 65 million pesos of new capital issues destined for Argentina were floated in London. Argentine Government, Department of Agriculture, *Argentine International Trade, 1914-15*, p. 13.

[31] Tornquist estimates these remittances after the War at not less than 15 million gold pesos.

[32] H. E. Peters, *op. cit.*, p. 96.

[33] "Handbook of American Underwriting of Foreign Securities, 1914-29,"

(millions of U. S. dollars)

Aug. 1916, International Portland Cement Company	2.5
Mar. 1917, Central Argentine Railway	15.0
Total	17.5

According to Tornquist's balance-of-payments data for the years 1914-17, total new private foreign capital invested in Argentina other than British was not over 20 million pesos during the first three years of the War, a large part of which presumably came from the United States. Combining these various loans, we arrive at a total of approximately 85 million dollars as follows:[34]

(millions of U. S. dollars)

Total as of 1913	40.0
Argentine Government Short-term Loans	25.0
Province of Buenos Aires	2.8
Private Corporate Issues	17.5
Total	85.3

If our previous estimate of 3,350 million pesos for total foreign investments in 1917 is accepted, there is thus a remainder of some 565 million pesos attributable to investments of other nations in Argentina.

No compilation of total foreign investments in Argentina between 1917 and 1923 is known to the writer. Early in 1924 Martinez estimated the total at 3,470,960,000 gold pesos (3,360

Trade Promotion Series No. 104, United States Bureau of Foreign and Domestic Commerce, Washington, D.C., pp. 68-69.

[34] Since these data are at best rough estimates, the figure of 85 million dollars is used, although conversion into gold pesos would give 88 millions.

Halsey estimated the total United States capital invested in Argentina in 1916 at 100 million dollars. See United States Bureau of Foreign and Domestic Commerce, *Special Agents Series* No. 169. If the Argentine Government short-term loans which totaled 80 million dollars in December 1916 were included in Halsey's figure, his total of 100 million dollars, in view of the estimate of 40 million dollars for 1913, appears too low.

Robert Dunn cites an estimate of 40 million dollars by W. R. Ingalls in *Wealth and Income of the American People* (second edition, York, Pa., 1923) as representing "the total American investment in Argentina at the end of 1920." R. W. Dunn, *American Foreign Investments*, 1926, New York City, p. 61.

million dollars).[35] In 1924 Bunge brought Schwenke's figures up to date, and estimated the total, however, at only 2,640 million gold pesos (6,000 million paper pesos).[36] Further reference to these two estimates is made below.

Since 1920 marked the end of the period of war and post-war prosperity during which Argentina was reducing her foreign obligations, however, the writer has made a rough estimate of her total external obligations at the end of 1920. This figure of 3,150 million gold pesos (see Table VI above) was presumably the low point, since in every succeeding year the international accounts have shown a gross increase in Argentina's foreign indebtedness.[37] This reduction in total foreign investments of 200 million gold pesos from the 1917 figure is based primarily upon an analysis of Tornquist's balance-of-payments statements for the years 1917/18-1919/20 inclusive. According to these statements there was an estimated decrease in Argentina's long-term obligations of slightly less than 200 million gold pesos.[38] According to the statement by Bunge in 1923 as Director of the Argentine National Bureau of Statistics, previously referred to, Argentina reduced her external obligations between 1915 and 1920 by more than 880 million gold pesos (2,000 million paper pesos),[39] and this estimated reduction, presumably, was the basis of Bunge's statement that the total foreign investments in Argentina in 1924 amounted to 2,640 million pesos, in contrast to

[35] *Barron's*, New York, March 17, 1924, p. 7; cited by Dunn, *op. cit.*, p. 61.

[36] *Review of the River Plate*, January 20, 1928, p. 25.

[37] Cf. Table I, "International Income Account of Argentina, 1913-1935," Appendix I, opposite p. 238; also, Table II, "Estimated International Capital Transactions of Argentina, 1913-1934," Appendix II, pp. 240-41.

[38] See Table II, pp. 240-41. During the same period, however, as Table II indicates, there was an estimated net increase in short-term foreign obligations of 202,480,000 gold pesos. This figure includes some 240 million pesos of unaccounted-for, or residual items in the Tornquist statements. In the writer's opinion, this large residual item must have been partially accounted for by overstatement in certain debit items, i.e., losses on imports suffered by foreign sellers, as well as omission of certain other credit items, rather than short-term borrowings abroad. Paucity of data prevents, however, any substantiation of this opinion.

[39] *Analisis del Comercio Exterior Argentino en los años 1910 a 1922*, *op. cit.*, p. 10.

Martinez's estimated total early in 1924 of 3,470 million gold pesos as stated in the preceding paragraph. In the writer's opinion, Bunge's estimated reduction of foreign obligations during the period 1915-20 was much too large. According to Tornquist's balance-of-payments statements the gross repayments of foreign long-term capital between 1915 and 1920 was only 316,780,000 gold pesos. Even by adding gross new long-term loans by Argentina of 250,370,000 pesos to foreigners, the total is still less than 600 million pesos. And these figures do not include estimated new long-term foreign borrowing by Argentina of 115,300,000 pesos nor repayments by foreigners of long-term capital of 59,400,000 pesos. When these figures are all combined, the total net reduction in foreign long-term obligations equals 201,480,000 pesos; and the estimated reduction in Argentina's net long-term foreign debtor position is only 392,450,000 pesos (i.e., including adjustments for loans to foreigners and repayments by foreigners), as indicated in Table VIII.[40]

TABLE VIII

ESTIMATED CHANGES IN ARGENTINA'S LONG-TERM INTERNATIONAL FINANCIAL POSITION

1915–1920

	(in millions of gold pesos)
A. Borrowings:	
1. Borrowing from foreigners	115.30
2. Repayments to foreigners	316.78
3. Net decrease	201.48
B. Loans:	
4. Loans to foreigners	250.37
5. Repayments by foreigners	59.40
6. Net increase	190.97
Net Change (3 plus 6), i.e., estimated decrease in net foreign indebtedness	392.45

[40] This is exclusive of net change in short-term credits which increased by some 150 million gold pesos from 1915 to 1919. As previously stated, however, these data on short-term capital movements probably have little validity, since they are composed largely of the residual figure which very possibly is due to errors and omissions in other items.

In further support of a much smaller reduction in Argentina's external indebtedness during the war and post-war period than Bunge's estimate of 880 million gold pesos, *The Statist* (London) of October 30, 1920, p. 31, estimates the reduction in British investments in private undertakings in Argentina "during and since the war" at only 103,600,000 gold pesos. The total reduction in Great Britain's investments in Argentina from 1917 to 1920 is estimated, therefore, at 125 million pesos, or a total in 1920 of 1,825 million pesos.[41]

Total United States investments in Argentina in 1920 are estimated roughly at 75 million pesos. By the middle of 1920 all of the short-term loans made by the Argentine National Government in New York during the War had been repaid. Based on Tornquist's estimates of new foreign capital invested in Argentina, the writer puts at 15 million gold pesos the estimated increase in United States investments in private undertakings in Argentina between 1917 and 1920. This, added to the estimate of 60 million pesos in 1917 (excluding Argentine Government short-term loans of 25 million dollars), gives a total United States investment as of 1920 of 75 million gold pesos.[42] Lacking precise data for other countries, excepting Martinez's estimates for 1923, the remainder of the total foreign investment is allocated according to the figures in Table VI above.

As already indicated, Martinez estimated total foreign investments in Argentina early in 1924 at 3,470 million pesos, which was considerably above Bunge's estimate of 2,640 million

[41] A large portion of British holdings of Argentine Government securities were taken from private investors by the British Government and pledged as collateral in the United States. According to the United States Federal Reserve Board, *Federal Reserve Bulletin*, June 1920, p. 595, securities valued at 300 million dollars were so acquired. Presumably, however, they were never sold outright in any large quantities. The *South American Journal* for August 19, 1916, p. 141, lists those securities requisitioned by the British Government for a period of five years. According to Tornquist, the repatriation of Argentine securities by Argentina during this period was roughly only some 65 million gold pesos.

[42] Dunn's figure for 1920, as already indicated, was 40 million dollars, which figure is also used by Bunge. Cf. Dunn, *op. cit.*, p. 61; Bunge, *op. cit.*, p. 25.

pesos. In the writer's opinion, the correct sum was somewhere between these two figures, and probably nearer the former than the latter. The estimated total used in Table VI above is 3,200 million pesos, although this may be as much as 100 million pesos too low.

An analysis of the capital items in the Tornquist balance-of-payments statements shows that the net decrease in long-term foreign investments in Argentina between 1917 and 1923 was roughly 200 million pesos which, if deducted from the 1917 figure of 3,350 million pesos, gives a total of 3,150 millions in 1923.[43]

Martinez estimated total British capital invested in Argentina in 1923 at 1,967 million gold pesos (1,900 million dollars).[44] The *South American Journal* figure for 1923 is 1,996 million gold pesos. The writer places the British figure, therefore, at 1,975 million pesos. On the assumption that French and German investments increased but slightly between 1920 and 1923, Martinez's figures for 1923 of 425 million dollars for France and 375 million dollars for Germany[45] are reduced to 400 million dollars and 275 million dollars, respectively, or in gold pesos, 415 millions and 285 millions.

The United States Department of Commerce estimated total United States capital in Argentina in 1924 at 243 million gold pesos (234,500,000 dollars) of which 100 million dollars was industrial investment, mostly in meat, oil, and cement.[46] Of the remainder, according to this estimate, 117 million dollars was in government bonds and 17,500,000 dollars in municipal bonds. At the end of 1923, however, the only Argentine public dollar obligations outstanding in the United States were 95 million

[43] See Table II, "Estimated International Capital Transactions of Argentina, 1913-1934," pp. 240-41. As shown in Table II, this figure of 200 million pesos excludes again an estimated increase in short-term borrowing of nearly 500 million pesos. This figure of 500 million pesos is made up again very largely of the residual, or unestimated items, for these years, which very possibly were not short-term borrowings but omissions of other credit items in the balance of payments or overstatement of debits, as previously suggested.

[44] Cited by Dunn, *op. cit.*

[45] *Ibid.*

[46] Dunn, *op. cit.*, pp. 62-65.

dollars of short-term loans of the National Government.[47] This sum, added to the estimated total of private investments, approximates 200 million pesos, which is the figure used in Table VI.[48] This leaves a remainder of 325 million pesos for other countries, a reduction from the previous estimates which may be unwarranted; possibly the total of 3,200 million pesos should be increased by at least another 100 millions, as already indicated.

In 1928, Bunge revised his estimate of foreign capital in Argentina and obtained a figure as of October 31, 1927, of 3,091 million gold pesos as representing total foreign investments in Argentina. In the writer's opinion, this estimate was (as also was his 1924 estimate, see above, p. 254) much too low. This conclusion is reached from a comparative analysis of other estimates by individual foreign countries as of 1927, as well as subsequent estimates of total foreign capital in Argentina. Furthermore, Tornquist's annual balance-of-payments statements indicate an increase in net new foreign long-term borrowings from 1923 to 1927 of approximately 400 million gold pesos,[49] and we have just shown that total foreign borrowings in 1923 must have been at least 3,200 million gold pesos. The total foreign investments in Argentina in 1927 are estimated, therefore, at not less than 3,600 million gold pesos, and even this figure may be an understatement by as much as 200 million pesos.[50]

With respect to investments by individual foreign countries for 1927 given in Table VI, the estimates are based upon the following data. Total British investments as estimated by the *South*

[47] Peters, *op. cit.*, p. 127.

[48] According to *Kimber's Record of Government Debts, 1923*, however, large amounts of Argentine external bonds which had been previously repatriated by Argentina from Europe were resold in the United States, on the basis of which it was estimated that a total of 400 million dollars of United States capital was invested in Argentina in 1922. The writer is unable to justify such a large estimate, although his figure of 200 million dollars may be too low by some 50 to 100 million dollars.

[49] There was an additional estimated increase in short-term borrowings of 100 million pesos, the accuracy of which is again problematical.

[50] In an article in *Current History* for September 1927, Dr. H. T. Collings placed the total foreign investments in Argentina at 3,600 million dollars.

American Journal for 1927 were roughly 2,075 million gold pesos. Bunge also uses this figure, [51] as does the writer. The balance of the estimated increase of 400 million pesos over 1923 is attributable largely to the United States. According to Bunge, "the greatest part of the increase in foreign capital since 1920 . . . comes from the United States," and he estimates the total of United States capital in Argentina as of November 1927 at 505 million gold pesos.[52] Another estimate, however, places the total United States investment at the end of 1928 at 647 million pesos.[53] Total new United States investments in Argentina during 1928 were approximately 90 million pesos (according to the United States Department of Commerce) which, subtracted from 647 millions, gives some 557 million pesos as the total as of the end of 1927, in contrast to Bunge's figure of 505 millions.

Presumably, there must have been some increase in the investments of other countries during this period, which, as already indicated, would augment this total for 1927; but lacking other data, the investments of Germany, France, and other countries are left at the 1923 estimate.

In 1931, the total foreign capital in Argentina was estimated at 4,032 million gold pesos (800 million pounds converted at par).[54] In 1932, another estimate placed the total at 4,273 million gold pesos (4,125 million dollars converted at par).[55] The writer uses, roughly, the average of these two estimates, or 4,100 million gold pesos.

The statistical problem with which one is confronted in a study of this nature is well illustrated in the estimates of British investments in Argentina in 1931. Estimates of total British capital invested in Argentina in that year, which the writer has encountered, vary from a low figure of 1,752 million gold pesos

[51] *Review of the River Plate*, Jan. 20, 1928, p. 25.

[52] Bunge, *op. cit.*

[53] *Kimber's Record of Government Debt, 1931*, Overseas Statistics, Inc., New York City, p. 28.

[54] *The South American Handbook (8th edition), 1931*, p. 97.

[55] G. Butler Sherwell, "Latin America's Balance Sheet," *Comments on Argentine Trade*, official publication of the Chamber of Commerce of the United States of America in the Argentine Republic, June 1932, p. 21.

to a high of 3,024 million gold pesos. *The South American Handbook*[56] uses the figure of 432,710,000 pounds which approximates that compiled by the *South American Journal* of 429,700,000 pounds. Converted at par, these estimates approximate 2,100 million pesos which seems a reasonable figure in view of the 1,752-3,024 million range just cited.[57]

With reference to United States investments in Argentina in recent years, we are fortunate in having the carefully prepared estimates of Dr. Paul Dickens, of the Finance Division of the Bureau of Foreign and Domestic Commerce, as well as those of Dr. Max Winkler and others. Presumably, United States investments in Argentina reached their peak in 1930. As of December 31, 1930, they were estimated at 836,860,000 gold pesos (807,780,000 dollars).[58] Three years later the same author's estimate of total United States capital investments in Argentina was 780 million gold pesos (753 million dollars).[59] Although United States public loans in Argentina declined approximately 60 million dollars during 1931, an estimate by Dr. Max Winkler as of December 31, 1931, places the total amount of United States capital in Argentina at 886 million pesos (855,340,000 dollars).[60] Sherwell's estimate placed the United States total at 777 million pesos (750 million dollars).[61] In Table VI the writer uses the figure of 807 million gold pesos.

Total French investments in Argentina in 1931 were estimated at 428 million gold pesos (85 million pounds).[62] Assum-

[56] P. 97.

[57] According to *The Statist* (London), January 4, 1930, p. 16, the total Argentine issues of new capital floated in London from 1927 to 1929 inclusive were 20,727,270 pounds, or 104,466,440 gold pesos. The estimated increase from 1927 to 1931 in Table VI of only 25 millions is, perhaps, therefore, too conservative. Sherwell's estimate for total British capital in Argentina in June 1932 was 2,285,800,000 gold pesos. Sherwell, *op. cit.*

[58] Paul Dickens, "A New Estimate of American Investments Abroad," *TIB* No. 767, United States Bureau of Foreign and Domestic Commerce, Washington, D.C., 1931, p. 16.

[59] "The Balance of International Payments of the United States, 1933," *TIB* No. 819, United States Bureau of Foreign and Domestic Commerce, Washington, D.C., 1934, p. 56.

[60] For a discussion of the reasons for the discrepancies between the estimates of Winkler and those of the Department of Commerce, see *TIB* No. 767, pp. 22-23.

[61] *Op. cit.*

[62] *The South American Handbook*, p. 97.

ing that German investments may have increased slightly, they are estimated at 300 million gold pesos, leaving a remainder of 500 millions for other foreign capital, provided the estimated total of 4,100 million pesos is accepted.

According to the above estimates, then, the total foreign capital in Argentina increased by 500 million gold pesos between 1927 and 1931. An analysis of Tornquist's balance-of-payments statements for the same period, however, reveals an increase in net long-term investments (i.e., new borrowing less repayments) of approximately 240 million pesos.[63] Whether this difference is due to understatements by Tornquist, with corresponding understatements in outgo items in the balance of payments (or overstatements in other income or credit items), or errors in the direct estimates enumerated, the writer is unable to say. One possible explanation of the discrepancy is, of course, the fact that the changes in capital as reflected in balance-of-payment data do not include capital gains or losses which may be included in the direct estimates, and which, in this period, were no doubt gains and not losses. Bunge, in discussing his estimates for 1927 emphasized the fact, however, that, at least with respect to railway capital, he used original investment figures, and not "reproduction" or present "actual" values.[64]

The estimates in Table VI for 1934 were derived as follows:

1. The British figures are based upon the estimates of the *South American Journal*.[65]

2. The United States figure is based upon data obtained from the files of the Bureau of Foreign and Domestic Commerce and from Sr. C. Alonso Irigoyen, Financial Attaché, Argentine Embassy, Washington, D.C. The decline in the value of United States investments since 1931 was due largely to sales of Argentine securities by Americans to foreigners, plus amortizations since that date. Of a total of 272,136,122 dollars of Argentine

[63] Short-term borrowings are estimated to have increased some 50 million pesos during the same period.

[64] *Review of the River Plate*, p. 25.

[65] According to figures obtained from the United States Bureau of Foreign and Domestic Commerce, the Argentine Exchange Commission was reported to hold exchange in London as of March 1935 totaling 132 million gold pesos (300 million paper pesos), which would reduce the estimated net foreign indebtedness to Great Britain.

National Government dollar securities outstanding in 1935, some 45 per cent were estimated to have been held outside the United States.[66] Furthermore, amortization since 1930 accounted for a reduction of 79,337,298 dollars. The total "repatriations" (presumably this includes all sales to foreigners by Americans, but not necessarily to Argentinians) of all types of Argentine securities publicly offered in the United States, national, provincial, and municipal, as well as private securities, was estimated at the end of 1934 to equal 175 million dollars.[67] Offsetting these decreases was an increase of approximately 27 million gold pesos resulting from the funding of blocked pesos.

3. The increases in the estimates for the other countries are based upon the funding of blocked pesos during 1933, plus the estimated amount of blocked pesos still waiting remittance, and thus invested in Argentina, at least at short term. The increase of approximately 200 million gold pesos for the investment of "other" countries includes the amount of Argentine securities purchased from Americans during this period referred to above, and estimated at from fifty to seventy-five million pesos. The increase in estimated total foreign investments is based upon the increase in new borrowings, largely in the form of funding of blocked pesos, less amortizations and estimated repatriations since 1931.

The growth of foreign investments in Argentina by types of investment which is summarized in Table XVII, Chapter V, page 108, are estimates based upon the sources previously cited in this appendix in connection with Table VI. These figures in many cases are presented as only rough approximations, since detailed data were not available. In some cases it was possible to find estimates for certain types of investments for certain countries, and by using these estimates as a starting point, to derive the figures to complete the table for that year; the figures for other countries than Great Britain and the United States were nearly all computed in this manner.

[66] According to the returns of a questionnaire sent out by Sr. Irigoyen.

[67] Data obtained from United States Bureau of Foreign and Domestic Commerce.

APPENDIX III

Argentine Note Circulation, Gold Reserves, Total Gold Stocks, and Gold Imports and Exports 1910–36

(millions of gold pesos)

Year[1]	*Monetary Gold Reserve* Conversion House	Legations Abroad	Total	Notes in Circulation	Per cent Reserve	Gold Holdings, Private Banks	Total Visible Gold Stocks	Gold Imports	Gold Exports
1910	186.0		186.0	315.0	59.0	67.5	253.5	37.0	1.7
1911	189.0		189.1	318.1	59.4	62.5	251.6	12.8	3.0
1912	222.9		222.9	351.9	63.3	68.8	291.7	36.1	0.6
1913	233.2		233.2	362.2	64.4	61.7	294.9	47.9	44.4
1914	224.4	2.7	227.1	353.4	64.3	50.3	277.4	18.0	31.3
1915	237.3	68.3	305.6	434.6	70.3	26.9	332.5	4.2	[2]
1916	260.3	56.5	316.8	445.8	71.1	33.4	350.2	25.9	0.3
1917	261.6	55.3	316.9	445.8	71.1	57.0	373.9	26.8	0.5
1918	279.5	99.6	379.1	508.0	74.6	54.1	433.2	17.9	0.1
1919	310.0	79.0	389.0	518.0	75.1	65.9	454.9	32.4	0.1
1920	466.5	4.1	470.6	599.5	78.4	45.9	516.5	143.0	[2]
1921	466.5	4.1	470.6	599.5	78.4	35.8	506.4	0.1	[2]
1922	466.5	4.1	470.6	599.5	78.4	34.7	505.3	[2]	[2]
1923	466.5	4.1	470.6	599.5	78.4	33.8	504.4	[2]	5.6
1924	451.8		451.8	580.7	77.8	17.9	469.7	[2]	22.9
1925	451.8		451.8	580.7	77.8	24.3	476.1	8.4	—
1926	451.8		451.8	580.7	77.8	24.2	476.0	2.0	—
1927	477.6		477.6	606.5	78.7	82.4	560.0	86.6	—
1928	489.7		489.7	618.6	79.2	151.5	641.2	99.4	12.3
1929	419.6		419.6	548.6	76.5	41.6	461.2	[2]	174.4
1930	425.8		425.8	554.7	76.8	9.9	435.7	[2]	25.2
1931	260.9		260.9	547.8	47.6	3.3	264.2	0.2	171.7
1932	256.9		256.9	589.0	44.0	2.1	259.0	0.1	5.0
1933	246.8		246.8	534.1	46.2	2.1	248.9	0.1	10.1
1934	246.8		246.8	515.5	47.9	2.7	249.5	[2]	2.9
1935	538.7[3]	56.9[4]	595.6	432.0	137.9	[5]	[5]	0.3	3.6
1936	538.7[3]	133.4[4]	672.2	481.3	139.7	[5]	[5]	2.6	1.5
				(millions of paper pesos)					
1935	1,224.4[3]	129.3[4]	1,353.7	981.8	137.9	[5]	[5]	0.7	8.2
1936	1,224.4[3]	303.2[4]	1,527.7	1,093.9	139.7	[5]	[5]	6.0	3.4

[1] All figures as of December 31 of each year, except export and import figures which cover calendar year.

[2] Less than 50 thousand gold pesos.

[3] Under the new banking legislation of 1935 the Conversion Office was abolished as of May 31, 1935, and all its assets and liabilities including gold were transferred to the new Central Bank. In accordance with the Central Bank Law and Article 6, Decree No. 61,127 of May 18, 1935, the gold holdings so taken over by the Central Bank were revalued at the rate of 0.2929 grams of fine gold per paper peso as contrasted with the former gold equivalent of 0.6397 grams fine gold per paper peso. This represented a devaluation of 54.213 per cent, although the National Government has stated that it is not to be considered as a definitive stabilization rate, but merely as a transfer rate. Definitive stabilization of the paper peso will not be attempted until the leading world currencies have been stabilized.

[4] Includes gold held abroad and foreign exchange.

[5] Not available.

Source: *El Comercio Exterior* (annual); *Revista de Economía Argentina.*

BIBLIOGRAPHY

GOVERNMENT PUBLICATIONS

Argentina

Dirección General de Estadística de la Nación, El Intercambio Económico en la República Argentina en 1916 (informe), Buenos Aires, 1917.

——, Intercambio Económico de la República en los Años 1910 a 1917, Buenos Aires, 1918.

——, Noticia Sumaria del Comercio Exterior Argentino de 1910 Hasta 1923, Informe No. 11, Serie C, No. 6, Buenos Aires, 1924.

——, Anuario del Comercio Exterior (annual).

——, El Comercio Exterior Argentino (quarterly or semi-annual).

Memoria del Departamento de Hacienda (annual report of the Ministry of Finance).

Ministerios de Hacienda y Agricultura de la Nación, El Plan de Acción Económica Ante El Congreso Nacional, Buenos Aires, 1934.

United States

Bureau of Foreign and Domestic Commerce, Foreign Commerce and Navigation (annual).

——, Statistical Abstract (annual).

——, World Economic Review, 1933, 1934.

——,The Balance of International Payments of the United States (annual since 1922).

——, American Underwriting of Foreign Securities, *Trade Promotion Series* No. 104, 1930.

——, American Direct Investments in Foreign Countries, *Trade Information Bulletin* No. 731, 1930.

——, A New Estimate of American Investments Abroad, *Trade Information Bulletin* No. 767, 1931.

——, The Economic Position of Argentina During the War, *Miscellaneous Series* No. 88, 1920.

——, Bulletins and Special Studies Regarding Argentina (see footnote, p. 175 of text).

——, Latin-American Financial Notes (mimeographed), bi-weekly.

Department of Agriculture, *Yearbook on Agriculture* (annual).

Federal Trade Commission, Report on Trade and Tariffs in Brazil, Uruguay, Argentina, etc., 1916.

United States Tariff Commission, The Argentine Customs Tariff and Other Trade Restrictions on Imports from the United States since January 1, 1922 (mimeographed), 1934.

——, Commercial Treaties and Agreements of Argentina in Force March 1, 1935 (mimeographed), May, 1935.

——, Reciprocity and Commercial Treaties, 1919.

——, Extent of Equal Tariff Treatment in Foreign Countries (mimeographed), 1936.

Great Britain

Department of Overseas Trade, Economic Conditions in the Argentine Republic (annual since 1919, excepting 1932 and 1934).

Board of Trade Journal and Commercial Gazette.

Committee on Finance and Industry Report (MacMillan Report).

Economic Mission to Argentina, Brazil, and Uruguay, Report, 1930 (D'Abernon Mission).

Sheffield Industrial Mission to South America, Report, 1931.

Commercial Mission to South America. Reports received from Mr. T. Worthington, Special Commissioner, Third Report, The Argentine Republic, 1898 (Cmd. 9101).

Canada

Department of Trade and Commerce, *Commercial Intelligence Journal.*

Spain

El Comercio Exterior Argentino y El Intercambio con España: Analisis detallado de nuestra importación y exportación en la Argentino—Medios de aumentarlos, 1916.

League of Nations

Memoranda on Balance of Payments (annual since 1924).

World Economic Survey (annual since 1931).

Monthly Bulletin of Statistics.

Statistical Yearbook.

BOOKS

Bain, H. F. and Read, T. T., *Ores and Industry in South America*, New York, 1934.

Bunge, Alejandro E., *La Economía Argentina*, 4 volumes, Buenos Aires, 1928-1930.

——, *Riqueza y renta de la Argentina, su distribución y su capacidad contributiva*, Buenos Aires, 1917.

Davies, A. E., *Investments Abroad*, New York, 1927.

Dunn, R. W., *American Foreign Investments*, New York, 1926.

Emiliani, R. P., *Reorganización Económica Política y Social*, Buenos Aires, 1920.

Garcia-Mata, Rafael and Llorens, Emilio, *Geografía Económica Argentina*, Buenos Aires, 1936.

Gifford, J. L. K., *The Devaluation of the Pound*, London, 1934.

Haberler, Gottfried, *The Theory of International Trade*, London, 1936.

Hansen, Emilio, *The Argentine Financial Emergency Measures on the Outbreak of the European War*, Buenos Aires, 1915.

——, *La Moneda Argentina*, Buenos Aires, 1916.

Haring, Clarence H., *South America Looks at the United States*, New York, 1928.

——, *Southern American Progress*, Harvard University Press, 1934.

Iverson, Carl, *Aspects of the Theory of International Capital Movements*, Copenhagen, 1935.

Jefferson, Mark, *Peopling the Argentine Pampa*, American Geographical Society, 1926.

Kimber's Record of Government Debts, 1916-1934 (annual).

Kirkpatrick, F., *History of the Argentine Republic*, Cambridge University Press, 1931.

Klein, Julius, *Frontiers of Trade*, New York, 1929.

LaFond, G., *L'Argentine au Travail*, Paris, 1929.

Lestard, Gaston, *La Establización Monetaria Argentina*, Buenos Aires, 1933.

Lewis, Cleona, *The International Accounts*, Washington, D.C., 1927.

Martinez, A. B., *Annuaire Economique et Financier de la République Argentine*, Premiere Annee, Barcelona, 1913.

Martinez, A. B. and Lewandowski, M., *The Argentine in the Twentieth Century*, London, 1911.

National Industrial Conference Board, *Trends in the Foreign Trade of the United States*, New York, 1930.

Normano, J. F., *The Struggle for South America*, New York, 1931.

Norton, H. K., *The Coming of South America*, New York, 1932.

Ohlin, Bertil, *Interregional and International Trade*, Harvard University Press, 1933.

Patterson, E. M., *Tests of a Foreign Government Bond*, New York, 1928.

Peters, H. E., *The Foreign Debt of the Argentine Republic*, Baltimore, 1934.

Phelps, D. M., *The Migration of Industry to South America*, New York, 1936.

Rippy, J. F., *Latin America in World Politics*, New York, 1931 (revised).

Ross, Gordon, *Argentina and Uruguay*, New York, 1916.

Soares, Carlos F., *Economía y Finanzas de la Nación Argentina*, Buenos Aires, Tomo I, 1916; Tomo II, 1922; Tomo III, 1932.

The Argentine Yearbook, J. Grant and Son, Buenos Aires.

Thompson, Wallace, *Greater America*, New York, 1932.

Thorp, W. L., *Business Annals*, New York, 1934.

Times Book on Argentina, Times Publishing Company, London, 1927.

Tornquist, C. A., *Economic Development of the Argentine Republic in the Last Fifty Years*, Buenos Aires, 1919.

Willcox, W. F. (editor), *International Migrations*, National Bureau of Economic Research, New York, 1929-31.

Williams, J. H., *Argentine International Trade Under Inconvertible Paper Money, 1880-1900*, Cambridge, Mass., 1920.

Winkler, Max, *Investments of United States Capital in Latin America*, World Peace Foundation, Boston, 1928.

ARTICLES AND MONOGRAPHS

Bacon, Nathaniel, "America's International Indebtedness," *Yale Review* (Nov., 1900).

De Witt, Paul, "The Commercial Relations Between the United States and Argentina," *The Southwestern Political and Social Science Quarterly*, XI (Sept., 1930).

Gibson, Herbert, "British Interests in Argentina," United Empire,

The Royal Colonial Institute Journal, Vol. 5, new series, 1914.

Hanson, Simon G., "The Argentine Grain Board," *Journal of Political Economy* (April, 1936).

Haring, C. H., "Depression and Recovery in Argentina," *Foreign Affairs* (April, 1936).

Hipwell, H. Hallan, "Trade Rivalries in Argentina," *Foreign Affairs* (Oct., 1929).

Institute of International Finance, "Credit Position of Argentina," Bulletins No. 8 (Nov. 26, 1927); No. 31 (Jan., 1930); No. 86 (June 1, 1936).

Jones, Clarence, "Argentine Trade Developments," *Economic Geography*, Clarke University, Worcester, Mass. (July, 1926).

Klein, Julius, "The Competitive Situation in South American Trade," *Harvard Review of Economic Statistics*, Vol. III (1921).

——, "Economic Rivalries in Latin-America," *Foreign Affairs*, Vol. 3 (Dec. 15, 1924).

Lamb, Eric, "The Argentine Recovery," *Economic Forum*, New York (Spring, 1935).

Lees, Wm. Clare, "Some Aspects of Trade with South America," *Journal of Royal Society of Arts*, London, Vol. 78.

Leguizamon, G. E., "Argentine View of the Problem of Exchange Restrictions," *Journal of the Royal Institute of International Affairs*, London (July, 1933).

McCrea, R. C., VanMetre, T. W. and Eder, G. J., "International Competition in the Trade of Argentina," *International Conciliation*, Carnegie Endowment for International Peace, No. 271 (June, 1931).

National Foreign Trade Council, "Survey of the Financial and Trade Problems of the Argentine Republic in their Relation to the United States of America," New York (1933).

Nelson, Ernesto, "Argentine Commerce with the United States and Europe," *Annals of the American Academy of Political and Social Science*, Philadelphia (July, 1903).

Paish, George, "Great Britain's Capital Investments in Individual Colonial, and Foreign Countries," *Journal of Royal Statistical Society*, Vol. 74 (Jan., 1911).

——, "Great Britain's Capital Investments in Other Lands," *Journal of Royal Statistical Society*, Vol. 72 (Sept., 1909).

Pasvolsky, Leo, "Bilateralism in International Commercial Relations," *Harvard Business Review* (Spring, 1936).

Pratt, E. E., "Trade Conditions in Latin America as Affected by the European War," *Annals*, Vol. 60 (1915).

Robertson, Malcolm, "The Economic Relations between Great Britain and the Argentine Republic," *Journal of the Royal Institute of International Affairs* (Mar., 1930).

Schoff, W. H., "Investments of American Capital in Latin American Countries," *Annals* (May, 1911).

Sherwell, G. B., "Trade Barriers in Their General Relations to Our Latin American Policy," *Comments on Argentine Trade* (Sept., 1934).

Smith, Lawrence, "Suspension of the Gold Standard in Raw Material Exporting Countries," *American Economic Review*, Vol. 24 (Sept., 1934).

Speare, C. F., "Foreign Investments of the Nations," *North American Review*, Vol. 190 (July, 1909).

Stewart, W., "United States-Argentine Commercial Negotiations of 1825," *Hispanic-American Historical Review*, Vol. 13 (Aug., 1933).

The Times (London), Supplement, Special Argentine number on the occasion of the visit of the Prince of Wales and the Centenary (Aug. 17, 1935).

Tornquist, C. A., *The Argentine Republic of Today* (Feb., 1916).

——, *El Balance de Pagos de la República Argentina*, Buenos Aires (1914-1931).

——, *La República Argentina, su situación económica y financiera, perspectivas para 1915*, Buenos Aires (1914).

Tornquist, Ernesto y Cia, Ltd., *Manual of Argentine National, Provincial, and Municipal Loans*, Buenos Aires (1913).

Williams, J. H., "Latin American Foreign Exchanges During the War," *Quarterly Journal of Economics* (May, 1919).

——, "Foreign Trade Balance of the United States Since the Armistice," *American Economic Review* (Mar., 1921, supplement).

——, "Argentine Foreign Exchange and Trade Since the Armistice," *Harvard Review of Economic Statistics*, Vol. III (Mar., 1921).

——, and Vanderlip, "The Future of Our Foreign Trade," *Harvard Review of Economic Statistics*, Supplement (April, 1920).

Wythe, George, "The New Industrialism in Latin America," *Journal of Political Economy* (April, 1937).

PERIODICALS AND NEWSPAPERS

Argentina, Argentine Bureau, New York City (*Review of Argentina* since Sept., 1933).

Bank of England, *Statistical Summary*.

Bankers Magazine, Bankers Publishing Company, New York City.

Bulletin of the Pan-American Union, Washington, D.C.

Business Conditions in Argentina, Ernesto Tornquist and Company, Buenos Aires.

Comments on Argentine Trade, Chamber of Commerce of the United States in Argentina, Buenos Aires.

Commercial Pan-America, Pan-American Union, Washington, D.C.

Current History, The New York Times Publishing Company, New York City.

Commercial and Financial Chronicle, New York City.

The Economist, London.

Federal Reserve Bulletin, Federal Reserve Board, Washington, D.C.

Foreign Policy Association, *Reports*.

Hispanic-American Historical Review, Duke University Press, Durham, N.C.

Monthly Review of Business and Trade Conditions in South America, Bank of London and South America.

Revista de Economía Argentina, Buenos Aires.

Review of the River Plate (weekly), Buenos Aires.

Revista Económica, Banco de la Nación (abbreviated English edition—*Economic Review*), 1928-1934.

Revue de l'Amerique Latine, Paris, 1910-1932.

South American Journal (weekly), London.

The Americas, National City Bank (monthly), New York City, 1915-1921.

The Buenos Aires Herald, Buenos Aires.

The South American, New York City, 1914-1922.

The Statist, London.

INDEX

www.ingramcontent.com/pod-product-compliance
Lightning Source LLC
LaVergne TN
LVHW011820200926
848484LV00005B/1254